Diminished
—————————
Faculties
—————————

Diminished

Faculties

A POLITICAL PHENOMENOLOGY

OF IMPAIRMENT

Jonathan Sterne

DUKE UNIVERSITY PRESS   *Durham and London*   2021

Printed in the United States of America on acid-free paper ∞
Designed by Matthew Tauch
Typeset in Garamond Premier Pro, Roboto, and Roboto Mono
by Copperline Book Services

Library of Congress Cataloging-in-Publication Data
Names: Sterne, Jonathan, [date] author.
Title: Diminished faculties : a political phenomenology of impairment /
Jonathan Sterne.
Description: Durham : Duke University Press, 2021. | Includes bibliographical
references and index.
Identifiers: LCCN 2021013326 (print) | LCCN 2021013327 (ebook)
ISBN 9781478015086 (hardcover)
ISBN 9781478017707 (paperback)
ISBN 9781478022329 (ebook)
Subjects: LCSH: Sociology of disability. | Disabilities—Philosophy. |
Disabilities—Social aspects. | Voice disorders. | Phenomenology. |
BISAC: SOCIAL SCIENCE / People with Disabilities | SOCIAL SCIENCE /
Media Studies
Classification: LCC HV1568 .S698 2021 (print) | LCC HV1568 (ebook) |
DDC 362.4—dc23
LC record available at https://lccn.loc.gov/2021013326
LC ebook record available at https://lccn.loc.gov/2021013327

Cover art: *Front:* Dork-o-phone in its faux-leather case,
with lanyard attached. *Back:* Dork-o-phone microphone
in windscreen, 3.5 millimeters mono plug. Photos by
Carrie Rentschler.

For Carrie

EULA BISS

"The Pain Scale"

The sensations of my own body may be the only

subject on which I am qualified to claim expertise.

Sad and terrible, then, how little I know.

MICHAEL BÉRUBÉ

"Autism Aesthetics"

There must be no performance

criteria for being human.

CONTENTS

01
—

Degrees of Muteness

Begin again.

Then: "Breathe, Jonathan!"
"Breathe!"
"Can you breathe for me?"

I can see the lights of the surgical theater arrayed above me. The lights are out of focus; they have halos, like they are doubling out from themselves. I see the blurry outlines of bodies in surgical outfits around me. People are mostly standing still. There are machines making sounds. I hear Dr. Q's voice imploring me to breathe.

I cannot breathe.

I can move the muscles in my diaphragm, but no air is coming in or out.

I think he walks around toward my head. "Breathe, Jonathan!"

There's a weird throttling sound that comes out of me. Or maybe it goes in.

Someone says to put me back under.

Everything fades.

I wake up, and it's sometime in June 2012. Or maybe even June 2011. Or 2013. I just know how it came to me, and that it was June, when the light leaks out from behind the bedroom shades early in the morning. Whenever it is, that memory of supervised, experimental asphyxiation explodes in all my senses, radiating through my body, as the early morning light peeks into the bedroom. I cannot stop it. I did not dream it. I know it happened to me, and yet for months or years, I had no recollection until I awoke in those early morning hours. The attempt to have me breathe on my own probably occurred during a completion thyroidectomy that happened on February 12, 2010. But I can't rule out the fifteenth either, which was the day I received my temporary tracheostomy. This is not one of those tales of patients waking up during surgery by accident.[1] My brief return to consciousness was intentional on the part of the surgeon and the anesthesiologist—there was really only one way to find out if I could breathe on my own. Breath is life.[2]

The experience and the memory begin from two different kinds of unconsciousness. As I have learned, surgical unconsciousness feels more like being dead than asleep. But the experiences of coming to consciousness share a certain morphology: one awakens both from anesthesia and from sleep, or one hopes to. What do I do with this memory, only available to me some time after the fact? It seems to enact two totally different temporalities, two different relationships to consciousness. Generations of thinkers have asked after the condition of possibility for experience. Is it consciousness, the body, culture, divinity, or something else?[3] This story starts instead with conditions of *im*possibility: What does it mean that I can never really know what happened and that, as a result, neither can you?

Did the awakening *happen* to me in the surgical theater in February 2010? Or did it happen *to me* some undetermined time later, when I consciously experienced it? Is it *happening to me* again as I am recalling it on the page? It happened, but when it happened depends on what it means to say that it happened. Am I talking about consciousness, consciousness of consciousness, or retrospection of consciousness? From what vantage point is it possible to account for this consciousness? Is it the materiality of my body and its sudden inability to access the air in an operating theater? Is it my experience of that fact? Which one?

This opening chapter is the story of an acquired impairment in my voice that followed from this series of surgeries—a paralyzed vocal cord—and its implications for my experience of vocalization. I cannot tell you when the story of my voice begins. But in this text, it has already begun in one of the least likely places, at least for me: phenomenology.

INTRODUCING IMPAIRMENT PHENOMENOLOGY

Phenomenology tells its practitioners to begin again. As Cressida Heyes explains, phenomenology is a philosophical method that "attempts to identify the essential structures of consciousness, starting from a first-personal perspective [with the goal] to shift our attention from what is experienced to how it is experienced, and what makes this experience possible."[4] Most phenomenologies of sound, and of voice, have been untenable for me in the past. In *The Audible Past*, my first book, I critiqued and provided an alternative to the problematic tendency to universalize and naturalize a certain kind of white, male, bourgeois, Christian experience of sound (and voice). But as Heyes points out, there are actually two completely different things called phenomenology (and a third, which simply uses the word *phenomenology* as a fancy term for the word *experience*). To greatly oversimplify: the tradition of phenomenology that just calls itself "phenomenology" refers back to the work of Edmund Husserl, who reflected on structures of consciousness and how objects in the world present themselves to consciousness. To achieve this, Husserl built his method around the suspension of judgment—*epoche*—and believed that through it, a subject like him could produce a transcendental account of consciousness and its possibilities. Martin Heidegger would later critique Husserl, arguing that existence was more fundamental than consciousness, and Maurice Merleau-Ponty problematized perception as something that mediates between consciousness and the world.[5] However, this tradition of phenomenology is still usually transcendent and universal in its aspirations. As Heyes explains, today a second, parallel line of phenomenology draws from feminist, queer, Black, Latinx, and disability traditions that began from the politicized analysis of experience outside university settings and only later directly engaged with phenomenology as a method or tradition. This work uses the methods of phenomenology to "critically reveal the naturalization and contingency of subjectivity"—which is quite different from the projects of Husserl or Heidegger.[6] A critique of naturalization is especially important for the phenomenologies of impairment, illness, and disability, which are defined by their contingency and situatedness but often treated as naturalized. As Havi Carel writes, for a phenomenology of illness to work, it must abandon its transcendental pretensions. Every body (and everybody) is situated historically, ecologically, and politically. I will call this bundle of "posttranscendental" approaches *political phenomenology*, to highlight their common thread and interest.[7]

I borrow the phrase *political phenomenology* from an early essay by Jody Berland.[8] She does not define the term but performs it as a method, combining her analysis of listening with talk of history, policy, and space. If political phenomenology sounds like other critical methods such as genealogy, historical materialism, or reflexive ethnography, that is because it shares some of the basic concerns about the origins and mechanisms through which experience becomes possible: how people come to act and intend, but mostly in conditions not of their own making. Like these other approaches, political phenomenology is fundamentally interested in power. Phenomenology provides some useful methods and traditions for interrogating experience of the self; it is not unique in this respect— ethnography and hermeneutics are other paths in. But since this book begins with consciousness of unconsciousness (or is it unconsciousness of consciousness?), and since I will be speaking to the way humanists narrate experience in our own writing, phenomenology is a good place to start because it is an approach that requires such narration in order to work.[9]

Diminished Faculties fleshes out a little corner of political phenomenology that I am going to call *impairment phenomenology*. Impairment phenomenology is different from other kinds of phenomenology in that it does not assume a subject in command of their own faculties. Most phenomenologists describe their experience to you as a reader, and you are asked to believe them. But I am an unreliable narrator. For instance, I "begin again" by telling the story of waking up in surgery. Except I don't have a solid foundation for a beginning. And to do phenomenology, do I need to be in control? Because I am clearly not in control. How am I supposed to tease out the foundations of my own experience when I don't even know what it is? My impairment phenomenology therefore cannot be self-sufficient. In writing this chapter and this book, I depend on other approaches, other scholarship, and other experiences. I frequently make recourse to work in disability studies, media studies, cultural studies, art history, science and technology studies, and anthropology in these pages. A successful impairment phenomenology should by definition produce an indisciplined text.

I am also drawn to political phenomenology because I no longer fully know my own voice. That's just weird for someone who has had a powerful voice in the past in both the physical and metaphoric meanings of the term: I could be loud and take up a lot of sonic space with my voice in a gendered and raced way, and things I said seemed to have efficacy in the world. Against every critical impulse in my body, my own voice was tied up in my own self-conception, even though I had repeatedly critiqued the idea in my prior writing. As my voice changed, so did my relationship to it. Please resist the impulse to read this as a tragic story of loss of an ability, or a tale of overcoming. Of course there was fear in going into surgery, in not being able to breathe, and in the prospect of never speaking again. But this is really a story about how to exist in a changed body and how to negotiate that change. It is not meant to be offered as a lament or a form of mourning. I experienced a change in orientation, and phenomenology is *all about* orientation.[10] The research on disability and self-acceptance is pretty clear: people who accept and incorporate their disabilities are as happy as (or happier than) anyone else. As Christina Crosby explains, "Whatever chance I have at a good life, in all senses of that phrase, depends on my openness to the undoing wrought by spinal cord injury, because there is no return to an earlier life."[11] This was my plan from the moment the possibility of a total loss of the ability to speak was explained to me by Dr. Q in a presurgery consult: whatever happened, I would experiment with it and make it work for me. But even in accepting a new vocal condition, I still had to learn to live with it, and analytically, living with and through it is the interesting part. My working hypothesis is that this experience is actually so common that it could be the founding basis of phenomenology. Living means changing, and often in fundamental ways. Many traditional phenomenologies treat time as continuous and contiguous: a person exists because of some historical continuity, an unbroken line in time. But that continuity has more to do with conventions of storytelling than with the experience it represents. Thus, many of the stories I relate in the first two chapters of *Diminished Faculties* can be read as experiments. Some worked, some did not.

As a method drawn from political phenomenology, impairment phenomenology amplifies four challenges for writing and thinking: (1) how to account for an experience of self that is unstable and ultimately not fully available; (2) how to account for selves, subjects, and experiences while presupposing the constant possibility of impairment, error, breakdown, and incommensurability; (3) how to represent that experience in writing and thought; and (4) and what to do with the implications of that experience. It aims to connect the personal and the political but always in relation to a terrain of "unknown unknowns," to borrow from Danielle Spencer (who borrowed from former U.S. defense secretary Donald Rumsfeld). It recognized "ignorance as the basis of knowledge."[12] Impairment phenomenology is what a disability simulation fails to be. Disability simulations aim to simulate the experience of disability for nondisabled people through such techniques as temporarily blindfolding sighted people and then asking them to complete a task. These simulations have been used as philosophical and teaching tools for a long time, and widely criticized by disability studies scholars. For example, in the 1968 article that coined the modern use of the word *soundscape*, Michael Southworth began from disability, using characterizations of blind, Deaf, and wheelchair-based experiences to build his theory of sonic space.[13] He took twenty people around the city: "People loved that, and they were blindfolded and I pushed them through on a wheelchair. . . . As a control, we had normal people who could see and hear. And then I had people who could see but not hear. Everyone had a tape recorder so they could talk into it so they could discuss what they were experiencing." He then used reports from the studies as the basis for his analysis of urban sonic space in Boston, a move that would come to influence subsequent uses of the term *soundscape*. Similarly, Don Ihde blindfolded himself in *Listening and Voice* in order to get a better sense of how sound works. Both Southworth and Ihde use a trope that Georgina Kleege criticizes as the "hypothetical blind man," which substitutes a stigmatizing account of blindness by the seeing for an account of blind people's experiences given by blind people themselves. The wheelchairs in Southworth's experiment probably have more to do with sighted people's absence of blind navigation skills than anything about mobility impairment. Blind people who are not mobility impaired can navigate urban space on foot, whereas sighted people pretending to be blind do not instantly acquire those skills by covering up their eyes.[14]

In my impairment phenomenology, the experiment does not involve taking on a condition temporarily (though impairments can be temporary); it involves the incorporation of impairment into the self, which is the opposite of what happens when someone puts on a blindfold they can take off. One of the ironic results of disability simulations is that they produce too much stability in accounts of experience—"this is how it really works"—because they have not spent enough time to acquire the variety of experiences that come from living with an impairment or disability. A political phenomenology of impairment should be more unstable, because it takes more time; and while it may traffic in hypotheses and fictions, those are generated from real conditions of impairment.

A PREVIEW OF DIMINISHED FACULTIES

Diminished Faculties is my attempt at an impairment phenomenology. It makes no deliberate gesture toward an integrative subject or a coherent narrative. Instead, I begin from a set of impairments: vocal impairments, hearing impairments, and fatigue; I will mention many others but those are my big three. (The original plan for this book included a chapter on visual impairments, but it didn't pan out.)[15] *Diminished Faculties* thus undertakes a maneuver I have been half-jokingly calling the "reverse Laura Marks." In her wonderful book *The Skin of the Film*, Marks constructs a theory of cinematic sensation and "living between cultural regimes of knowledge" by focusing on vision, taste, smell, and touch while briefly mentioning a host of other capacities.[16] *Diminished Faculties* constructs an impairment phenomenology (which also involves living between regimes of knowledge) by examining three faculties she deemphasized in that book: speech, hearing, and embodied apperception; it considers many others in passing, including seeing, moving, touching, remembering, sleeping, fighting, teaching, and tasting. By its very nature, such a project must be empirically incomplete and inadequate to the plurality of experience. But since that is the case for all theory by definition, I use these partial accounts to ask big questions about impairment, subjectivity, power, and experience.

In an academic book, it is probably impossible to produce a truly unstable or fragmented authorial voice to match the rendition of impaired experience. It would be especially difficult for me since I have already published a lot of other material under my own name and it is invested with all sorts of significations I do not control. Like my sonic voice, my authorial voice in *Diminished Faculties* will vary from time to time. Right now you are reading the "Jonathan Sterne talks didactically" voice; it will show up repeatedly. But other voices appear in other chapters (along with callbacks to voices that have already appeared on the playbill). Chapter 1—you are here—shuttles between narrating my experience of vocal transformation and interrogating it. The somewhat ponderous phenomenological style feels appropriate for representing the exploration that goes with acquired impairments—or at least it does to me. Chapter 2 introduces the dork-o-phone, a personal, portable speech amplifier, and revels in the traditions of crip humor, play with stigmatizing terms and self-deprecation (and a touch of artist or design research, or, as it's called in Quebec, research-creation), while engaging with ongoing conversations about voices, design, prosthesis, and disability. Chapter 3 stages alternative figurations of voice through an imaginary exhibition, and is written mostly in the second person in the form of a guide and a spatial narrative, moving you through the exhibition. Throughout, it challenges commonly assumed connections among voice, ability, intention, and agency. After these first three chapters, a more didactic scholarly tone takes over. Chapter 4 deals with a suite of normalized auditory impairments, often grouped under the misnomer "hearing loss," and is written somewhere near the intersection of Deaf studies and science and technology studies, with a bit of anthropology, music, and cultural studies thrown in. Coining the term *audile scarification*, it treats the transformation of hearing as something normal and desired in many cultural contexts, using that case to develop a more general theory of normal impairments. Chapter 5 is an account of fatigue. It offers a genealogy of its various permutations as a normal impairment and a kind of energy depletion in industry, science, medicine, disability politics. It then assembles an alternative approach to fatigue that begins from understanding fatigue as a presence rather than an absence. If it is tiring to read, please be assured that it was exhausting to write. The book ends—or begins again—with a user's guide to impairment theory, complete with sample applications and troubleshooting instructions. It comes at the end because so few people start using something by reading the manual, if they ever read it at all.[17]

A book-length impairment phenomenology also requires abandoning recourse to two overused pronouns in humanities writing: *we* and *our*. Impairment phenomenology gives the lie to the idea of an unimpaired phenomenology, that a *humanities we*—a common experience assumed to be shared between author and reader, usually framed in terms of affects and desires—could be the source of coherent descriptions of the world, felt relations to it, texts, aesthetic experiences, and political crises alike. The problem with the *humanities we* is that it is its own bizarre universalism and assumes a fixity of experience. If I use those pronouns, it will be in reference to a specific group of which I am a part, and which you may or may not be a part. There is no unified *we* here because the *me* is only available in multiples. As Édouard Glissant puts it, "It is possible to be one and multiple at the same time; . . . you can be yourself and the other; you can be the same and different." W. E. B. Du Bois, Paul Gilroy, and others have developed the idea of a "double consciousness" that speaks to the coexistence and disjuncture of a physical "fact" that is not actually a fixed fact—skin color—and its experience in consciousness. Consciousness of impairment is not consciousness of race, because their real manifestations do not follow matched paths, even if they often intersect. But the idea of a multiple consciousness is exceptionally generative, even as it can also be painful.[18]

To this end, descriptions of my experience are presented as texts to be interrogated rather than truths rendered in testimony. Like all authors, I will exercise some sleight of hand and will also slip in some experiential claims not in brackets. Most extended descriptions of my experience are already reflections at a distance: blog entries as I was trying to make sense of what was happening to me the first time around, or drawn from field notes and other disorganized but written reflections, or written versions of stories I've repeatedly told friends over the years (which is its own kind of textualization). In contrast, I tend to trust others whose experience I quote. Trusting others is not standard humanist hermeneutics (or social-psychological hermeneutics for that matter)—the goal is usually to uncover what is hidden in discourse. But as an exercise, I thought it useful to invert the standard scholarly approach of trusting one's self over trusting others.[19] This move is partly the product of the standpoint from which I'm producing this text—one need only ask which perspectives are generally treated as trustworthy in halls of academe to see where this goes. But, as someone who has benefited from that system, it seemed worth trying it the other way around. I have, of course, carefully curated the list of others I have chosen to trust (also not a bad thing to do in life). Everything in the narration of experience is a distortion. That is a well-established fact in literature, poetry, music, painting, and even some branches of psychology. What would it mean to treat it as a basis for phenomenology?

A Telegraphic History of This Chapter in Eight Parts

"*How ironic!* You write about sound, and something happened to your voice."[20]

(How come nobody says that to people in art history or film studies who wear glasses?)

"You should *definitely* write about your voice."

I had been writing about my voice constantly since 2009 on my blog, and in correspondence with friends and family. I had talked about it virtually nonstop in social settings.

"Your voice sounds good," say friends on the last day of a cattle call conference—the kind with thousands of academics crammed into a hotel conference center—when my vocal cords were shot and I was the most Lauren Bacall version of myself possible. Yes, it sounds good because *I've trashed it.*

To *write about my own voice*, to make a point about it, that was a different proposition. Do I really want to be on display like that? I am not a private person, and yet I always tell my students not to share their experience in class discussion if they don't want it debated. Or if they do and then decide that they don't, they can retract it. A published book is hard to retract. Also, I am really uncomfortable with the ways that writers in disability studies claim epistemic authority through claims to disability. Sure, I get that as a moment in history, but why can't it be more like feminism or queer theory, something where it's an epistemology informed by standpoint but where standpoint doesn't produce closure? What happens when two people claiming the epistemic authority of experience disagree?

I read Ann Cvetkovich's *Depression,* Lochlann Jain's *Malignant,* Georgina Kleege's *Sight Unseen,* Lauren Berlant's *Cruel Optimism,* and think about it some more.

Shit! To do it right, *I am going to have to debate myself.* That's going to be awkward.

Does this mean I have to resettle my accounts with phenomenology?

Sometime around 2012, I began a file on my hard drive with the name Degrees of Muteness. I knew it was about my voice. Ideas and notes got poured in. I watched as public figures like Adele and Joe Buck acquired paralyzed vocal cords. This was not going to be something I could practice by giving public talks. It just had to be written. How else would I gain enough distance from my own voice?[21]

TURNING THE TABLES ON PHENOMENOLOGY

As Sara Ahmed explains, the foundation of traditional phenomenology is a certain luxury (and apparently a love of question marks).[22] Reading the standard phenomenological texts, I am struck by an aesthetic of immense quietude, and a satisfaction of basic desires and needs. I do not mean actual silence or quiet but the conditions of peace and space for reflection that silence and quietude are meant to signify. Phenomenology's original conceit is that it can identify a universal horizon of experience from the fixed, coherent point of a contemplating subject. Philosophers contemplate tables and hammers; sighted writers bang around rooms with blindfolds and canes or imagine hypothetical blind people; hearing theorists are able to hear far enough to outline horizons.

Consider the table: phenomenologists talk a lot about tables. They contemplate them, sit at them, maybe read or write at them. My phenomenology starts on a table too, except I'm the object on the table being contemplated by everyone and everything else in the room. The traditional phenomenologists seem to be in command. They declare that they have agency, or at least that they can discern when they do and do not have agency. In writing *The Phenomenology of Perception*, Merleau-Ponty repeatedly uses the figure "I can" to describe bodily intention. But his use of "I cannot" is equally revealing because it demonstrates that he believes he has a position to apperceive the limits of his own perception. He is in enough control to delineate the line between "I can" and "I cannot."[23]

I cannot.

I have the material privileges of the philosophers, and better gear, but not the agential luxury that affords the quiet contemplation of a table, a room, or a blindfold, to build my account of perception. A political phenomenology of impairment is therefore phenomenology minus one, minus unity, minus wholeness, minus quietude, minus a stable beginning.[24] It is a phenomenology plus power, plus gear, plus policy—but only because those things were already there in the first place, just not recognized. It must be founded on ambiguities, contradictions, fragments, webs: a subject who is somewhere and someplace, unsure of itself; a subject that oscillates between self-assertion and self-abrogation, between agential audacity and claiming its radical dependency and situatedness. As Susan Wendell has explained, "It seems possible to pay more attention to impairment while supporting a social constructionist analysis of disability, especially if we focus our attention on the phenomenology of impairment, rather than accepting a medical approach to it. Knowing more about how people experience, live with, and think about their own impairments could contribute to an appreciation of disability as a valuable difference from the medical norms of body and mind."[25] At the same time, impairment should not only be thought of as a limit. As Simi Linton writes, "The explication of impairment should in no way be confined to experience that has a negative valence. A phenomenological approach to the study of impairment will yield [a] rich array of descriptions of experience."[26] To be a phenomenology, and not just a recounting of experience, it must also reveal the conditions of possibility—and impossibility—for the experiences it describes. To do so means, as so many authors have argued in recent years, moving beyond the split between a medical and a social model of disability to a conception of biology as having historical dimensions, and history as having biological dimensions. It is possible to contest the compulsory medicalization of people with disabilities, without dismissing the reality of bodily and subjective differences that have physical, physiological, somatic, or perceptual aspects and implications. But how to address experience as it emerges from this dense web of causality?

If phenomenology often begins from an agential subject, the standard rhetorical road in disability studies is also to claim an agential voice against a death-fearing world, one that treats disability as an unwelcome reminder of an imperfect present, an imperfect future, and the certainty of finitude. The agential subject of disability theory emanates from the hard-won affirmative demands for space and recognition made by disability rights movements around the world. Alison Kafer tells the story of another person in her rehabilitation facility who recommended that she consider suicide as an alternative to life in a wheelchair after an accident; she also tells of the teacher who told her she needed to "heal" rather than to study disability academically. Michael Bérubé retells the story of a nurse's commentary on his and Janet Lyon's reaction to their son being born with Down syndrome: "Parents seem to be intellectualizing." Margaret Price asks, "If you are crazy, can you still be of sound mind?" M. Remi Yergeau begins *Authoring Autism* by relating a story about her childhood shit-smearing exploits to mock the ways in which autistic subjects are rendered as unreliable narrators of their own experience. Tobin Siebers writes that disability is the "master trope of human disqualification."[27] All these accounts offer glimpses of an impairment phenomenology. They all question the scene in which people around people with disabilities are revealed as unreliable phenomenologists. As well they should. But there is another radical reading of these foundational scenes. Yes, disability studies and disability activism need their agential subjects. But philosophy's agential subject has yet to reckon with what Siebers calls *the ideology of ability*—the unstated preference for ability over disability—and the necessity of dependency, and therefore has also never really understood the meaning of independence or transcendence despite its lofty claims.[28]

An engagement with the vast literature on disability puts a different spin on an imaginary humanist subject, describing its own perceptions and experience, as I am doing here. In response to her parents' narrative of her own childhood, Yergeau plays with the idea that she is an unreliable narrator of her own experience.[29] But in doing so, she also turns around the critique. The ideology of ability masks the prevalence of disability-like difference throughout the human variety. If people with disabilities are cast as unreliable narrators because of their disabilities, because they do not conform to imagined universals, then stories like Yergeau's show how the most universalist phenomenologists are the most unreliable ones. Every simple description of "I see," "I hear," "I say," "I can," and "I feel" requires its own questioning from a standpoint of a critique of the ideology of ability. How does phenomenology work when its subject begins from impairment rather than from an imagination of itself as agential and whole?

The ground for phenomenology—and perhaps for all descriptions of experience—is more like sand than a floor. If there's a table in the room, it's going to sink and rock a little. Existentialists have long argued that Western philosophers have not fully reckoned with the question of finitude; and when they do, they have often done so in ableist terms. But as Amanda Lagerkvist has shown, even finitude has its own historical conditions.[30] Disability theory advances this way of thinking while correcting its ableist error: many writers have claimed that fear of, and revulsion at, disability is precisely rooted in a subject's refusal to confront its own finitude.

Two concepts from Iris Marion Young's feminist phenomenology are especially relevant here: *ambiguous transcendence*, the inability to fully "transcend" as an embodied woman; and *discontinuous unity*, or the experience of one's body as divided between subject and object.[31] She uses an account of women's embodied experience in order to at once critique the effects of patriarchy and undermine the phenomenological imperative toward transcendence. While contemporary readers might challenge a unitary category of women, Young has identified a condition well known to many minoritized subjects. Experience like this ought to be the foundation rather than the exception for giving an account of experience. This is the founding contradiction of phenomenology: an agential, self-knowing subject that wants to claim enough mastery of its faculties to describe the world around it, even as no subject ever has full access to that world. As with Young's account of gendered embodiment, accounts of impairment also subvert transcendence and render bodies as objects to themselves. Crosby describes her own experience of her big toe after a spinal injury:

> My spinal cord was not severed, so I still have sensation all over my body, and can feel the pressure when someone touches me. When I was first injured, in intensive care at Hartford Hospital, he took hold of my big toe, told me not to look, and instructed me to tell him whether he was bending it up or down. So I did. I reported exactly what I felt. The problem was, I was wrong much of the time. It seemed so odd to me then, and continues to seem so today that I could be so misinformed by a part of my body I'd taken for granted always. My big toe! How could it be telling me the wrong information? Dr. Seetherama was testing my proprioception, and I failed the test. If the "felt sense" of my body is unreliable, how am I to think about the "bodily ego" that psychoanalysis theorizes is necessary to all of us, an image of the body that emerges internally through the differentiation of bodily parts and zones, and externally through relations with others. What becomes of my "self"? This question has haunted me from my earliest efforts to somehow grasp what had happened to me. How can I not be fundamentally different, estranged from myself?[32]

Crosby's story depicts a body divided against itself as subject and object. Crosby's account reflects what Siebers calls a "complex embodiment."[33] She is at once confronting the physical fact of not being able to read the "felt sense" of her body, and the institutional and political condition of disability. Alongside Young—in her account of why cis women (generally) take up less space than cis men as they move through the world—Crosby offers an impaired theory of motility.[34]

AGAIN: BEGIN AGAIN

It is November 2009. I am at a different hospital, in the recovery room. Consciousness rises following an irregular orbit, as it dizzily wanders around the twin poles of lucidity and haze. I can hear; then I can see light, then the edges of bodies again as people and my surroundings fade into view. Dr. Q addresses me by speaking my name. He tells me that they could not find my right recurrent laryngeal nerve. They had to stop my thyroidectomy halfway. I would have a paralyzed vocal cord on my right side.

By the time I had that first surgery, the cancer had been in me for years. It first forced me to notice it while delivering a talk at the University of California, San Diego, in the spring of 2009. One minute, I was standing up, delivering a talk on my MP3 project to an interdisciplinary audience, in a full seminar room. All of a sudden, it was not a normal talk: I was out of breath and the room was spinning, like I was going to faint. I grabbed the podium, kept talking, and powered through. I thought maybe it was just a stuffy, hot room with too many people and not enough oxygen, so I went on to dinner. But back in the hotel that night, I couldn't shake the dizziness or the shortness of breath. I wound up in La Jolla's very fancy hospital, where they did a series of tests. A computed tomography (CT) scan showed a large goiter on my right side, compressing my trachea. They found nothing else. I was cleared to return home and told to see my doctor, or rather doctors. Months of referrals, tests, more referrals, and more tests ensued, but they yielded more questions than answers. My heart was fine; I was diagnosed with asthma. Finally in the early fall, I had a biopsy. I remember it clearly, because as the needle went in, Dr. Q asked me to explain Noam Chomsky to him. I failed, but it was good for a laugh. The test came back positive for papillary thyroid cancer, and that is how I wound up in a recovery room in November 2009.

That light-headedness I felt in San Diego was probably caused by the tumor wrapping itself around my trachea. In the months leading up to the diagnosis, I couldn't quite figure out the bundle of symptoms—light-headedness, sudden dizziness, shortness of breath, weird feelings in my throat. The cancer diagnosis was actually a relief because it offered an explanation for my otherwise unexplainable symptoms: I was being slowly-but-not-so-gently strangled. That is why every time air pressure changed, it had felt like a gerbil was slowly rotating inside my neck.

It is not a surprise that the surgery wasn't easy. As a fat person, I am hard to operate on in the best of circumstances, and the cancer had been in me for a long time, growing undetected as I went around living my life.[35] By the time Dr. Q first encountered it in person, the tumor on my right side had calcified into some kind of hard, jagged form with sharp edges—sharp enough to cut his glove—and was about seven and a half centimeters in size (figure 1.1). It had taken up a large portion of the right lobe of my thyroid gland and wrapped itself around my trachea. The "average" papillary thyroid cancer tumor is about one centimeter in diameter and soft. I wish I had a picture. Dr. Q had to carefully scrape it off, in thin layers, so as not to puncture my windpipe. Then, after removing the tumor, they couldn't find my right recurrent laryngeal nerve. Normally when a nerve like that is cut, the surgeon at least sees the ends flapping around. But there was nothing. Between the scraping and the searching, the surgery stretched on for hours. Eventually, with no sign there ever was a recurrent laryngeal nerve there (other than that I had clearly needed one to talk and swallow for all those years), they closed me up.

Right after Dr. Q gave me the news, I remember trying to talk and my voice betraying me. "Hearing oneself speak is not the inwardness of an inside that is closed in upon itself; it is the irreducible openness in the inside," says Jacques Derrida. Sure enough, my insides had a new kind of openness, and I could feel myself not quite speaking. I don't think that's what Derrida meant, but it illustrates the problem.[36] The interior voice is at least as much imagined as a reflection of external phenomena, and if you have a voice and have heard a recording of yourself speaking, you probably know that the auditory perspective between your ears is like nowhere else. Now, imagine that that perspective is not available as a stable foundation for self-regard but changes from day to day and hour to hour. Imagine you are attuned to sound and have grown up in a culture that hears voices as indices. A shifting interior voice is an index of something very different from a stable interior voice. The vocal cords are essential for talking, swallowing, and breathing. They open and close the aperture of the throat, directing air, liquid, and solid to the right destinations, serving as a kind of gatekeeper of the body. The recurrent laryngeal nerves carry signals to the muscles of the

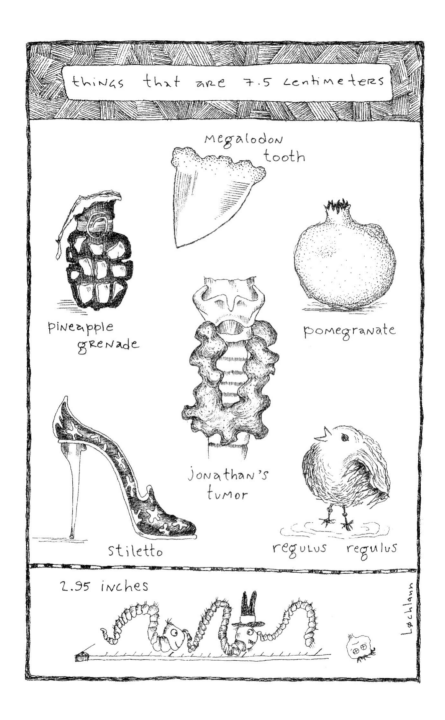

1.1 *Things That Are 7.5 Centimeters*, original illustration by Lochlann Jain.

vocal cords, which shuttle between voluntary and involuntary action. Or sometimes both. One of the strange things about paralysis is trying—and failing—to do something voluntarily that one had previously done involuntarily. It is strange to lose control over something over which I never had conscious control in the first place. Crosby's misplaced toe, my misplaced voice: a body aware of its own faculties but aware of them in a wrong way.

Within a day or two of my first surgery, I was home and recovering. Now there was going to be a lot of talk about what to do next, while I learned how to live with an ever-changing voice. A loss of both recurrent laryngeal nerves would, I was told, mean a total loss of control over my vocal cords, and I would have to have a tracheostomy in order to be able to breathe. Trach or no trach, my voice was already altered, though, just not *visibly* so. In a blog entry from December 12, I describe my voice as sounding "somewhere between Tom Waits and Marge Simpson" and improving somewhat from there. But I could not talk on the phone, and for a while I had to swallow while turning my head to the right to make sure food and liquid did not get into my lungs. The ensuing months led to a lot of people worrying about my voice.

JANUARY 5, 2010

At least once a day when I'm out or get a phone call, someone asks what is wrong with my voice. So I tell them that I've got a paralyzed vocal cord from thyroid cancer. I don't know who said that coming out is a constant, ongoing process, but again I feel that there is some kind of parallel between what disability studies scholars sometimes call normalism [2019 edit; ableism is actually the preferred term] (you can guess what that means) and heterosexism. In both cases, you're assumed to belong to a dominant category until suddenly, you do not. And when you do not, you must explain yourself.

Voices are always indices: caused by interiors exerting effects on themselves and in concert with their environments, they are heard as signs. For those asking, my voice was a sign of an uncertain future, or perhaps an uncertain future that had already arrived. Here was an audible difference immediately converted into a disability—the word *wrong* in the question "What's wrong with your voice?" declares as much. As Kafer explains, the dream of a future without disability is a dream of a future without the ills of the present, a fantasy world where the value of people with disabilities is disavowed, and where disability is reduced from a political category—that can be contested, that has a history—to a simple physical or biological fact.[37] My vocal disability did contain a fact that my voice worked differently than it had, and that it was no longer in harmony with a world constructed for a certain kind of voice, whether that world featured strangers listening to me or automated phone menus.

In their critique of text-to-speech technologies, Graham Pullin and Andrew Cook write about tone of voice being fundamental for meaning: "A lack of variation in tone of voice can never be neutral. A lack of expressiveness can itself send out a false message that the person is emotionally impaired as well as speech-impaired, or perhaps socially unsophisticated."[38] By expressiveness here, they are referring to controlled variation, where unexpected timbres can also signify a subject out of control or otherwise impaired to an uninitiated auditor. Ideas of expressiveness have probably manifested in all the arts, but in designing assistive technologies for speaking, expressiveness is directly related to ideas of an interior, intending subject that manifests itself through the speaking voice. Think of all the moving parts in that scenario: a subject whose body cannot match its will; but also auditors struggling to align themselves with whatever techniques the speaker is using. Everyone is trying; nobody is quite succeeding.

Disability Studies 101: Saturday Night Practicum

JANUARY 11, 2010

This is a post about some issues I encountered at someone else's birthday party, which makes it inherently pathetic and self-centered. But then, this *is* a blog, so I get to be pathetic and self-centered once in a while, right? I apologize up front. For the record, it *was* a fun party and any non-fun issues are strictly my own and not the responsibility of my hosts or friends. I was totally glad I went.

So, on to the story.

As I have mentioned here, my voice has not been the same since the surgery. Assuming that there isn't further damage in the next surgery—if there is a next surgery (or from the cancer itself)—I will get back about 70–80% of what I have. I've been going to an excellent speech therapist (it's like singing lessons) and every few weeks there is some improvement.

But for all that, I am functionally disabled in the meantime. I used to have much more vocal power than other people. Now I have considerably less, and what is projected is harder to hear. That said, I am not the kind of person who wants to sit at home and be depressed about a disability or being in the middle of treatment. If I feel good on a given day, I should do something. There's a Quebec saying that is something to the effect of "you have to live your life." And so I am trying to figure out how to do that.

Since the surgery, I hadn't been out to anything more than a dinner party, and even dining out has been kind of fraught because even moderate restaurant noise makes it difficult for my voice to be heard. It is easily masked. Carrie and I dined recently at Bombay Mahal and while she could hardly hear anything I said, I had an entertaining time watching her try to eat the "extra spicy" dosa she'd ordered, so that sort of made up for it. (The waiter said, "Have you had our food before?" She answered, "Yes, but I still want it extra hot.")

Anyway, Saturday night was a party celebrating two of my friends turning 40 so I thought it would be a good time to give this whole outside world thing another try. Sooner or later I have to, so if not now, when? The party was held at a bar, starting at 8:30 and then migrating upstairs two hours later for dancing. I figured I can at least dance if I can't talk, right? And I was clever—or so I thought. This whole being disabled thing means I've got to experiment and figure out something that works for me in the big bad normalist [ableist] world. So I took some index cards and a Sharpie, and came up with a series of stock phrases that I could flash at people, such as:

"Hi, how's it going?"
"My voice is messed up so I made these cards."
"Cancer sucks. I feel fine. Thanks for asking."
"I don't know yet. I'll know more Monday or Tuesday."
"Tell me how YOU'RE doing."
"Yes, please. Water."
"Great party!"
"Happy 40th birthday!"
"Tell me more."
"That's awesome/I agree/I'm happy for you." (select whichever one is appropriate)
"That sucks/I disagree/That's too bad." (select whichever one is appropriate)

"If you could hear me, I would have a clever 1-liner right now."

and so on. I brought my Sharpie and some more blank cards to improvise on the spot.

My hope was that with a little prompting, other people would talk and I would listen, aided by the cards. But two things happened.

First, people were self-conscious about asking me stuff. So I tried to talk. Today I was incredibly hoarse as a result. I should know better. They were trying to be nice. And I *do* like to talk, so the temptation is great.

Second, it turns out I wasn't the only disabled person at the table. In more than a few cases, each time a card came out, friends had to reach for their reading glasses in order to be able to see them. Foiled! Some disabilities, like farsightedness, are "normal" but I obviously didn't even consider them, since they are not my own. Others, like my voice, are "abnormal" and therefore marked. Though marked disabilities are equally unconsidered by those unaffected—I always hated phone menus that require you to speak; now they do not even recognize my voice as a voice.

As the disability studies motto goes, "Someday, you will join us." That is what is so difficult in thinking about anything like systematic accommodation. Bodies fall apart or are "absent" in different ways, and accommodations may themselves introduce new issues into play.

I still plan to get some kind of portable voice amplifier (or, more likely, buying whatever is out there as a template for something more advanced that I help design). But first we have to have some decisions about my course of treatment. I don't want to drop a few hundred bucks on something I won't be able to use.

I am happy to report that I can still dance. If by dancing we mean "semi-rhythmic movements on a dance floor." I was never very good at the whole "particular-body-part-in-a-particular-place-at-particular-time" thing.

Postscript: I learned that film critic Roger Ebert is a thyroid cancer survivor, though he's had a particularly rough go of it. He's written a few things about it, but they're pretty sobering, since he no longer eats or speaks with his own voice.[39]

One common trope of acquiring a disability is that you wake up in a different body. But the process of negotiating that body is more like a process of awakening than one that happens in a particular instant. This entry is a textbook case of the ideology of ability in action. My friends and I fetishize and exclude disabilities and impairments from discourse even though they are right in front of us (or inside us); we treat disability as private and individualized matter. My entry mobilizes the idea that loss of ability translates into loss of sociability; the idea that to focus on disability is self-centered; and that "nondisabled people have the right to choose when to be able-bodied. Disabled people must try to be as able-bodied as possible all the time."[40] I even end the blog entry with a tale of impairment that I don't want to have. Though it remains funny to me, I would write the story differently today. But to do so would be less useful for my argument. An anecdote in a blog entry shows that there is no pure, ideal, or perfect position from which to negotiate disability and impairment. One must always start somewhere in the imperfect world.

DEFINING IMPAIRMENT

What counts as disability, or impairment, or normal? Glasses have a history as a marked prosthetic, socially diminishing the wearer.[41] This is why, for instance, the British National Health service issued pink glasses for women in the early 1960s: they were supposed to be "skin" colored and not call attention to themselves (nor, apparently, to the racial presuppositions behind assuming that pink would blend into the color of "skin").[42] Today, at least in my social milieu, eyewear is a kind of fashion accessory, and I wear glasses that frequently draw compliments and comments—though reading glasses appear to inspire ambivalence for others (and I know people in other social milieus who still feel some stigma around any kind of glasses). The borderline status of mild visual impairment—and the historical and emotional weight it still carries for some people—illustrates how difficult it is to draw a line around impairment, especially against disability, and how the politics normally ascribed to disability seep out into the borderlands marked by ambiguous, or even mild, impairment.

I have been shuttling between these two words—*disability* and *impairment*—because they are difficult to parse, and because in the stories I am quoting, my own status is ambiguous to me (it is no longer). But what is the difference between impairment and disability, and what is the meaning of that difference? The easy first attempt at an answer would be that *impairment* is the physical reality of *disability*, which is a social construct. This answer treats impairment as a purely material substrate for disability, which is then considered as a hybrid discursive and material phenomenon. But other theories of the subject have already been around this block: sex and gender, skin color and race, and on and on.[43] The putatively material term—sex, skin—that is supposed to be a substrate of the other turns out not to be. Impairment and disability are no different: they are historical, contested categories that fall in on themselves, inextricably linked to bodily or intellectual differences, or experiences like pain and fatigue, but always more than that as well. Much work has been done to explore the political ramifications of disability as a variable, contested, and political mode of classification, as in Wendell's classic question: How far does one need to be able to walk to be considered able-bodied?[44] The answer varies contextually and environmentally. Communities that have grown up around autism or Deafness struggle with the label, often rejecting it. Visible bodily differences, for instance the absence of a nose, often bring social stigma that operates like disability even though they do not otherwise reduce a subject's abilities in most ways. Racial differences have at different times been coded as disabilities as well, but the rejection of disability as the basis for racial advancement itself has a complex and vexed political history. Conversely, legal pushback against corporate responsibility for environmentally caused illnesses, including cancer, results in new constructs like "fear of cancer" as legal placeholders for actually debilitating or deadly conditions.[45] Disability is a notably slippery category, central to identity construction and political organizing but difficult to pin down definitionally. In chapter 4, I have much more to say about the construction of norms, following the work of Georges Canguilhem, who argues that the norm comes after its infraction.[46] For now, it is enough to consider that norms are those things against which impairments and disabilities are defined.

In discussions where impairment is rendered as the substrate of a disability, it might be understood simply as the diminishment of a faculty, as in the UN's language from the 2006 "Convention on the Rights of Persons with Disabilities and Optional Protocol": "Persons with disabilities include those who have long-term physical, mental, intellectual or sensory impairments which in interaction with various barriers may hinder their full and effective participation in society on an equal basis with others."[47] But a faculty is defined as a kind of ability or agency—and therefore etymology gives us nothing but a recursive, self-referential loop. According to the entry in the *Oxford English Dictionary*, the term *faculty* has a long and varied history in the English language related to power, agency, and function: the power to do something or a virtue; an ability or branch of art and science (including the people who populate a university); conferred power, authority, or privilege.[48] A faculty is a fundamental capacity of a subject, whether that subject is a human subject or a body of knowledge. If impairment is simply a diminished faculty, then faculty sounds an awful lot like "ability" and impairment sounds an awful lot like "disability," down to the use of "ability" in the definition. The ability to affect the world is conflated with virtue or goodness; it is connected with prestige, and then elevated into the abstraction of systematized knowledge. Impairment is no more brute fact of the body than disability, which is to say that it both is and is not.[49]

The recent history of impairment is considerably more enlightening than its etymology. As Mara Mills has shown, early twentieth-century U.S. medicine and engineering took up the English-language term *impairment* as a preferred term to *defect*. As Mills demonstrates, impairment was tied both to a rehabilitation model of disability—could a person work?—and to the possibility of repair, of a person or a system. *Impair* may be an individualizing term, since it focuses on the machinic capacities of an individual— impaired movement, speech, hearing, cognition—but it is also subindividual, focusing on particular faculties in relation to particular tasks rather than the whole being. The concept of impairment doesn't even have to refer to a person. Mills shows that "transmission impairments" were formalized in communication engineering around the same time as medical impairments, as engineering problems in communication systems, not all of which were ever meant to be overcome. Interestingly, while the ideology of ability would cast impairment as something to be either overlooked or overcome, the engineering discourse highlighted by Mills assumes the inevitability of transmission impairments, some of which might be repaired, but not all. Perfect communication might have been an imagined ideal for engineers or philosophers, but actual engineering practice assumes every system will have some kind of impairment, if for no other reason than that perfection is simply too expensive.[50]

A theory of impairment built around a pragmatic, economistic, or existential acceptance of limits is a very different frame from the recent history of the concept in disability theory. As many writers in the field have noted, the social model of disability was important for overcoming the idea of disability as a defect inherent in an individual, but it had a difficult time dealing with pain, fatigue, and chronic illness, where subjects are in some sense divided against themselves, where a subject's lived experience of the body prevents them from embracing a constructivist account of its disability story, or simply where access to care requires strategic medicalization. The irony of the social model of disability is thus that in its critique of disability as something in need of repair or overcoming, *impairment* came to work semantically more like *defect*, even if disability activists and theorists would never use that term, and even if ultimately the politics of disability aimed for a utopic horizon where the human variety would not be spread out on a grid of abilities and disabilities.[51]

In life, impairment works in a shady place between function and non-function. Nowhere is this clearer than in the theory and practice of communication: a mobile phone or a videoconference connection is glitchy; a spam filter lets through some spam, or filters out correspondence the recipient desires; radio waves come with static and noise; an online video never stops buffering; books and photos age and change color; the meaning you take from these written words never perfectly lines up with my authorial intent; what you heard or read on my lips is not what I said.[52] Sometimes those distortions are even fundamental to how things mean: electrified and recorded music is full of harmonic distortions—textbook transmission impairments—that come to signify the depths of meaning and that countless digital devices have sought to re-create or simulate. When digital video came along, filmmakers sought ways to reproduce the noise on the screen that accompanied analog film stock. Digital synthesizers sometimes include a parameter with a name like "slop" to reproduce the tuning variances of analog oscillators.[53] In speech, accents signify all sort of things about the subjects who speak with them (and every speaker has an accent to someone else).[54] Impairment may be a blockage, a failure, a defect, but it is also a supplement, rich with texture and potential meaning. If impairment is at the center of communication, then it is already at the center of experience.

Nothing works exactly like it is supposed to—machines, media, models, conversations—and least of all, people. If almost everyone and everything has some degree of impairment (though not in the same way), then impairment is a quality of experience. Impairment is always already there. Drawing a sharp line between *impaired* and *not impaired* would then obscure the ways in which one impairment or another conditions almost every human action, reaction, and relation.[55] But of course these lines are drawn and lived—the lines *must* be drawn or the term has no meaning at all. A phenomenology of impairment is also a phenomenology of policy.

Institutions define impairment and disability all the time—who requires accommodation and who does not; who is judged "able to work" and who is not; what even qualifies as work; who needs extra time on a test; whose impairments even matter and under what conditions; what differences must be accounted for in the design of a building, website, or broadcast system; how and by whom: "The very fact that so much energy is funneled into defining disability and impairment suggests the fundamental instability of the terms."[56] Policy wades into practical philosophy—it has to operationalize a classificatory schema even if it claims to bracket ontological debates—and policy segments impairment and disability so that they can be commensurated with money one way or another.

There is a long history of attempts to quantify and make sense of disability and impairment in some aggregate form for the purposes of policy making. As Sarah Rose writes of disability policy in the early twentieth-century United States, what might be considered a disability in one context might be considered within the realm of normal in another: "Early twentieth-century Pittsburgh steel mills were so dangerous, for example, that missing a finger was considered normal and did not prevent laborers from finding employment."[57] Part of the drive to quantify disability came from policy makers' varied motivations: they at once sought to create a common basis to comprehend the sheer variety of things that come under the sign of impairment or disability, and to deal with the ways they intersected with race, class, gender, age—and, in the United States, occupation.[58] In fact, it could be said that disability was part of the drive of modern states to quantify: from Lambert Adolphe Jacques Quetelet's scientific racism and ableism, to emerging bureaucracies' use of statistical aggregation of their self-constitutions, to nineteenth-century public health discourse as a medium for state anxieties about and interventions in its populations.[59] Today, this legacy lives on in institutions like the Educational Testing Service, which began as a "Census of Abilities" and still produces tests that sort out American children ostensibly according to ability, despite their tests' cultural biases being well documented. Quantification of disability has become an issue in global attempts at policy making as well. Measures like the Global Burden of Disease (GBD) and Disability-Adjusted Life-Year (DALY) are used in health policy, both as a tool for allocating World Health Organization (WHO) funds and by epidemiologists analyzing WHO policy.[60]

The idea of a pristine subject—body or mind—that is then impaired or disabled is of course a raced, classed, historical, and geographic construct as well. Before its twentieth-century bureaucratic existence in liberal democratic states, disability was part and parcel of the disqualification of women, racialized or Indigenous people, and people who did not conform to gender or sexual norms. But the nondisabled, able-bodied, nonimpaired, or otherwise "whole" subject against which these differences were compared was also always a fantasy. As an alternative to disability and its liberal institutional history, Julie Livingston has posed the concept of *debility*, which "illuminates how fundamental social, moral, and biological dynamics are grounded in experience as people struggle to marshal care and rework meanings and lives within and around bodies that are somehow impaired or different. The relationships between bodies and persons, history and meaning-making are highlighted and transformed in the context of debility."[61] Based on her fieldwork in Botswana, Livingston's use of *debility* includes both impairment and disability, but does not exhaust either. It foregrounds the networks of familial and community care as well as fraught relationships with medical institutions and practices, and it is inextricably tied to what she calls the "moral imagination": "stark reminders of the physical dangers of moral uncertainty and reaffirming the long-recognized fact that the human body does not exist as somehow separate or abstracted from the complex lives of persons."[62] In other words, for the Tswana people with whom Livingston worked, *debility* was inseparable from the experiences and constructions of subjects in time and space: the history of colonialism and postcolonialism in Botswana; increased independence for young women following political independence for the country; the rise of industrial capitalism, which affected both work opportunities and the practice of biomedicine; and of course the experience of work and embodiment itself.

One major difference between debility and the conception of impairment advanced by Mills, and as I describe it in my experience, is that the body-machine analogy—between human impairments and system impairments—is distinctive to a Western, bourgeois context, as explained by Livingston: "Despite the fact that some Batswana have begun to invoke mechanistic imagery when describing the human body, they by no means liken impaired bodies to broken machines, nor do they envision a world in which technological fixes will obviate the need for grappling with difference through benign sentiment and healthy social relationships."[63] In the Tswana context, the concept of communication impairments wouldn't work at all as a foundation for thinking about impairment and disability. For Livingston, *impairment* as well as *debility* facilitate thinking across disability, illness, and aging: "Reduced mobility and physical strength, as well as blindness and a range of other infirmities, have long marked understandings of senescence. These were not regarded as disability: indeed, they were 'normal' and in some cases even expected impairments."[64] I will take up the idea of "normal and expected" impairments, specifically of hearing and fatigue, in chapters 4 and 5.

But even my *unexpected* vocal impairment raises this issue of classification between impairment, illness, and disability, especially the uneasy relationship between disability and chronic illness: "Recognition of impairment is crucial to the inclusion of people with chronic illnesses in disability politics. Chronic illness frequently involves pain, fatigue, dizziness, nausea, weakness, depression, and/or other impairments that are hard to ignore."[65] Strictly speaking, my vocal cord paralysis is the result of cancer. Because modern medicine has developed ways to deal with papillary thyroid cancer, I exist in an ambiguous space. The word *cancer* is a conversation stopper. But even with the metastases in my lungs (technically stage IV as of this writing, though that is being actively debated in the medical literature), I experience myself as chronically ill, not in imminent danger, because of my access to the Canadian medical system, private insurance, and the various privileges that follow me into the hospital.[66] Diane Price Herndl writes that "most people in the disability community do not want to be considered ill, and most people who are ill don't want to be considered disabled"; this mutual resistance is partially about the intersecting politics of stigma and classification, and the differential institutional histories of *impaired*, *ill*, and *disabled*.[67]

The problem of chronic illness as (or and) disability is also about the different work of metaphors—especially in its punctual (nonchronic) form, a concept of illness as "globally incapacitating" would be more acceptable to activists than a concept of a disability being globally incapacitating.[68] I move between these terms in my daily life: reassuring friends that I am chronically ill when telling them about new cancer treatments (as I just did for you, dear reader, in the previous paragraph), claiming the right to disability accommodation for my vocal cord impairment when teaching or giving talks, and passing for nondisabled (but fat) in many public spaces (because it would be too much work to come out in each and every situation).[69] Chronic illness fits neither category: it is illness that will not kill me, but from which I will not recover.[70] The semantic ambiguity among impairment, disability, and illness remains a constitutive feature of all three categories. They move through the same space and bump into one another, sometimes overlapping, sometimes repelling. All three are conditioned by a divergence from medical or social norms. All three are conditioned by an ideology of ability and a preference for ability and health. Indeed, phenomenologists of illness have even defined it in terms of "a loss of wholeness," a condition of "bodily doubt."[71] These preferences may be political and ideological, but they are also orientational: they are felt, lived, and negotiated.

The *loss-of-wholeness* thesis runs right up against another category problem: impairments that are acquired versus those that are not. The loss-of-wholeness thesis is not even really adequate to my experience of impairment as more of a change in orientation than a loss per se—it's not just about blockages and where I don't go, but where I now want to go and what I want to do. The experience of impairment and its relationship to self and to orientation can be very different depending on whether a person knew themselves differently before. I can tell you a whole lot about my life before acquiring a vocal impairment. My partner, Carrie (who will repeatedly appear in this book as a character), was diagnosed with type 1 diabetes at twenty months of age and has never known anything else. We experience our impairments differently in that she did not experience its acquisition—or, rather, her body certainly did, but the subject Carrie did not. I experienced a moment of acquisition.

Impairment is only a loss or lack if it is experienced that way. As Geyla Frank writes in her cultural biography of Diane DeVries, a woman born without arms and legs: "The clinical term *congenital amputee* has been applied to Diane. But to call up an image of Diane in the company of people who have had an arm or leg cut off leaves something to be desired. Her arms and legs can only be postulated. They exist in a state of potential as much as a state of loss."[72] In other ways, my experience is the same as Carrie's or Diane's: our bodies don't work like bodies are supposed to work, and none of us fit the cultural script for the unified, continuous, whole subject. But our relations to something like phenomenological integration or wholeness may be different: I am more likely to experience my impairment as a challenge to integration; had I been born with a paralyzed vocal cord, maybe it would be different. But this is not just a question of experience: some impairments are minoritized, some are dismissed, some are disbelieved, others are attributed when they are not present. Impairment phenomenology is political phenomenology because impairment is a term that always has multiple references that exist in relation to one another. Something cannot be impaired unless something else is not impaired. The meaning of that difference may be something left to an individual to resolve, but more often, like all meanings, it is situationally variable and a place for contestation.

For some disability writers and activists, and for some culturally Deaf people who may entirely reject the labels of impairment and disability, an experience of wholeness and personal integration is essential to claiming identity. On an operative level, a sense of personal integration is also essential to all sorts of everyday actions. In this text, I am trying to thread the needle of holding on to that possibility, while producing a theoretical account that does not demand of impaired subjects that they position themselves in respect to (or aspire to being) an idealized, whole, integrated, self-consistent person. It's a very different thing if you come to it on your own than if others are making the demand that you do it. Make yourself a whole person if you want to; just don't demand that others do it to themselves.

SPEECH REQUIRES CLOSURE

Even though I keep insisting that the story of my voice is a story about orientation, that doesn't mean the fear of loss never appears. In December 2009 and January 2010, we were at a crossroads in my treatment. I'd lost the use of one vocal cord. I didn't want to lose another. As Tom Shakespeare has written, "Those of us born with our disabilities are used to our form of life, and we rarely bother worrying about it—we cannot imagine any other way of being. But ask any disabled person how they would feel about losing further abilities, and most would be less sanguine, I think."[73] At first, we thought I could perhaps go straight into radioactive iodine therapy, which works by starving the body of iodine, then adding radioactive iodine, which the thyroid cancer cells soak up. If this treatment sounds medieval, that's because it is: the only known cause of thyroid cancer is exposure to radioactivity. The poison is the cure! Enter the pharmakon! Or don't: the problem with that option turned out to be that a dose high enough to kill the tumor would also kill me. A second surgery was scheduled for February 12. The goal was to save the nerve, but not at the cost of leaving cancer in my body. To do that, the doctors would attach my nerve to a device that electrified it, sort of like the old buzzer-and-tweezers game Operation. If they got too close to the nerve, an alarm would sound. In addition to Dr. Q, my neck surgeon, a thoracic surgeon came on board. But my nerve could still go: if it was wrapped in cancer, then it could not be saved.[74]

We all knew a possible outcome of the surgery was losing the nerve, or that it could go into spasm temporarily. It was the latter experience with which this chapter began. Unable to breathe on my own, I was intubated, put into the recovery room for the weekend (the ICU was full), and kept in a state of sedation so I did not instinctively pull the tube out. Since I was still unable to breathe on the following Monday, they installed a temporary tracheostomy, and by Tuesday I was in my own hospital room.[75] By the following Sunday, I could not speak for myself, but I could write (the following post has been edited for usefulness).

FEBRUARY 21, 2010

Didn't Foucault say something about hospitals and jails?

Anyway, I have been gradually coming back to personhood over the past few days. 2 days in pants. 24 hours narcotic free now, though the trade-off is, well, pain. My neck feels like it has been re-arranged. Because of course it has. There's a new hole in my head. It's hard to describe the "new tracheostomy feeling" but I can offer an exercise that probably works for any major body modification. Imagine a range of things that you would find it disturbing for others to do to your neck. Now imagine that you've become comfortable with half of them. Congrats, you have accepted your new trache.

I still can't talk at all. In my head, it's all logorrhea.[76]

To say that I could only communicate by writing is to assume that everybody could read. By this time in the story, your protagonist should theoretically have known better. If writing to speak didn't even work on my overeducated social scene, why would it work on hospital staff who might have very different histories with and relationships to writing, and who occupied very different class positions? In a way, it's miraculous—and a testament to the commitment of most of the nurses and orderlies—that in a large part it worked and I was able to communicate with the people around me (better, in fact, than at that fortieth birthday party). It also probably helped that Carrie went on a campaign of bribery, bringing in baked goods from the Portuguese bakery around the corner from our apartment a couple of times a week. But one orderly in particular who seemed not to like me at all may well have formed that attitude *because* I kept writing stuff to him. It's entirely possible he couldn't read whatever I was writing him, which added frustration to our interactions for both of us. Years later, I have taken his side in our conflict: I was stoned out of my mind on Dilaudid for the first few days of interactions with him—and everyone else in the ostomy ward. Who the hell knows what I wrote and what it meant?[77]

Two days later, I would have my trach tube replaced with a smaller one, which meant that I could talk and swallow. When the possibility of a trach was first presented to me, it was explained as a total loss of voice. But as I learned firsthand, having a trach can mean many things, from no speech at all, to speech that is altered in one of many ways. Trach voices are highly variable from person to person, depending on the condition of their throats and chests. Some are hoarse sounding, some are whispers, some produce robotic, metallic, or inharmonic timbres because of the particular prosthesis they use. As with accents, the visible and audible differences may well combine in the hearer: just as a sighted auditor might see brown skin and "hear" accented English where there is none, a trach voice might collapse into the sight of a trach on a body for an auditor.[78]

Every person who has spent time as an inpatient probably has their story of hospital dehydration, but what I remember most profoundly from the smaller trach was not the recovery of speech but the discovery that I could swallow little bits of water.[79] Sometime around 2 a.m. the night before I was to be tested to see if I could swallow well enough to eat or drink, I learned that I could swallow, and I proceeded to fill a tiny cup with water over and over again, sipping and sipping until I was too exhausted to continue. It also allowed enough air through my throat for speech. I had spoken a "1 2 3 4" under sedation on February 12 or 15, but on the twenty-third, I was able to cover the hole in my trach and talk. That was *also* a euphoric feeling, and I talked myself hoarse in short order. About what, I do not recall; logorrhea demanded its satisfaction. With the smaller tube, I had one of those hoarse trach voices. It sounded like "me" in my head, but after a lot of yelling in a smoky bar.

Another two days later, I was "taped" for twenty-four hours to see if I could handle a closed trach. The challenge turned out not to be breathing in or talking but exhaling, which simply had to do with the bulk of the tube. The next day, my trach was removed, and the hole was imperfectly sealed. I wrote, "It feels good to be back 'in' my nose and mouth."[80] I have lost the memory of that particular feeling, but today I would read it as a reflection on breath more than anything else. That is the dynamic I have been playing throughout this chapter: every time I give an account of experience, I also give an account of how it is not fully available to me.

The project of interpretation often relies on *ethos*, on the production of the interpretant as a vessel through which the reader can access the world. This is one of the most important, and one of the most difficult, insights that disability theory offers to hermeneutics more generally. But it is a description of consciousness that few scholars in the humanities—never mind philosophy, psychology, or cognitive science—would recognize as plausible if applied to any party other than the authorial voice in a scholarly text. Few serious scholars believe that a subject's discourse simply reflects a real condition or an unmediated experience—not ethnographers, not lawyers, not psychologists, not philologists, not literary critics, not historians. Yet academic texts and criticism perform all the time as if this were the case for them, even if for nobody else. Even writing in disability studies often relies on the power of testimony as a mode of access to reality. But to subject disability theory to disability theory's critique of experience is hard, and it's possible that my inaccessible-to-myself-self constructed in this chapter is more annoying than satisfying. So be it! This is the challenge: to include the testimony of disability while subjecting the very category of testimony to a critique. While there is a rich literature on the politics of testimony, it is still rare to critique the term from the standpoint of impairment or disability. This chapter has been one attempt; there should be more.

02

Meet the Dork-o-Phone

This is a dork-o-phone (figures 2.1–2.4). My dork-o-phone is essentially a transistor radio with no radio, attached to a small wearable microphone, that lives inside a vinyl pouch (with fake-leather cowskin embossing) that can be hung around my neck. Its real name is the Spokeman Personal Voice Amplifier. Other, similar devices can be clipped to a belt, or are built into belts themselves, or can be laid out on a table. I own two Spokemans (Spokesmen? No: two dork-o-phones!), each of which cost about US$300 total, though it seems the prices have dropped since I purchased them in 2012. I am not sure why it costs that much given what transistor radios go for these days. It could be an artifact of how medical insurance works in the United States, but it could also be a question of the economy of scale (there is not a huge user base) combined with the smallness and frankly impressive personal service of the company from whom I bought it. I have had both my units repaired more than once. They are clearly not designed for the abuse I inflict on them, though at the same time I have developed a respect for their durability and ruggedness.

Spokeman is either a misuse of "spokesman" or more likely an unsuccessful riff on "Walkman," which, it must be noted, was not named the

2.1 (*overleaf*) Dork-o-phone top view, with power, LED, and mic input. Photo by Carrie Rentschler.

2.2 Dork-o-phone rear view, with charging instructions. Photo by Carrie Rentschler.

2.3 Dork-o-phone rear interior, showing wear, corrosion from aged rechargeable batteries, and a hidden gain switch. Close to half the interior space is taken up with rechargeable AAA batteries; a "power" switch sets the gain for the microphone. Higher gain is louder but is more prone to feedback. Photo by Carrie Rentschler.

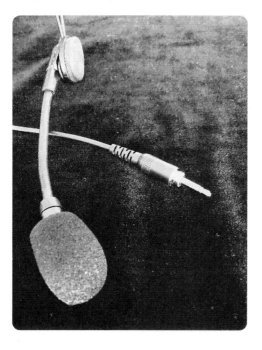

2.4 Dork-o-phone microphone in windscreen, 3.5 millimeters mono plug. Photo by Carrie Rentschler.

"ListenMan" or "listen, man"—probably for good reason.[1] Rather than signifying the mastery of speech or the coolness of mobile music, the name *Spokeman* represents the social oddity of personal voice amplification itself. Of course, voices are amplified all the time. Public address (PA) systems, microphones, and speakers are common objects all over the world, and in many places it is a daily experience to be serenaded by a host of voices meant to refer to distant bodies. Contemporary audio culture in most of the world is *speaker culture*. Here *speaker* refers to the technical devices, not the person, but the ambiguity is central to the story of this chapter: speakers (devices) are everywhere, but a speaker (person) is not supposed to *need* a speaker (device) on their body.[2] Even though my dork-o-phone is technically *the same thing* as a PA system, just smaller, it is socially set apart. Its oddity is socially produced. As design object, one might expect it to fall under the category of audio wearables: MP3 players, earbuds, smartphones, and now even boom boxes, thanks to lighter batteries, computer-assisted cabinet design, and different elements in the magnets. But categorically, it falls on the side of artificial limbs, insulin pumps, and crutches. If they have to be experienced as a prosthetic, I wish dork-o-phones were more like eyeglasses, once a stigmatizing object and now a fashion accessory. Instead, they share a set of technical and cultural problems with hearing aids and cochlear implants. Hearing aids introduced issues of portability and miniaturization in microelectronics, while generations of users have had to negotiate the relationship among social appearance, stigma, and their needs and desires for the technology.[3]

The Spokeman is one example in a genre of voice amplifiers, a genre without a shared name or a defining brand but whose names all point to a weird gray area of voice and techne that it occupies: speech amplifier, voice amplifier, personal public address system, personal voice amplifier; Chattervox, Amplivox, Sound Pocket, Zavox, Zoweetek, VoiceBuddy, SoundBuddy, Zygo. They are marketed to people like me, with vocal impairments, but a quick internet search will also see them depicted in pictures of happy businesspeople, teachers, exercise instructors, and tour guides. Disability is not, in fact, a marketing point. Here is the SoundBuddy pitch:

> The Perfect solution for: Teachers—Presenters—Tour Guides—Out Doors—In Doors—Music—Story Telling—Theaters—Group Gatherings—Karaoke
>
> In fact if you need to amplify your voice . . . The SoundBuddy is your new Best Friend and Soul Mate.[4]

The irony is that the company selling it actually is an assistive technology company, but it also describes its products as "workplace ergonomics." This repeats a recurring thread in the history of disability, where disability activists agitate for a particular alteration to the technological world, which, once mainstreamed, is no longer associated with disability. Activists in wheelchairs fought for curb cuts, but today they are also useful to people moving wheeled suitcases, strollers, furniture on dollies, groceries in wheeled baskets, double basses on wheeled endpins, and anyone else with wheels to push on and off a sidewalk. The same story could be told about closed captioning, which took years of Deaf activism to realize for broadcast and is now a staple of fitness clubs, airport waiting rooms, and a handy tool for language learners. Graham Pullin argues that design should aim to make objects for purpose rather than for kinds of people. This absolutely makes sense in the case of the dork-o-phone but also shows how the marginalization of disability (or, rather, the upholding of disability stigma that leads to its exscription from public life) can be an unintentional side effect of the mainstreaming of an assistive technology. In fact, disability is nowhere to be found in the ads for the other speech amplifier technologies. In my travels through dork-o-phonedom, I have only found direct mention of vocal disability in catalogs, like that of Luminaud, the company from which I bought mine.[5]

> Helpful for people with soft voices whatever the reason—Parkinson's, ALS, MS, PSP, laryngectomy, vocal nodules, partially paralyzed vocal cords, limited breath support, etc. With the Spokeman you can be heard more easily whether talking to one person or a small group—up to twenty-five depending on surrounding noise level. Useful in the car, bus or train, at family gatherings, parties or meetings, in a restaurant, in a small class or seminar, etc. Ideal when talking to someone with a hearing loss.[6]

Note here the classic assistive technology language: yes, it can amplify your voice, but here is a list of the *kinds of* people who might need voice amplification. Since all technologies are "assistive" in one way or another, the *assistive technology* context is defined in terms of its users. Specifically, the technology is defined as assistive because its users are defined as *people who need assistance*. Whether marketing talk is oriented toward or away from disability, the connection between disability and technology is a fraught and contradictory corner of discourse.[7]

It is one thing to consider the dork-o-phone as a device in itself and another thing to consider it on my body, or anyone else's. Out in the world, the thing that marks me most as a person with a disability is my attempt to compensate for it in institutional contexts.[8] In this way, I am not very different from others with physical disabilities and, increasingly, certain mental or intellectual disabilities. My attempts to influence my environment through asking others for help—for instance, in the rider I provide for my talks or in my requests for a stool on which to remain seated while lecturing in a class—mark me as different. They force me to declare that difference in relation to environments that are putatively designed for "everyone" who would have cause to use them, though in fact they enact many interlocking assumptions about what a normal body or person is and can do. If you are indoors, consider the room in which you are reading or listening to this text: What assumptions about height, scent, light and dark, comfort and discomfort are built into your space? When a space makes demands and people have to make demands back, it marks a person as different, irrespective of their self-concept. I can imagine myself as impaired, as disabled, or as nondisabled, and the prosthesis will do its semiotic work on my body. In terms of the perceptions of others, G. W. F. Hegel and his followers explain that identification is not just an individual choice: the politics and phenomenology of disability have an irreducible relationship to the politics of recognition. And so, every time I ask for accommodation, or provide it myself, I call my voice—and "the" voice—into question.

The simple choice of where to position a speaker on the body raises the question of under what conditions a person has a voice to speak with, and from where it truly comes. The dork-o-phone's speaker cannot be positioned over the mouth, and yet the mouth is supposed to be the visual and sonic point of origin of the voice, even though technically mouths are just modulators. In wearing a dork-o-phone, suddenly my voice is somewhere it's not supposed to be, and my mouth is *not* doing something it is supposed to do. The dork-o-phone thus creates a distance between me and my voice (even though there already was one); the mic on my head and the box hanging from my neck call attention to this distance, destabilizing ideologies that naturalize voices and speech. It performs that distance for others who see and hear me, who are then dealt a rich hand of philosophical questions about voice, intention, and embodiment, which they can either confront or work to ignore.

For instance, you are not supposed to put the speaker for a vocal prosthesis directly in front of your mouth. Your voice is supposed to come from your mouth; putting the speaker directly in front of it makes it harder to imagine that the voice is speaking without supplement. This simple prohibition—don't hide your mouth with a prosthesis when speaking—initiates one of the most demanding conceptual exercises in voice theory.[9] "The voice may extend the range of the body by returning us to the mouth," writes Brandon Labelle. "In this regard, is it truly possible to separate the two, voice and mouth?"[10] I will call this close coupling of mouth and voice *oral voice*. The oral voice is everywhere in writing about voices and the voice. While clearly understanding—and accepting—the ethical necessity to write in support of the human variety, many contemporary voice theorists still too often return to how voices *are supposed to work* and a universalist conception of *the* body, of a *we* and an *us*, and of what a voice is and where it comes from. They begin from a normative voice and a normative mouth. I cannot imagine contemporary work that engages with coloniality, sexuality, gender, or race from the standpoint of a positionless writer—performing a "god trick," which in this case is both a seeing from nowhere and a hearing from everywhere.

A fantasy of an idealized-subject-pretending-to-be-a-materialist-subject appears to remain the lamentable status quo in many theoretical discussions of voices in many disciplines. "Materialism" is a position with almost no opposition in contemporary theory, which means that it may be approaching the status of an empty signifier, ironically arriving at the state of free-floating signification that its invocation is supposed to disallow. If everyone is "for" materialism, but nobody agrees on what it means, does it have any useful analytic value? It would, if the term *material* has a specified value. But even in their most reductively materialist definitions, voice and sound are not "things" in the world. Sound always requires a medium and at least two causes, and it is not a sound (or a voice, which among other things is a kind of sound) unless there is some kind of percipient, though the percipient could be animal or machine. Absent that, it is not sound.[11] In other words, the challenge is both political and epistemic, and the political problem cannot be solved by simply being "more materialist" (whatever that means) or less ableist.[12] The epistemic challenge requires acknowledging that the body often functions as point of identification in social life but that these identifications are often misattributed and mixed.

In this way, the epistemology and politics of the voice are related to those of passing and coming out. As Ellen Jean Samuels explains, *coming out* really refers to multiple moments and at least two different things: *coming out* as a changing process of self-understanding, and *coming out to* a particular person or group in a particular setting; both have presented challenges for me.[13] As Wendell has written, the paradigmatic model of disability is a person who is "predictably impaired." Those of us with chronic illness, meanwhile, "have to remind people frequently of our needs and limitations. That in itself can be a source of alienation from other people with disabilities [and nondisabled people] because it requires repeatedly calling attention to our impairments."[14]

I have been trying to understand the relationship between voice, subjectivity, and power on a theoretical plane since shortly after I began my postsecondary education, but I have been trying to integrate it into my self-understanding in a different way since 2009. It is one thing to know—experientially or intellectually—the critiques that feminism, postcolonial and decolonial theory, critical race theory, sexuality studies, disability studies, and standpoint epistemology (among other traditions) bring to the idea of a universal theory of the body and the subject. It is another to apply that knowledge to one's own shifting existence. To claim a universal power or mechanism of voice in cultural theory is an inherently conservative project, for it demands conformity to the author's imagination of *the* subject, *the* voice, *the* body, and *the* mouth in order to work. What if I don't conform to the author's theory of the subject, or what if someone's insides refuse to conform with their own theory of the subject?

I do not deny the force of the visual metaphor between mouth and voice, but the first step in a political analysis of voice is to recognize its link with the mouth *as metonymic*—a substitution of a part for a part, both of which play a role in subjects' self-constitution but not always the same role. Andrea Gyenge has probably gone further than any other writer in building a conceptual edifice for thinking mouths and voices separately, arguing that "we do not need a theory of the voice to think the mouth." She challenges "the assumption that research on the mouth is necessarily research on the voice," and by extension, that discourse on the mouth is discourse on the voice. Here, I build on Gyenge's thesis by advancing its converse: if her decoupling of the mouth and voice shows how the mouth works separately from the voice, that requires a theory of the voice separate from the mouth.[15]

In the case of the dork-o-phone, its problem is that suddenly my voice appears to emanate from more than one place: it issues from my mouth (and, if I am honest, also my resonating chest and head) but also from a speaker. My voice *comes out of two places at once*. But now there is a problem: What is the *best* non-mouth place for my voice to be fixed in others' visual and auditory fields? And what are my criteria? None of the waist-level or tabletop speech amps worked well for me. Waist-worn technologies go with the American predilection for standing while engaging in public or group speech; they are not designed for interpersonal conversation. In 2016 a friend at a university in a sunnier place saw undergraduate tour guides using the belt-worn Chattervox and wrote to me, saying, in essence, "Hey, these dork-o-phones are actually fashionable when they are on these undergrads." I have heard of the Chattervox also being used by fitness instructors. Of course, it's the people, not the technology, that make a difference here. But belt-worn amplifiers just don't work for me. For one thing, I'm fat, and as you might imagine, all the people in the pictures created to sell these devices are slim. For another, I have been known to speak while sitting down at a seminar table, and a voice coming from under the table is not an ideal prosthetic scenario for most people. As in the starting point for so many phenomenologies, the table becomes a platform for reflection: Where to put my voice so that it may do its work? This is a very different kind of hearing-oneself-speak than what Husserl or Derrida wrote about: here the voice and body are separable, and the object from which one's voice emanates can be held in the hand, wrapped around the waist, or set on the table.

Placement matters in most social situations. Standing close together at parties or sitting next to someone at an event also require a speech amp that is on my upper body. According to that criterion alone, the Spokeman worked best for me compared with other devices. The microphone that comes with it could be worn in multiple positions and could be wrestled onto my larger-than-the-standard-deviation head. Its position around my neck and on a lanyard also makes it easy to manipulate and gives me a tiny supercrip power: I can speak in directions that I am not facing. For instance, once at a loud sporting event I was able to hold it up to a friend's ear to yell in their ear while keeping my eyes fixed on the game. Human mouths and eyes usually move together.

In its black fake-leather-looking vinyl pouch (figure 2.5), the dork-o-phone is a kind of reverse-fashion statement, possibly "cool" in a crip-tech way, or a few steps beyond "chunky jewelry" into "Flava Flav Clock" territory (look it up, kids), but not cool in a high-tech way. This is why I call it the *dork-o-phone*. It isn't all that dorky, but any coolness it has is off-key, just as calling anything an "o-phone" today conjures up visions of a high-tech future that belongs to the past, like the sound of a vocoder in a song, or the mise-en-scène of a spaceship in a 1960s movie. My only mode of en-

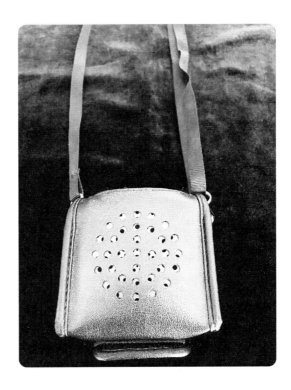

2.5 Dork-o-phone in its faux-leather case, with lanyard attached. Photo by Carrie Rentschler.

gaging with it aesthetically is through retrofuturism, treating its imagination of its own technicity as a style.[16] In this sense, it follows the history of the word *dork* in the English language: its etymology uncertain, "perhaps a variation of the word *dick*." Its most common usage today is similar to how the word *nerd* is used, to denote a person with excessive or obsessive interest in a subject, especially a technical one. *Nerd* or *dork* could follow the phrase "science fiction" or "A-V Club" and convey the same meaning. However, like *nerd*, *dork* has undergone a bit of recoding in recent years, and there is no better rendering to explain it than the *Oxford English Dictionary*'s dorky definition: "a person (esp. a student) ridiculed as socially awkward, unfashionable, overly studious, or odd. Now also: a person in whom these qualities are regarded as endearing."[17] All these meanings fit perfectly with voice amplification, which is perhaps why I was moved to use the word *dork* in my very first encounters with the dork-o-phone. I am also not alone. As I discuss in chapter 4, terms like *daggy*, *nerdy*, *dorky*, *not trendy*, and *not cool* have also been associated with earplugs, suggesting a general positionality of prosthetic aesthetics in relation to mainstream design aesthetics and fashion.[18]

The dork-o-phone's dorkiness is not an accident. Prosthetic fashion—and, by extension, the user's affective relationship with the device—has often been the *last* concern for designers.[19] Where it has been a concern, it has often been more about employing normative ideas of simulation or stigma avoidance, as in the mimetic appearance of prosthetic limbs or the endless quest to miniaturize electronics for hearing aids.[20] As Jaipreet Vidri explains, when industrial capitalism and medicine merged in mid-nineteenth-century Europe and the United States, some aural prosthetics, like ear trumpets, were "designed to be conspicuous," but those were the exception: most aural prosthetics were marketed for discretion.[21] Regardless of its visibility to others, any user of a prosthesis can attest to its deep affective resonance both for the user and for others around it. As Vivian Sobchack writes, the fluctuating line between "the" and "my" prosthesis makes for all sorts of give-and-take around meaning. In her case, "there is significant figural movement from metonymy to synecdoche, from *the* prosthetic viewed abstractly to *my* prosthetic leaning up against the wall near my bed in the morning to *my leg*, which works with the other one and enables me to walk."[22] In my case, the dork-o-phone *assimilates into* my voice and action. Let's follow Sobchack's arrow of figuration: *the voice* as an impossible abstraction, *my* dork-o-phone charging on my desk, *my voice*. What makes the dork-o-phone noticeable, and sometimes uncanny, is its proximity to the physical generation of sound in my diaphragm, throat, and mouth. This is its defining technocultural feature. It audibly and visibly marks my vocal system as in need of supplementation when it's supposed to be self-sufficient. It is weird because it is both a small distance from where it is supposed to be and too close to where it is supposed to be. This also marks its difference from Sobchak's leg: her leg is *where her leg is supposed to be*, whereas the dork-o-phone doubles the point-source location of my voice, which is now visually rooted to my mouth and from a speaker on my chest (even though in any reverberant space, it comes from other places as well). In honor of Derrida's critique of the metaphysics of presence, let us call this process of techno-vocal doubling *dork-o-phonè*. Leg and voice prostheses may present themselves differently: as subjects we adjust to them differently and legs and voices tend to represent different things; absent the prostheses, Sobchak's disability is visible to others, while my impairment is not visible and only sometimes audible. But walking and speaking are both operations of faculties, and the diminishment of voices and legs alter the imagined unity of the nondisabled body.

I may have been a bit preconditioned to like the Spokeman: the dork-o-phone was not that far from the first speech amp I ever used. Despite years of studying sound technologies (and becoming known as the kind of person who will be interested in that weird sound technology you just learned about), I had no idea speech amplifiers even existed or that I could use one. That was something I learned from my speech therapist. And speech therapy was, itself, a challenge.

The Loaner

MARCH 21, 2010

I had a killer speech therapy session on Wednesday, in the sense of "difficult" and "exhausting." Speech therapy is a cross between physical therapy (moving stuff around) and singing lessons, more or less. It's pretty fun, but there was a lot of trial and error. My speech therapist suspects that my trachea still isn't fully closed and was actually able to make me make myself dizzy doing certain exercises—which we promptly stopped—but that suggests there is still a leak somewhere in the system. Also, my voice is still weak enough that talking at normal volume for me is sort of like yelling at full volume for you. Now imagine trying to have a normal conversation for an hour or two.

Thus, while I'm not depressed, you could call me impatient and slightly frustrated. I am lucid enough and energetic enough to take visitors, but I can't really do a whole lot of socializing yet because the temptation to talk is too great and too taxing over time. So clearly I need a technological solution. I need a cane for my voice.

I spent time Thursday and Friday researching portable voice amplifiers, and next week one and possibly two may arrive for me to try out. They universally look lame, but they do seem to work. I know this because my speech therapist kindly lent me a "loaner." It's reminiscent of the kind of "loaner" you get when a car dealer fixes your car and has to wait a week for a part—not the nicest unit on the lot, but it works [figure 2.6].

Both the mic and the speaker are over twenty-five years old as far as I can tell. Radio Shack no longer exists in Canada and while "The Source" has countless things into which you can plug your iPod, there are no electronic nerd amplifiers like this for sale anymore. Which leaves me in considerably more pricey medical supplies markets. Anyway, the voice amp does really help, though I have to watch out for feedback. Friday night I was able to go out to dinner with friends, and while I was considerably less loquacious than I might be under better circumstances (pick up the mic to talk), I was able to make myself heard while more or less speaking at whisper volume. Of course I look like some dork televangelist sitting at a table with a mic and speaker, but I could make myself heard and participate in real time, as opposed to writing notes, which has been established as inferior. The units I ordered come with head- or neck-mounted mics (you could use a lapel mic but since I want the speaker near my chest, the opportunities for feedback are too great) so I'll look more like a call center worker and less like a televangelist. For a pretty penny, I can upgrade to one of the slightly more discreet mics that Broadway actors use. Yes, I might seriously consider doing that if this is going to be a long-term thing.

I should note that while whisper volume is my normal voice volume right now, I am not in fact whispering. Yet I noticed this winter when my voice was in similar shape that people would whisper back at me. Which it turns out is super annoying because they probably aren't consciously doing it—it's that thing where people raise or drop their voices to match your levels (useful knowledge if you ever want to defuse an escalating conflict: speak more quietly and flatly). But I don't *want* to be whispered to. I kind of feel like I'm being addressed like a child. Which is not really how I want to be addressed.[23]

There is a lot to unpack here. My desire to look like a call center employee or a Broadway performer instead of a televangelist is an aesthetic preference having to do with self-presentation. But to understand my speech therapy experience and what followed, you should know that I began with an excess of vocal force to lose. I had a lot of power and projection before my cancer—lecturing to two hundred undergraduates in a hall without a microphone. (To this day, my laryngologist tells me that I have unrealistic expectations for my voice.) As a big person with a big voice, I leaned into this as a form of self-presentation. It worked for me as a teacher and professionally, and probably interpersonally as well.[24] There is of course also a gendered and raced dimension to this, since I was negotiating everything from a position of relative privilege where I could exercise the enti-

2.6 Realistic Micro-sonic Speaker-Amplifier and Sennheiser Dynamic Microphone, aka "The Loaner." This may have originally been a kludge, similar to those described by Bess Williamson in *Accessible America*. Photo by the author.

tlement to take up space. But regardless of my prior status, a vocal impairment meant that I had to reposition myself with respect to my own voice. I had to learn how to speak again, which I did over months of speech therapy. And shortly after I began speech therapy, my voice would be battered one more time by external beam radiation. If the voice is supposed to be the ground of subjectivity, then mine was more like the ground during an earthquake, which is to say more like the swelling and dipping sea.

Starting six weeks after the end of radiation doses, I began giving academic talks again. I scheduled my first-ever sabbatical for 2010–11, before I had known about the cancer diagnosis, which meant that I had a year to figure out how to teach again. In my attempts at public speaking in 2010 and early 2011, I first tried to deliver talks while standing: I had to grip the podium for support as I pushed hard. Sure, wind was escaping my lungs, but the exhaustion felt more like my personality leaking out of my fingers.[25] During a question-and-answer session in 2011 at the Pop Conference at UCLA, I took my questions while seated (as all the other panelists did) and discovered—thanks to Carrie and an unexpected compliment from the writer Ann Powers—that I was much more able to manifest my skills as a speaker in that position. I began doing all my public speaking while seated, and now ask for a seat for any talk over five minutes in length. But even so, it is easy to blow out my voice, and so to this day my voice—perhaps as all voices truly do—requires supplementation.

I also have to learn how to negotiate the fact of using a vocal prosthesis. For example: an arrival at one of our house parties in 2011 looked me up and down right after I opened the door to greet him, then smiled, pointed, and asked, "What the fuck is that?" I offered the shortest explanation I have been able to muster—glasses for my vocal cords ("a cane for my voice" works well too)—and within minutes we were talking like nothing was out of the ordinary.[26] This is how the assimilation works: prosthesis is noticeable at first, but because the dork-o-phone hangs around my neck, my prosthetic voice is physically close to my other voice, and over time the two can blend into one. The principle upon which it works is not that different from placing dialogue on a center channel in film or television sound: voices seem to be coming from the mouths of people depicted on the screen even when they are actually coming from behind, beneath, or next to the screen. Michel Chion describes this phenomenon as images "magnetizing" sound in space and frames it as a part of what he calls the *audio-visual contract*, a specific kind of suspension of disbelief, where sounds are causally "mapped" onto images even though their real relationship is a much more tangled web.[27] In the case of the dork-o-phone and my voice, it is more like an audio-visual *contraction* of sonic space, where the difference between the voice coming out of my mouth and the voice emanating from a speaker on my chest ceases to matter. Once the social question the dork-o-phone presents is answered—"What the fuck is that?"—it retreats into my voice. It simply becomes part of me in the course of social interactions. The magnet in the dork-o-phone's speaker may pull things like paper clips to it when I carry it in my backpack, but its social magnetism moves in the opposite direction: my voice climbs back up to my face for those who see and hear me speak.

It can also disappear in social contexts where I am being ignored. My first public outing with it was a crowded exhibition at the Musée des Beaux Arts in Montreal on March 27, 2010. According to my notes, and my blog entry after the visit, my companion Carrie and I registered no stares or reactions at all. People were minding their own business. While a body-mounted speaker stands out, a head-mounted microphone may not. I was just another dorky guy with a Bluetooth headset, perhaps anticipating an urgent call that was definitely not destined to arrive. But this is the exception rather than the rule. If I hold a book or paper or menu in front of the speaker and microphone (for instance to read something), the dork-o-phone can produce mighty, shrieking waves of feedback. This is because the microphone and speaker are so close together, and because of the gain structure inside the dork-o-phone.[28] Once I was at a restaurant, and when I absentmindedly brought the menu up to my face to read it, the wave of feedback produced was so powerful it actually interacted with the restaurant's PA system, overwhelmed the piped-in music for which the PA was supposed to be used, and silenced a hundred-odd diners for a moment. It (or I?) performed an act somewhere between guerrilla, site-specific performance art and one of those cheesy undergraduate sociology projects where the student does something awkward in an elevator and then notes other people's reactions like it's a controlled experiment. A moment of confusion, followed by the termination of the feedback, and then back to meals and chatter. This is particularly unfortunate for me, since I live in a city where fashionable restaurants are very loud and crank up the piped-in music. But even in class, I have to be careful when lifting a book or photo-copied reading. The class of object as "book" or "menu" is less relevant than its length, width, and position: if it is tall and wide enough and placed in front of my body, parallel to my mouth and my chest, the sound coming out of the speaker bounces into the mic, and the feedback loop takes off. I live with my dork-o-phone in classrooms and at talks where I am in charge, but the screeching means I probably use it less at restaurants and parties than I would if it had better feedback rejection.

If I give an academic talk with the dork-o-phone, say to a small seminar mostly composed of strangers, and do not explain it, it has a definite effect. Since I am often invited to talk about sound (and often oblige my hosts), the audience reads my unexplained use of the dork-o-phone as a profound comment on the mediality of the voice. If I choose not to explain the speaker-box hanging from my neck, it becomes part of a different kind of feedback phenomenon. As someone who has published a lot on sound and media, and as the special invited guest or the teacher, my presence at the front of the room or the end of the table signifies sound and media theory, and perhaps some kind of eccentricity, and as a result, *the dork-o-phone on my body actually does effect a metacommentary on the mediality of the voice*, as if all by itself, without me saying a word about it, all because of how signifying chains and academic speech acts work. A voice, slightly displaced, calls into question the nature of its source; "all sounds are severed from their sources—that's what makes sound sound."[29] In the context of sound scholar Jonathan Sterne giving an academic talk on sound while wearing the dork-o-phone, as a speech act, the dork-o-phone announces the fundamental impossibility of perfect identity between body and voice. Conversely, if I come out as a speaker in need of supplementation at the beginning of a talk, that has a whole other apodictic effect, moving us from the abstract philosophy of the voice to the technological and environmental politics of disability, which can range from meditations on stigma (dork-o-phone versus eyewear) to meditations on the value of interdependence and collaboration in the construction of experience (when I have audience members read out long quotations at my talks). In the context of public performance with the dork-o-phone, my voice demands commentary. It is an "intermaterial vibrational practice" that enfolds my body, the room and its listening subjects, the dork-o-phone's transducers, and the social and technical prescriptions of the speaking situation.[30] But it does more than that, because voice out of place, whether on my chest, unexpectedly emerging from an oddly placed speaker, or bouncing around underwater instead of in the air, reveals the intermateriality of all voices and all subjects.

This is a return to the problem of passing and coming out, this time in the sense of "coming out to." Most vocal impairments are invisible, and mine has the interesting feature of being something one has to learn how to hear. It *can* be heard, but to the uninitiated, my voice sounds *fine*. In fact, under conditions of vocal strain, my voice can sound *better* in the same way that voices conditioned by years of smoking can sound sultry. If I give a presentation with the dork-o-phone and do not come out as needing it, it is assumed to be a performance of mastery of theoretical discourse by virtue of my institutional position (as I discussed earlier, it doesn't necessarily work this way at parties or restaurants). If I do come out, it is rendered as a performance of impairment that has one meaning at the front of a seminar table and another among strangers in public. As Samuels writes, this is the predicament of all those who live on the ambiguous edges of visible (and I would add audible) difference, whether that difference is primarily shaped by disability, sexuality, gender identity, or race: passing is not a willful act so much as a default, which leads to people making all sorts of assumptions about the person who has passed. Invisible and inaudible disability becomes a set of contradictions between "tools, behaviors, and social expectations."[31]

Aimi Hamraie has defined "crip technoscience" as a process through which "misfit disabled users, for whom estrangement from the default norms of the built environment is already a pervasive experience, draw on the sensibilities of friction and disorientation to enact design politics."[32] A focus on impairment forces disability theory to consider what happens to its theoretical reach in the murky margins, and extends its critique of norms beyond the obviously crip world. At the same time, the lived experience of impairment is a shuttling between ability and disability. A vocal impairment both estranges me from my own voice and binds me with it in new ways. A prosthesis like the dork-o-phone is supposed to have a compensatory dimension, allowing me to focus on a task, rather than my voice, when speaking through it. But in actual use, the dork-o-phone both estranges me from my own voice *again* and unifies itself with me on a different plane. The ways in which this estrangement and unification play out can be different for me, and for every person with whom I share a speech situation. This is why I consider my vocal condition experimental in the sense of experimentalism in the arts: every day, every encounter is an experiment where my voice, once a constant in my self-conception, is now a variable, a search "for an otherwise."[33]

OF OTHER DORK-O-PHONES

My relationship with the dork-o-phone has also been experimental in a more old-fashioned way. Thanks to great work on disability and design by scholars Graham Pullin, Aimi Hamraie, Bess Williamson, and Sara Hendren, I have thought a lot about the possibility of *other* dork-o-phones that might serve me better than the Spokeman does. Over the years, I have had many conversations with designers about alternative approaches. Only one custom dork-o-phone has come to fruition so far, built in 2014, by Montreal artist L. Alexis Emelianoff.[34] Among her practices, she works on alternative transducers: metal plates or massive sheets of wood made to vibrate and disperse sound into air the way the cone of a speaker might, or rather, instead of the cone of a speaker. It is hard to describe their sound; it is open and clear, somehow less *speaker-like* and more *there* in the room, less directional than a traditional speaker. They also look really cool. I liked the idea of wearing wood; as a material from nature, it feels like close kin to the natural fibers in the clothes I wear to teach and conduct seminars. Alexis came up with the idea of a pair of speakers that sit on my breast bones. These would have to be connected to a microphone, an amplifier, and a battery pack to power the amp and the microphone (figure 2.7).

The wood panels she built were beautiful and thin, with a small transducer element ingeniously attached to the back. I chose a particularly good headset microphone by DPA known for its rejection of feedback—as predicted in my early blog entry on the subject, I chose the kind that pop stars and Broadway performers have been known to wear. The Spokeman was a single unit plus a headset, and plugged into an adapter to recharge. My custom dork-o-phone was much more involved to manage. I now had to carry around an assemblage of things with four separate parts, which weighed

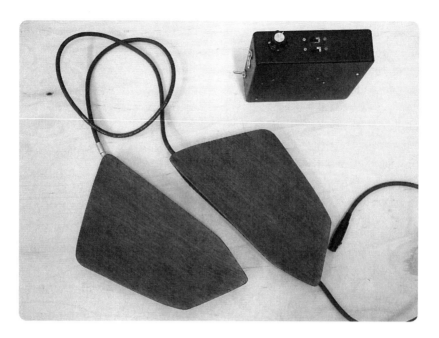

2.7 Experimental dork-o-phone transducers and amplifier. Photo by L. Alexis Emelianoff, used with permission.

considerably more, in order to give off the appearance of weightlessness and sleek natural design in the speakers and mic on the front of my body. The batteries were rechargeable but had to be removed to be recharged. In other words, it produced a visual effect of sleekness in one area at the expense of effort and bulk in others. While this device was meant to be more like a fashion accessory and less a matter of concealing my impairment, its many parts made it less likely to disappear to me in use—there was too much for me to attend to. I could not exercise an instrumental relationship with it in the way that I wanted. Its articulated parts remind me of the vacuum tube hearing aids from the 1920s and 1930s that Mara Mills writes about. One Sonotone ad from the 1930s shows a speaker clipped to the wearer's ear, attached to an amplifier affixed to a bra, and a battery pack tied to the user's leg. In a caption, it says that men also "wear Sonotone in many ways, for example: transmitter in vest pocket, or underneath shirt [*sic*], and the battery in the hip pocket or a leather belt case. So worn it can be less noticeable than glasses."[35] Part of the problem was my fault—I should not have chosen a microphone that required phantom power, and this was our first attempt at designing a dork-o-phone, so Alexis didn't know to anticipate the issue either. Part of the problem was the weight of batteries (in 2014, batteries were still pretty heavy compared to 2020, though very light compared to 1920), and yet another was the limited efficiency of the elements that drove the wooden "speakers." As I write in 2020, we are giving it another go—a dork-o-phone 3.0—with lighter Universal Serial Bus (USB)–rechargeable battery pack, more efficient transducers, smaller electronic components, and fancy bird's-eye maple speakers (figures 2.8–2.10). In discussing it, Alexis had one more request of me: "Maybe we can give it a more flattering name."

There are evolving commercial options as well. In correspondence with my speech therapist, I also learned that there were now Canadian dork-o-phones—though at this point I consider my Spokemen to be naturalized Canadians by immigration if not by birth. Assistive Listening Device Services of Canada offers a variety of products in its "voice amplifier" category (currently listed as "hot" on its website). Among these is the MiniBuddy Pro, which is a lot like the Spokeman but thinner, wider, and with much lighter batteries (figure 2.11). It also costs C$210, which is considerably less than what I paid for my Spokemen. It is rechargeable through a USB cable and charger (yes, the cable is too short like with every other electronics product). This makes it easier to charge in the short term, but in the long term more likely to wind up in a landfill sooner, since the battery is not user-replaceable.

Since I received it in 2020 during the COVID-19 quarantine, I will not have an opportunity to try it out at a seminar, party, or event for many months. In tests at home with Carrie and our cats, it does not cause feedback as easily as the Spokeman, but the vocal sound is perhaps a little more flabby and echoey. Because it is lighter, it feels more fragile (though it may not be). The unit itself is made of shiny black plastic, meant to be worn without the case, and new out of the box sports a branded sticker on the front (you can bet I will be removing or replacing that before appearing in public). While the vinyl on my Spokeman looks weathered, I am curious what kind of patina the MiniBuddy might develop. My main bass guitar is a glossy black and shows every scratch and fingerprint, but those signs of use are also somehow signs of authenticity—it's not a museum piece. Perhaps the most intriguing thing for me, however, is that the MiniBuddy has an option that did not exist on voice amplifiers when I first surveyed them in 2010: it has a slot for a TransFlash (TF) card, and a plug for a USB key (figures 2.12–2.14). It will play MP3s.[36] The jokes about the arc of my research career write themselves: sound studies author who developed a

2.8 New transducers in progress for an as-yet-unnamed voice amplifier, rear view, summer 2020. Photo by L. Alexis Emelianoff, used with permission.

2.9 Front and rear view of new transducers in progress for an as-yet-unnamed voice amplifier, summer 2020. Photo by L. Alexis Emelianoff, used with permission.

2.10 Side view of new transducers in progress for an as-yet-unnamed voice amplifier, summer 2020. Photo by L. Alexis Emelianoff, used with permission.

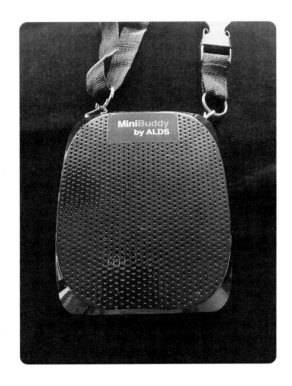

2.11 MiniBuddy front, with sticker still on, lanyard, and hooks. Photo by Carrie Rentschler.

vocal impairment and wrote a book about MP3s now plays MP3s through his vocal prosthesis, which is the subject of a chapter in his new book. But my dream for the device would actually be signal processing, not playback, so that I could add various effects to my voice and turn the foundational variability of my voice into an opportunity for performance and intentional expression (or at least unintentional expression of a different kind). But that fantasy will have to wait for now.

My confinement during COVID-19 has led to another voice amplification problem, one directly related to hearing oneself speak. While com-

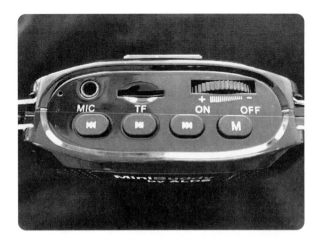

2.12 MiniBuddy top with MP3 controls, mute buttons, volume, and mic input. Photo by Carrie Rentschler.

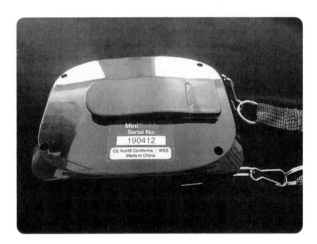

2.13 MiniBuddy rear: the unit offers no user-serviceable battery, but it does offer a shiny plastic surface. Photo by Carrie Rentschler.

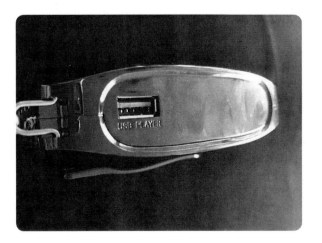

2.14 MiniBuddy side, with port for a USB stick and a fingerprint. Photo by Carrie Rentschler.

menters have reflected on the limited video and audio quality of Zoom meetings, or the problems of interacting with people through that modality all day, the main issue it has produced for me is one of interacting with my voice. On a landline telephone, the phone receiver plays back a little bit of your speech into your ear. This feedback mechanism is important for people like me who are trying to avoid vocal strain: put simply, people tend to talk louder when they don't hear their own voices; it is possible but difficult to unlearn this behavior, and I have not succeeded. Mobile phones do not have this feature, which was either engineered out as a nonnecessity, presented some practical engineering obstacle that was deemed not worth solving, or perhaps as with the audio track on the video compact disc, they simply forgot to include it. Voice over Internet Protocol (VoIP), which is the sound part of video chat protocols like Skype, Zoom, WhatsApp, Messenger, Teams, and all the rest, also does not have this feature built in, and neither do computer sound cards. This means that while I have no practical use for a regular dork-o-phone as of this writing (and won't until quarantine is lifted), the only way to get through many hours of video chats for work would be to construct an assembly of technologies and techniques for hearing myself speak. Let us call this assemblage the *auto-dork-o-phone*. As with the loaner I tried out, constructing such a device was a kludge that made use of a studio microphone, an audio interface for getting sound in and out of my computer, and a way of getting that sound into my VoIP.

On one level, this should be a simple proposition. Musicians routinely need this feature because microtiming matters when one is recording music to a beat. Audio interface companies market the feature as "zero-latency monitoring" or "input monitoring," and most modern interfaces have it. Unfortunately, these interfaces run on specialized software drivers that get installed in the deep nether regions of the computer's operating system. There was a glitch in mine that did not allow me to connect my microphone to my VoIP applications. I tried every troubleshooting trick I could think of. Then I contacted technical support, which is the problem-solving equivalent of that moment in a horror movie when the protagonist enters a dark basement: you know it will not end well. Sure enough, technical support for the operating system and technical support for the audio interface created an infinite, recursive loop where they blamed the problem on each other. I will spare you details on how I fixed it in the end, but I now have the ability to hear myself speak, so long as I use my external interface and an external microphone and wear headphones.[37] I also invested in one of those cool broadcast arms to move the microphone back and forth.

Because this setup uses a lot of gain on the microphone and is located in front of a set of speakers, it produces a noise music kind of feedback, at skull-ripping volumes, if I accidentally switch on the speakers while the microphone is on. The simple need to hear oneself speak over VoIP requires a kludge, and extra care. To my knowledge, nobody is clamoring for audio feedback mechanisms as accessibility features in computers and VoIP programs; however, I can't help but wonder if, like curb cuts, hearing-oneself-VoIP might be useful to other people as well.

While the title of this section is meant as an extended Michel Foucault joke, his "Of Other Spaces" essay is instructive in at least one important way. He contrasts heterotopias as places apart from utopias; the latter he calls no-places that simply exist as fantastical renditions of "society in perfected form," that are "fundamentally unreal," with the implication that it would be more helpful to focus on the real spaces of heterotopias rather than the fictional spaces of utopias. More often than not, the imagined function of voices, both in everyday discourse about voices and in philosophical ruminations on vocality, are much closer to the "fundamentally unreal" world of utopias than any description of what an actual human voice might be or do.[38]

The thing about my voice, or voices in general, is that the internal experience of a voice is also an experience of an imagination of a voice: "Its corporality, its materiality, makes up only half the story."[39] Scholars have turned to the term *vocality* to signal the broader cultural field of which the voice is a part but also the range of things that are not simply vocal that now exist inside the voice, "in its multiple manifestations."[40] In Katherine Meizel's review of the term's hundred-year history, she homes in on several key aspects of vocality for critical analysis: the voice as a sign or marker of difference, the voice as a cultural construct, the voice as a form of lived experience (which could refer to your experience of your voice, or your experience of others' voices), voice as a place where physics and physiology commingle with history and social contest, voice as a nexus of power. "The voice is often understood as a kind of sonic fingerprint, embodying a unique, unalterable, and authentic self," writes Meizel. But what is at stake when "one body generates many voices"?[41] And what is at stake when a certain number of voices generates a different number of bodies?

The only adequate theories of vocality begin from a founding disunity of subjects and voices and a founding understanding of *voice* that casts it in the plural. For me, but perhaps for anyone with an impaired voice, this is a personal, political, and philosophical project all at once. It might be better to focus on other vocalities instead, but fictions can exert a real force in the world. If the dork-o-phone has been at the center of an experimental vocal practice for me, these experiments still happen inside an ideological world filled with unreal voices that mystify the workings of real human and animal voices while pretending to reveal them. If vocal impairment has taught me anything, it has taught me what singers, elocutionists, and my speech therapists knew all along: I make use of my voice.

People are all at best vocal operators. Those operations happen in a world suffused by the ideology of ability, which says that ability is preferable to disability, and the ideology of vocal ability, where I operate a voice as if it were the carrier of my intent, as if it were my soul and will spilling forward out of my mouth with my breath.[42] What I seek from any dork-o-phone is a kind of instrumental relationship, a merger of subject and object, where the articulation of body, vocal practice, and device becomes "just my voice" in a moment of speech or vocalization. As in any tool use, this instrumentality requires practice and work. Like a musician who bonds with some instruments but not others, my problem with other dork-o-phones is that I don't know if I can *get to* this state of instrumentality.

Subjects, objects, instrumentalities: here we are, dear reader, at the standard blockage in Western metaphysics. Is subject/object best rendered in terms of a Cartesian dualism where an intending soul operates a compliant body that it animates? Is my desired synthesis between subject and object a kind of practical reason that reflexively operates on itself where my body's self-knowledge is itself embodied? Or am I talking about a situation in which a body folds in on itself in an act of autopoietic transformation? Any of these theoretical formulations of what a voicing subject "is" allows for an instrumental relationship between vocalizing subject and voice, and each has advantages over the other. I can identify three main strains: a Cartesian dualism, a second built around a theory of practice, and a third based on monism. (1) While René Descartes's dualism is not fashionable in the cultural theory world, it is actually the closest match to how people in my bourgeois world actually talk and write about voices, whether in everyday contexts or the specialized worlds of speech research or philosophy: there are subjects and there are objects. (2) The practice-based model of voice presents it as a historical and culturally located practice, connected to people's agency but also to cultural contestation—for instance, around history and memory, as Daphne Brooks shows with African American singers and as Dylan Robinson shows with the juridical function of Indigenous song. It also materializes voice and places it in the world of body techniques and tacit knowledges, as outlined by Marcel Mauss, Norbert Elias, and Pierre Bourdieu. That works better for me because it breaks down the problematic subject/object distinction and can take on critiques of dualism offered by writers from within and without the so-called Western tradition. But this approach replaces ontological dualism with epistemological dialectics, retaining the language of subject and object while refusing to resolve it. (3) The idea of an autopoietic body folding in on itself comes from a monistic philosophy that provides an inspiring alternative to the Christian theology behind Descartes's dualism. However zany Gilles Deleuze and Félix Guattari's metaphysics seem with their rhizomes, lobsters, and endlessly folding folds, it requires many fewer leaps of faith than dualism and dialectics. In terms of required assumptions, it makes fewer demands on its users than the philosophies it challenges. But in my experience, the aesthetic writing that has come out of this tradition sometimes leads to problematically doctrinaire avant-garde and avant-gardist descriptions of the world that, without a great deal of additional work, do not match up with how voices and vocal impairments are usually described, how most people (and peoples) narrate their own experience, only aligning with accounts people want to give of their own worlds in very special circumstances.[43] Thus, my invocation of subject-object must remain somewhat theoretically ambiguous, or at least pragmatic: vocal ideology is Cartesian; vocality seems best described through a model based in practice and history; and from a theoretical standpoint, the most believable model of the body and voice is monistic. So much for resolving theoretical contradictions in a grand synthesis!

The dork-o-phone references and deconstructs the idea of oral voice and the visual figure of the mouth as source-point for the voice, in its everyday use. In the shadow of the dork-o-phone, *"What the fuck is that?"* becomes a question for all voices; it is the verso of what Nina Sun Eidsheim calls the acousmatic question: *"Who is this?"*[44] Like all voices, mine is constantly redirected, short-circuited, negotiated, challenged. It is experienced ideologically as if it originates from one place, but in fact it originates from many all at once. The difference is that in the experience of a prosthetic vocality, I must attend to the multicausality of voice, explicitly and tacitly, from moment to moment. And in interacting with me and my dork-o-phone, the transparency, givenness, and agency of "the" voice as a universal phenomenon is challenged for others. This is the beginning of a crip vocal technoscience. Every speech act involving any audible or visible crip voice raises anew the relationship between intent and expression, interiority and exteriority, subject and object. As speech acts involve others, their sociability refracts these questions and adds layers of agential complexity. And there at the center of my public speech practice is the dork-o-phone: a quirky box that sounds one way and signifies another; a prosthesis that gives the lie to the still-pervasive belief that voice, subjects, and bodies can be easily linked or identified with one another.

Content Note: This chapter includes some medical photography, descriptions of plastic surgery on my throat, images of and references to self-harm, and discussions of cruel conditions endured by migrants and asylum seekers.

In Search of New Vocalities

AN IMAGINARY EXHIBITION

It is very difficult to make technologies that are capable of creating and enforcing desired configurations of power and authority, especially if those configurations are radically different from those that preceded them. / EDEN MEDINA / *Cybernetic Revolutionaries*

Welcome to "In Search of New Vocalities." This chapter takes the form of an imaginary exhibition.[1] The cost of admission is acquiring this text—if you're reading, you have already paid. If it is cold where you are, there is a coatroom to the right inside the front door, with cubicles for your bags should you want one. If it is hot outside, come on in—the temperature is perfect in here. Locks are not necessary for your belongings, since nobody will steal them. You may also bring your belongings with you, eat, talk, make noise, and touch the objects. Single-user bathrooms—accessible and gender-neutral—are off to the left, and do not contain high-powered hand dryers.[2] With one potentially tasty exception in the Signals room, the whole space is odor free, and the lighting technology can be instantly changed to accommodate any sensory sensitivities. There are so many advantages to an imaginary exhibition![3]

In the previous chapter, I introduced you to the dork-o-phone, one modality through which I have tried to experience, operate, and imagine my voice anew. "In Search of New Vocalities" broadens this exploration into a much more expansive conceptual exercise. It highlights some sources and materials that can go into imagining vocality itself differently. Like a nonimaginary exhibition, this chapter is an act of gathering and displaying things. And because it is an exhibition, there is a bias toward material artifacts, documentary practices, and artistic and experimental work. There are chapters and books on *other* other vocalities, for instance: sign language (which makes an appearance toward the end of the exhibition); interpreters, who translate speech into another language in real time; and singers whose voices change midcareer.[4] This is just one of many attempts and I encourage you to explore others.

Throughout the exhibition, you will find different materials. Approaches will be juxtaposed with one another, sometimes in the works themselves, and sometimes in my textual explication. As the map shows, the exhibition is organized into four rooms. You are currently standing at the entry. As you might expect, the exit is through the gift shop, but it is currently closed.[5] Just like with a nonimaginary exhibition, these exhibits are arranged in particular orders and spatial relationships, and the linear form of this chapter implies a path through. But you can move through it in any way you like. (Academic authors often forget that this is also the case with the text in academic books.) And just as with a nonimaginary exhibition, you might skip whole parts of it. Though it won't be because you encounter a crowd.

You are currently in the foyer, contemplating the Visitor's Guide. There are portable seats available to take with you through the exhibition, though there will also be some seating inside. From here, you will move through the other parts of the exhibition, though you will not spend an equal amount of time in each room.[6] Each room will begin with a description of the space and the things within it. Each exhibit—a single piece or a group of works or objects—has been given a museum label as well as a number that corresponds to an entry in the exhibition's audio guide. Sometimes there is also an option to learn more about the subject, which you can access by pressing the asterisk button [*] on your audioguide device. I have also provided the text of audiodescriptions for all exhibits. (There are also audiodescriptions for all images in the rest of the book; they should be available to screen readers via the alt-text field in the digital editions.)[7] If you would like to

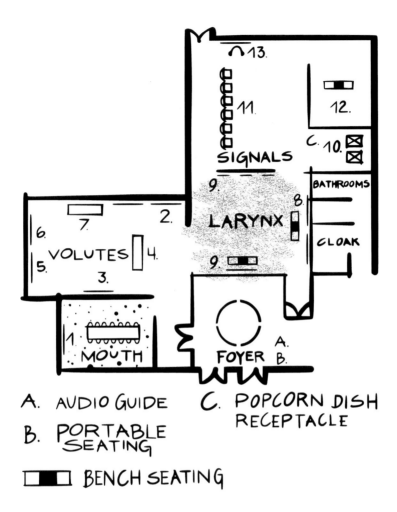

13.

11.

SIGNALS

12.

C. 10.

9.

LARYNX

8.

BATHROOMS

CLOAK

6.

7.

2.

VOLUTES   4.

5.

3.

9.

9.

1.

MOUTH

FOYER   A.
        B.

A. AUDIO GUIDE

B. PORTABLE SEATING

BENCH SEATING

C. POPCORN DISH RECEPTACLE

Exhibition map. Drawing by Darsha Hewitt; exhibition layout conceived by Zoë de Luca.

AUDIODESCRIPTION: You are standing in the foyer. There is a counter with some helpful and well-compensated staff behind it. Before you is a map of the exhibition, which consists of five rooms in addition to this one as well as a bathroom and a cloakroom. Throughout the chapter, there will be instructions regarding where to walk. However, we can also provide you with a tactile map of the space, or integrate an audio map into the audio guide, where each exhibit is assigned a unique sound. Just ask one of our staff and they will set you up.

learn more about the motivations behind the exhibition, press [*] now. Or just move forward into the Mouth room.

[*] BACKGROUND ON THE EXHIBITION

Why an exhibition on *vocality*? The purpose of this exhibition is to consider vocality as a kind of representational field and to ask after the stakes of locating voices on bodies—onto mouths, hands, prosthetics, larynxes—or outside bodies as objects in the world, or as attached to nonhuman objects. Scholars have used the term *vocality* to separate voice from language, in order to talk about the voice in itself, and as a field of practice (this is discussed further in chapters 1 and 2).[8] As a concept, vocality places singing, coughing, laughing, breathing, accents, stutters, wind instrument performance, and countless other vocal phenomena on the same analytical plane as the semantic dimensions of speech. By not holding up the semantic dimensions of speech or the expressive dimensions of singing as master frameworks from which voices should be understood, the concept of vocality expands the possibilities for thinking about voices.

Today, representations and mechanisms of voice are exploding across cultural registers. Much of this has to do with technical or technological forms—digital assistants, talking objects, spectacular software—but also the increased availability of sound-making and processing technologies for people to do things with; in recording and performance, the fashion for representing voice in contemporary art, the mainstreaming of gender transitioning and its attendant vocal skills, and the proliferation of vocal techniques in different disability communities. But despite this profusion of attention paid to various vocalities, dominant theoretical and political practices still seem to prefer a mapping of voices onto speakers' mouths. They still associate voices with ideas of interiority, selfhood, agency, and political power. As Mickey Vallee writes:

> It is an inveterate belief in cultural theory that the voice simultaneously indexes the body as it escapes the body, and, as a consequence is a vibrating intermediary between the body's first-order physical presence and second-order representational presence. The voice is a doubly valued laurel for people seeking to capture their own "inner voice," as

though it were a lighthouse to a hitherto-undiscovered confidence in inhabiting the world. [And] what to make of the voice estrangement/embodiment hypothesis that underlies voice theorizing and voice studies, an instrumental one which states that the voice must be embodied in order to enjoy the capacity for autonomy and power?[9]

Vallee's solution is to treat the voice as an "imaginary organ, insofar as it has come, through its imaging technologies, to be an effect built from the imagining of its causes."[10] What better reaction to an imaginary voice rendered through imaging techniques and technologies than an imaginary exhibition?

None of the examples I present should be taken to have any inherent political meaning or effect immanent in their very form. Too often, writing on aesthetics—whether high art or not—ignores context and writes as if representations have effects in themselves. This caution is equally warranted for the technological examples I offer, bound up as they are with histories of rationality and control, and medical examples, which carry exceptionally heavy baggage in a disability studies frame. All modes of vocal figuration have political histories; there is no politically pure figuration of the voice or vocality. To take three relevant examples: Jennifer Stoever has shown that the agential voice is deeply tied to ideas of race and gender; Bill Kirkpatrick has shown how the mediated voice is tied to an ideology of ability; and Caitlin Marshall has shown that the line between "normal" and "crip" voices is itself shaped by an auditory protocol of normalization.[11] Images of disembodied voices can suggest a materiality and autonomy of the voice as a thing in the world when it can only exist at a given moment in a given web of relations. Celebrations of sign language can too easily ignore d/Deaf experiences of sound and hearing, reenacting deaf marginalization in audist culture.[12] At the same time, the future utility of a practice, technology, or idea is rarely foreordained by its prior use. It is this tension I hope to bring out. An imaginary exhibit is a really bourgeois way to accomplish this, but then so is writing an academic book. I offer you some words and pictures, but not the last word or the full picture.

In the first two chapters, I systematically undermined my own authority to interpret experience in an attempt to demonstrate its fundamental nontransparency; I tried to perform a phenomenology through antiphenomenology. In this chapter, I invite you, dear visitor, to work with me to react to and interpret the materials presented here as occasions to imagine other, better, more inviting and varied figures of vocality. Voices can be made up of, and do, many things.[13]

I have chosen the materials here simply because they are good to think with, and because I was able to assemble them in the exhibition format. They are nothing more than cultural probes, presented to inspire and provoke reflection.[14] And this project already comes in a disability studies tradition of thinking through, with, and against technology.[15] A more capacious vocal theory requires breaking down the articulation between voice, mouth, and subject. But it also requires a more capacious vocal imagination, and the task of this chapter is to nurture that imagination.

THE MOUTH ROOM

The Mouth room is your standard white cube gallery space. At first glance, the room is almost bare; the white walls and ceiling are stark, open canvases. But look down and the floor is a well-reinforced mesh full of tiny holes (don't worry—it will support you). If you look through the holes, you can see some kind of spongy material below. Look up, and angled acoustic panels hang from the ceiling, and you can make out some kind of similar spongy material above and behind them. The room is not silent, but it lacks the characteristic echo and ambience of a gallery space. This room is quiet, very quiet. A single, well-lit photograph hangs on the wall. In the middle is a table with various Australian newspapers and periodicals covering Australia's treatment of migrants. Some are from 2002; some are from this year. Feel free to sit down and look through them.

[1] Closed Mouths

In visual representations of agency—or its absence—the mouth takes on a larger-than-life role. "Voice" is more a representational attribution than it is the power of a self-possessed subject. Often in visual representations, voices are mapped to mouths and, in the process, located as the site of agency, whether metaphorical or in fact. When it is used as a metaphor for agency—especially an as-yet-unmet possibility for agency—the loss of voice is often depicted as closure of the mouth.

[1] "An activist wears tape on her mouth while protesting in front of the Charles Schwab headquarters on October 4, 2018, in San Francisco, California. Activists and sexual abuse survivors staged a protest to show silencing of sexual abuse survivors outside of the headquarters of Charles Schwab and to demand that the company does not donate to the Republican Party" (Photo by Justin Sullivan).

Color print, on paper, poster paste.

Dimensions: 10.00 × 6.53 in.

AUDIODESCRIPTION: A young olive-skinned woman with straight, shoulder-length brown hair and brown eyes gazes into the distance. A rectangular, silver piece of duct tape covers her mouth and extends to the bottom of her nose. The photographer frames the shot close enough that the activist's full head is not in the picture, but her face is clear, and beneath the tape her lips are visible, locked in a resting pose. The tape looks very strong, and painful to remove.

Protest imagery is full of images of sealed mouths. Activists will tape their mouths shut to signify "silencing," by which they do not mean the elimination of *sound* as such but the elimination of agency that comes with the voice, as in this 2018 photograph of an activist outside Charles Schwab headquarters in San Francisco, where she is protesting the metaphorical silencing of sexual abuse survivors by the U.S. Republican Party.

It is not always tape. In 2002 a group of asylum seekers in the Woomera

Detention Center in Australia—located in the South Australian desert, two hours away from the nearest town, in forty-four-degree-Celsius heat—began sewing their lips shut to protest the horrific conditions they were forced to endure. This was part of a series of protests that included hunger strikes, suicide attempts, and eventually rioting. The Woomera facility closed in 2003, after an attempted escape.[16] Since 2002, lip-sewing protests have proliferated worldwide, occurring in France, Greece, Papua New Guinea, Turkey, and Italy, at the very least. They have become a form of mass movement, an extension of protest practices, a form of political withdrawal, and, as Banu Bargu argues, a form of truth telling that works through enactment rather than speech.[17]

In 2002 the mainstream Australian press reacted to the lip sewing with horror, as if to suggest that it was the protest that was excessive and not the prison-like conditions the asylum seekers were enduring. As Nithya Rajan writes, lip sewing was not only shocking to Australian journalists but incomprehensible within a management framework, thereby calling it into question: "Lip sewing has a phantasmagorical quality unlike any other form of protest. It symbolizes the reduction of refugees to their corporeality as well as the immense capacity for resistance they possess despite the overwhelming odds they face."[18] Australian politicians and shock-jocks reacted to mouth sewing as an un-Australian act. In Joseph Pugliese's terms, the act "stages the graphic disruption of the social contract" and "cleave[s] body from soul"; it also signals the refusal of food. It is a gesture of absolute political pathos, humiliating the liberal Australian state, exposing its lack of hospitality and ultimate brutality.[19]

Reading about Woomera in 2019, both the Australian asylum seekers (many of them originating from Iraq) and Pugliese are sadly prophetic. Hostility to migration has become a signature gesture of European and settler colonial liberal states in crisis, perhaps a dress rehearsal for the waves of climate migrants to come. Ramesh Fernandez, who survived the Woomera facility and went on to earn a social work degree and found a refugee survivors advocacy group, writes that Australia had the same number of people detained in camps—both offshore and onshore—ten years after Woomera's closing, and their treatment was no better.[20]

When separated from political urgency by the frame of institutionally consecrated art, mouth sewing can take on other meanings. Amelia Jones offers a list of artists who have engaged in mouth sewing or lacing as part of their performance practice: in addition to a 1976 performance ("Talking about Similarity") where Marina Abramović attempted to articulate the thoughts of her partner, Ulay, while he sewed his mouth shut, "artists from Americans David Wojnarowicz, Bob Flanagan and Sheree Rose, and Ron Athey to London-based Italian Franko B. and Australian Mike Parr have had their lips laced or sewn shut in performances that protest the silencing of victims of AIDS, censorship in general and the mistreatment of asylum seekers." Jones's analysis shuttles between artistic and political settings, at once careful to distinguish the experiences and actions of asylum seekers and artists, and simultaneously considering the discursive mechanisms through which they circulate and operate. She writes that the wound *"makes pain, and the body itself, into a representational field."* Most often this occurs through a visual register, and though Jones seems to reserve some power for the experience of being in a room with a self-wounding artist, she acknowledges that most of the political meaning of the work circulates because images of the wounds circulate.[21]

Jones's important move here is to situate the mouth alongside other orifices, and to locate wounding as something that may be experienced internally but is signified on surfaces—of bodies, of two-dimensional images. It turns out that the mouth is not a hole into the subject but yet another surface. As Amanda Weidman explains, "Ideas about the voice as a metaphor or trope of subjectivity, agency, power, and authenticity are bound up with the particular moment when, and the very material ways in which, voices become audible."[22] This relationship reveals something about audist and ableist ideas built into mainstream vocality: a certain construct of speech and hearing are required to establish the seat of subjectivity, and where muteness is tragedy or the loss of agency. I call this construct *the ideology of vocal ability.* Whether muteness is necessarily tragic is a question that Deaf scholars have already answered in the negative; whether silence is always an imposition to be avoided is a question to be revisited in a society of suraudience, where ambient surveillance is produced through forms of machine listening that aspire to ubiquity.[23]

The power of the asylum seekers' gesture and the analytic of speech engaged by Pugliese, Bargu, and Rajan is in how they present voice as the connection between a personal interior and public exterior world—a portal from the soul to the polis. If the voice is the guarantor of individuality and subjective self-presence, then its negation is a political act. Even Bargu's assertion—that the silence performed by lip sewing is a form of political participation—requires a connection between voice and an idea of agency.[24]

To learn more about the ideology of vocal ability, press * now. Or continue on to the Volutes room.

The ideology of vocal ability is a set of intertwined beliefs about voice, personhood, and agency: they may be stated explicitly; they may be operationalized implicitly; they may be experienced through processes or actions and not considered at all; they may appear in images, performances, recordings, or other representations of voice. The ideology of vocal ability includes the following propositions, any one of which can figure and enact the voice as a figure of agency (which I will call *the agential voice*):

1   There is such a thing as "the" voice, which is a universal faculty of human beings. The voice defines a person as a person.
2   To understand the voice is to understand a fundamental aspect of subjectivity.
3   The voice is a "natural" expression of an inner subjective self. As breath moves out into the world in the form of sound, so does agency.
4   Therefore, having a voice is preferable to not having a voice.
5   If the voice is a proxy for the effects of a subject on the external world, then agency consists in "having a voice."
6   While sonic and somatic metaphors are used to describe how vocal agency works, where the voice leaves the body and touches the world, actual sound matters less than the imagination of sound, its mechanics, and the message it carries.
7   Western culture is visual and subordinates sound. Voice is thus both a primordial extension of self in the world and at the same time a hallmark of subjugated Western or non-Western cultures.[25]

Remember: a list like this is both true and false and cannot be exhaustive. The term *ideology* refers to the fact that people live and feel these things, whether or not they believe them. Sometimes ideologies are especially effective when they are not believed or are actively resisted.[26] This contradiction is present in the Woomera story and my discussion of it: my feeling for the asylum seekers is driven both by their expression of desperation and by the symbolic work people do when they place their own voices under erasure, especially in the context of a liberal state asserting itself on people's bodies.

Even as it can be moving and powerful for all the right reasons, the role of this voice in the migrants' story—as an agential voice—also employs an ideology of ability. The sewed mouth represents a self-efficacy that the asylum seekers are supposed to have, one ostensibly guaranteed by liberalism's narratives.[27] It highlights the limits of the social contract—built as it is on a host of founding exclusions, from gender, to race, to indigeneity, to ability, to alterity.[28] Border zones are one of the places where those limits of the social contract are most violently enforced. The agencies of filtering at the border—shuttling between force and bureaucratic reason—have freely mixed markers of ability like intelligence, youth, and health with the signifiers of race, language, and ethnicity. The same can be said for extrastate territories.[29] So already there is a contradiction: the signifiers of liberal individualism—the voice as agent—reach out to liberal subjects from places where the expressed tenets of liberalism do not even pretend to obtain. Asylum seekers' self-harm challenges the legitimacy of the state. All this is to say that the ideology of vocal ability works, and that it can do work.

At the same time, the ideology of vocal ability marks an irreducible difference from the plurality of lived reality, or the actual workings of voices, for that matter. It mystifies and conceals dimensions of experience even as it gives name and shape to others that would otherwise remain unexpressed. As Wendy Brown writes, "Expression is cast either as that which makes us free, tells 'our' truth, and puts our truth into circulation, *or* as that which oppresses us by featuring 'their' truth." Both positions "equate freedom with voice and visibility, both assume recognition to be unproblematic when we tell our own story, and both assume that such recognition is the material of power as well as pleasure. Neither confronts the regulatory potential of speaking ourselves, its capacity to bind rather than emancipate us."[30] This is the power of the voice-as-agency metaphor: again, the fact that ideology is lived as true and felt amplifies its effect.[31] And yet power can just as easily demand a voice, demand speech, extract expression. In these cases, the voice-as-agency metaphor does not work. It also does not work when speech itself is felt as a form of struggle or labor, whether as a result of impairments, translation, interpretation, or other modalities where the safe, self-same home of subjectivity is put into question or distress.

An agential voice is figured visually as an *oral* voice, visually located in the mouth, an aperture between interior subject and external world. This helps explain the ubiquity and power of the sutured mouth as a protest gesture.[32] But to confuse vocality with what comes out of the mouth is like reducing the faculty of hearing to the *pinna*, the folded masses of flesh on the sides of people's heads. Voices are reduced to mouths because it makes it easier to picture the voice. But the voice does not actually have to be heard to do its work; and it does not need to be seen in order to be shut down, so long as the voice can be registered somehow as belonging to an individual. In some European languages, *voice* and *vote* are the same word, eliding the difference between direct, small-scale democracy in a polis and large-scale representative democracy in a modern state as if the former were synecdochic of the latter, as if scales of human interaction were homologies of one another. The agential voice is one configuration of voice and agency. There are others.

THE VOLUTES ROOM

Exiting the Mouth room the way you entered, turn left. You are facing a giant photograph of an ancient-looking stone tablet. Walk toward it and you will find yourself in the Volutes room. Turn left again and you are facing a case with some weird old dark paper in it. Some colorful framed works are hung on the back wall and to your left. Further in from the large stone object is some kind of small, lumpy sculpture suspended midway up a wall. In the Volutes room, you will confront objects and works that imagine voices as things that exist outside bodies, as physical forces in the world that can be visualized, and as singular events.

[2] Stela 13 at Seibal

Meso-American speech scrolls, pictorial representations of the voice outside people's bodies, are perhaps the oldest known volute representations. According to Gary Tomlinson, volutes take many forms and morph into many things in Meso-American representations: "seashells, feathers, precious stones, and especially flowers." In their physical form, they unify song and paint, operating as "presentations rather than figurations of the world." Volutes represent voices as material forces in the world, but they are materials that are not unique in their substance.[33] Tomlinson argues that the seashells and flowers were not ontologically separate categories from speech, which the volutes unified in metaphor. They were "always already connected." Volutes represented "a dovetailing of certain phenomena in the world between which Western modes of thought perceive gaps," specifically the gap between speech and song.[34] Further, writing systems from that time and region of the world were semasiographic *and* partially

[2] Stela 13, Seibal, Guatemala,
ca. 400 BCE–600 CE

Black-and-white photograph, 1975.

Original dimensions: 5.72 × 5.72 cm.

Gift of Ian Graham.

Peabody Museum of Archaeology
and Ethnology, Harvard University.

Exhibited work is a reproduction of a
photographic negative at scale of the
stela: approximately 201 × 120 cm.

AUDIODESCRIPTION: A large,
life-sized grayscale photo shows
an old-looking, unpainted, rectangular stone tablet covered with
engravings. A figure of a man of
unknown skin tone takes up most
of the space. Snakes and other animals emerge from his legs. Facing
left, a scroll and dots emerge from
his mouth.

phonetic, allowing speakers of regionally different languages to sound out personal and place-names, "giving them voice in their own language."[35] A loose coupling between speech and song rather than their separation; an understanding of voice as a thing in the world like birds and flowers; and a fluid understanding of language as related sets of writings and voicings that would both overlap and diverge: all these aspects of vocality are central to the volute.[36]

Volutes like Stela 13 at Seibal announce one set of possibilities for representations of the voice to be tied to people speaking or singing but not necessarily to bodies' interiority, their subjecthood, or their uniqueness. Rather, the vocal events in volutes appear to tie voices to a host of other manifestations of a multifaceted physical and spiritual world, while still allowing for a taxonomy of vocal actions and gestures. Context seems to be both heightened and extended in volutes, for vocalizations appear to have a material existence outside the body of the speaker, but inside a web of relationships and events.

[3] Banderole in an Early Modern Painting

Banderoles appeared in medieval European manuscripts as well as in sculpture, stained glass, tapestries, and paintings. Medievalists have connected banderoles to modern visual representations of speech, such as speech bubbles. Although there is a formal similarity between Meso-American volutes and early modern European speech scrolls or banderoles, they do not have any known shared history, and they are connected to totally different hermeneutic and metaphysical traditions. Prior to the use of volutes, speech was often signified in medieval European imagery through a raised index finger: "The pointing index finger was a universal sign of acoustical performance, the speaking subject."[37] When speech scrolls emerged, they were used to represent subjects' speech but also potentially their emotions or state of mind: "Figures usually hold their discourse, as here, but occasionally the band spurts directly from their mouths in a straight line. This occurs only in moments of extreme emotion." Or they point at the scroll, otherwise touch it, or—only occasionally—it emanates from a speaker's mouth.

Kathryn Kerby Fulton writes that banderoles were "the single most reliable medieval indicator of the performative."[38] Their semiotic significance came from both the words they contained and the formal, visual aspects of their composition.[39] Beholding it in an exhibit, it is easy to imag-

[3] Bernhard Strigel

The Annunciation to Saint Anne (detail), ca. 1505–10.

Oil on panel.

58 × 30 cm.

Museo Nacional Thyssen-Bornemisza, Madrid.

Inv. no. 380 (1978.48).

AUDIODESCRIPTION: In this detail of an early modern painting, a light-skinned man on the right speaks or sings to a light-skinned woman on the left. She is dressed in red, with a flowing white head covering. He is dressed in a brown robe and looks directly at her. A scroll with ornate words on it unspools from his mouth. She looks slightly downward.

ine a volute as somehow silent because it is a visual representation. But silent reading is a modern invention, and it is probably wiser to treat each volute—whatever its origin—as "a total experience of communication involving sight, sound, action and physical expression."[40] Visual resemblance also can be deceiving.

[4] Phonautogram

Of all the many modern techniques for inscribing sound, perhaps the closest relative to the banderole is not the speech bubble but Édouard-Léon Scott de Martinville's phonautograms. Phonautograms were visual inscriptions of audio, recorded on smoked glass or a piece of paper rolled around a spool. The device that made them was called a phonautograph. The phonautographer would turn a crank, a person would speak or sing into the horn, a diaphragm would vibrate, and an attached stylus would then inscribe vibrations on the paper as it passed by. Scott called the paper documents he produced phonautograms but also *épruves*, which meant "tests" or "trials" but could also refer to printers' proofs. This is important because, as Patrick Feaster has shown, Scott's submission of phonautograms to archives (which is how there are any to study today) was not to preserve his or anyone else's voice for posterity. It was to prove that his method of vocal inscription bore a correspondence to the vibrations of sound in the air that resulted from speech or song. In this way, phonautograms were multimodal: made up of speech, sound, sight, action, and physical expression. The phonautogram's technological correspondence to speech, like any other, had to be manufactured. For instance, in an 1859 phonautogram, Scott added a tracing of the vibrations of a tuning fork alongside the trace of the audio being recorded. This was meant to compensate for the variable speed of the rotation that resulted from hand-cranking the phonautograph. While today sound recording technologies are described as operating at constant speeds (33⅓ rpm, 256 kbps, etc.), the technology to accomplish that—called a governor—would not be applied to sound technologies for another three decades. (The governor was also important for sewing machines and other nineteenth-century mechanical inventions.) The tuning fork solution was a way to indicate a constant temporal benchmark against the variability of the recording apparatus in use.[41] In this way, phonautograms were one example in a long line of nineteenth-century apparatuses that subjected physical and physiological phenomena

[4] Édouard-Léon Scott de Martinville

"Au clair de la Lune," 1860.

Paper, unmounted, helical-trace-plus-timecode.

Approximately 22.5 × 50.5 cm.

Collection of the Academie des Sciences.

Scan by First Sounds. From Feaster, "Édouard-Léon Scott de Martinville," 69–70.

AUDIODESCRIPTION: A rectangular sheet of paper is laid out horizontally, appearing as if it had once been spooled. On the far right is a clean vertical strip with a red stamp and a "no. 5," alongside some handwritten text. The rest of the sheet is covered by a sooty black substance. Squiggly horizontal lines are inscribed in the black background.

to automatic, timed inscription.[42] But they also mark a shift in the status and meaning of voices.

Considered as visual representations, phonautograms are defined by several characteristics that would also appear in later technologies. First, they are defined by a two-dimensional representation of a three-dimensional event — so they connect later imaging practice with volutes and speech scrolls.[43] The phonautogram is also *unspooled*: the waves of recorded speech move from left to right and from top to bottom, like the scripts of European languages, so time follows a spiral that is flattened out as a line. Vertical movement in the lines of the phonautograph represent variation in pitch, timbre, and intensity over time. This waveform representation also treats voicing as a unique event, independent of the speaker. In fact, the phonautogram is defined by a complete absence of any visual depiction of the subject.[44] The air and the machine inscribe not the speaking or singing subject. In this way, vocality can exist entirely independently of a present body. As the next example shows, leaving the body out of the picture does not automatically mean that this mode of representation disembodies voice. Rather, it tethers a body to an event at the moment of transduction, and a proliferation of possible embodiments at the moment of reception, beholding, or playback (if it even happens).

For more on the phonautograms, hit [*], or continue on to the waveform and spectrogram.

[*] PHONAUTOGRAMS: INSCRIBING SOUND

In *The Audible Past*, I considered phonautographs important because they were *tympanic* technologies, built around a resonating diaphragm, loosely modeled on the human ear, that did not "care" whether the sound it was recording was speech, song, or nonhuman sound (though the ear on which it was modeled would eventually become a poorer instance of the general principle). In that sense, and in use, it was an example of how philosophical boundaries between speech and song and between the human voice and other sonic phenomena began to erode in nineteenth-century Europe and in some of its colonies and postcolonies. Almost all mechanical, electrical, and digital representations of sound today do not treat the inscribed or represented voice as anything special or ontologically separate from other kinds of sound.[45] And the vast majority use a vibrating diaphragm to transduce sound into energy or energy into sound at some point in their process. But the phonautograph is not the same thing as the technologies that followed it. While the phonautograph transduced sound into inscription, it was not designed to reproduce recorded sounds. Though Feaster and David Giovannoni have recently developed an audio-forensic method to "play back" recordings that were never intended for hearing, they are both quite clear that this is a modern aspiration and has nothing to do with how Scott understood his invention. That it is now possible to hear what may be Scott's voice singing "Au clair de la Lune" on a phonautogram from April 9, 1860, says more about digital audio epistemologies than technologies or ways of thinking from an earlier era. In that way, the direction of the transduction matters. If Scott transduced sound into a script, Feaster and Giovannoni *educed* script into sound. One operation does not necessarily imply or require the other.[46] The phonautograph was thus both a sound *transducer* and a machine to produce visual representations of sound.

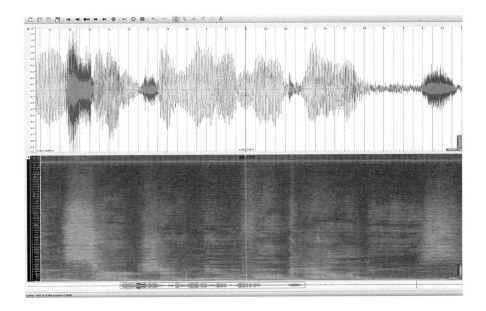

[5] Jonathan Sterne

Waveform Image and Spectogram of the Author Saying, "In Search of New Vocalities," 2020.

Taken with Sonic Visualiser software, color print, on paper.

Approximately 100 × 90 cm.

Collection of the artist.

AUDIODESCRIPTION: A rectangular image is horizontally divided into two panels. The upper panel is a white grid, with a green waveform made of oscillating lines emanating vertically from a central line. The bottom image is a field of green punctuated by yellow splotches, which are sometimes punctuated by little orange splotches inside. The spacing and color intensity of the splotches on the bottom roughly match the lines on top.

[5] Sound Waveform and Sound Spectrogram

Today the dominant technical visual representation of speech is the sound spectrogram, developed at AT&T Bell Laboratories in the 1940s. The idea was to produce something like a much more advanced phonautogram: a single, linear representation of sound where time moved from left to right, frequency moved from low to high, and intensities of different frequencies would be represented by intensity of ink—today represented by intensity of color.

As Xiaochang Li and Mara Mills write, "This new approach to the visual records of the voice at first aimed to reveal the contents of speech rather than the identity of speakers." It found applications in cryptography, linguistics, and communication engineering. Later, spectrograms would be important for speech recognition, allowing computers to compare a spoken utterance to a library of stored reference patterns for each word or phrase. Today they are perhaps the dominant visual representation of speech in engineering and computer science, while simple time-intensity graphs—waveforms—are the dominant mode of representation in software settings, from Digital Audio Workstations to the SoundCloud player.[47] As distant descendants of the phonautograms, waveforms and spectrograms represent voice as a phenomenon in the world bound up in a unique event, fusing any distinctive marks from a sounding body with the room, the microphone that recorded it, and the mode of inscription itself. They treat voice like any other sound, since a spectrogram or waveform is equally at home representing music, ambient noise, or a street scene. They unspool voice, rendering a three-dimensional phenomenon in two dimensions. And they separate recording and eduction as different moments of transduction: spectrograms are for human or machine reading, and may sometimes lead to playback (that is an option in the Sonic Visualiser software I used for the spectrogram) but may also be used for all sorts of things that do not require playback, from speech analysis to turning speech into commands, as in contemporary voice assistants.

[6] *Aldrich Ames with Someone in Russia*

This relationship between subjects, speech, dimensionality, and representation takes an interesting turn in Louisa Bufardeci's 2006 series of embroidered works, *13 Captured Telephone Conversations—All One Minute Long*, which mixes historical conversations, real conversations from the artist's home, and imagined conversations. Each piece is represented by a series of colorful, embroidered waveforms. Though the artist frames her project in terms of "warrantless, limitless, wiretapping," the effect is also three-dimensional, rendering voices as things that have touchable, variegated surfaces—even when represented as waveforms.[48] It suggests the dimensionality of sound writing. In a work on biosensing musical interfaces, Zeynep Bulut uses the term *tactile speech* to describe a technology of voice that "is

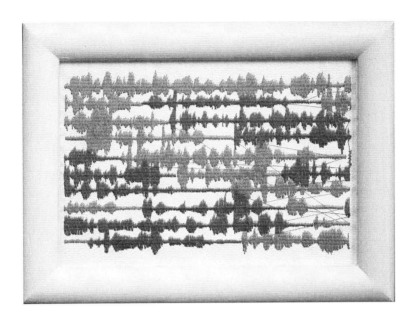

[6] **Louisa Bufardeci**

1994/01/21 08:21–08:22 Aldrich Ames with Someone in Russia, 2006.

From the series 13 Captured Phone Conversations—All One Minute Long.

Machine embroidery on linen.

13 × 18 cm.

Courtesy of the artist and Anna Schwartz Gallery, Melbourne.

AUDIODESCRIPTION: A white frame holds a white cloth. A series of ten colorfully embroidered waveforms move from left to right. Some are pink and some are orange. A few extra stitches are visible.

---

not limited to verbal language, the human body, or vocal cords." Through their embroidered surface, Bufardeci's waveforms accomplish tactile speech through an entirely different technical register, but to the same political end.

The colored waveforms imply that the voices of two speakers can be separated out, but the nature of *what* was said remains opaque, and the speaker identification, whether based on metadata or Bufardeci's imagination, remains incomplete. What is left is a unique vocal event—one with an implied dimensionality but also an implied tactility. The move to embroidery is also interesting: the use of machine embroidering rather than doing it by hand suggests the spectrogram's history as a command-and-control technology for things that have no inherent or necessary relationship to sound, like computer-controlled embroidery.

[7] *Volute #1: Au clair de la Lune*

The Volutes room comes full circle with Rafael Lozano-Hemmer's *Volutes* series, for which only one volute is currently available as of this writing. The term *volute* refers back to the Meso-American technologies and epistemologies with which this room began, and represents the phrase "Au clair de la Lune," referring back to Scott's phonautograph. Lozano-Hemmer's volute, however, is its own kind of high-tech art: using 3D printing, it offers a three-dimensional snapshot of sound in motion, or air disturbance in space. Like the objects in the room, Lozano-Hemmer's *Volutes* says nothing explicit about what happens inside the subject that uttered them. When voices are understood as sounds in space, their linkage to the interiority of a subject is tenuous at best.

Jason Stanyek and Ben Piekut use the term *rhizophonia* "for taking account both of sound's exteriority and the impossibility of a perfect identity between sound and source."[49] This is most apparent in subjects that are themselves difficult to place for auditors, especially in cases of ambiguous gender or race. As Andrew Anastasia writes, a trans* voice can "trouble and blur normative assumptions about sex and gender, human and creature. Trans* voices can fail to make sense in spectacular ways when our voices no longer provide adequate evidence for the bodies that emit them."[50] Lozano-Hemmer's *Volutes* could be understood as a critique of voice as interiority, as a celebration of high-tech vocal inscription through its explicit linkage back to other historical milestones, or it could even be understood as announcing its own kind of metaphysics of presence, one based on air in the room rather than the spirit inside the subject. However you want to read them, this volute and any more to come are an excellent way to consider how voices always must exist outside bodies. What would it take to presume nothing about the insides from where they came? How might you or I be able to speak differently about voices and subjects freed from that sometimes-painful tether? In the Volutes room, the possible effects of voices outside bodies have multiplied. It is now time to look back inside the subject to try to think beyond the tether of voice to personhood.

[7] Rafael Lozano-Hemmer

Volute #1: Au clair de la Lune, 2016.
3D-printed polished aluminum,
tomography video.

Sculpture: 65 × 19 × 21 cm.
Video: variable dimensions.

Photo by author; reproduced by
permission of the artist.

AUDIODESCRIPTION: An
abstract-looking, oblong, gray,
lumpy, hard mass, full of holes
and gaps, is mounted on a white
wall. It looks like it could be a
fossilized form of a biological
effusion. The light shining on it
casts a striking shadow.

THE LARYNX ROOM

Exit the Volutes room by walking toward the pink lights. When you cross
the threshold into the room, suddenly you can hear singing. Four light-
skinned women in black clothes are singing an a cappella piece, whose
legato tones take advantage of the reverberant acoustics of the gallery
space. Like the Mouth room, the Larynx room is also rectangular in shape,
though it is more square. On the opposite wall, you can see two photographs of something pinkish and fleshy. On the wall to your left is a series
of drawings and computer graphics; on the wall to your right is a giant
pink mandala-like image.

Even today, with high-resolution digital imaging, CT scans, and all the rest, laryngoscopy's scopic regime is essentially the same as it has been since the mid-nineteenth century: take a tube with a light on the end of it, pass it down the throat, and look.[51] (Happily, the tube is now thin enough to go up through the nose and then down into the throat.) The difference is that today, they are able to act upon the images in ways that were not possible until recently. The two images of my larynx were taken with a laryngoscope to check up on a vocal cord surgery I had in late winter 2016. They depict my own vocal cords opening and closing. But the cord on your left (my right) is paralyzed. So the closure is only possible because of the injection of some kind of goo. At first they used a substance that lasted only six months. More recently, they have switched to a substance that lasts eighteen months: calcium hydroxylapatite (branded as Radiesse Voice). Both the substance and the approach are essentially techniques of cosmetic surgery applied to the vocal cords.

It was somewhat ironic that, after spending time in Los Angeles, where I saw more white women with cosmetic surgery than at any other time in my life before or since, I began the surgeries. It is not just irony, but business: the injection medialization laryngoplasty has been rebranded as a "voice lift," and the rhetorical connection to both cosmetic surgery and the intensively normative bodily habitus that accompanies it are complete.[52] As with my speech amplifier (discussed in chapter 2), my voice lift may well have been developed for one or another form of prothesis or rehabilitation, but it is marketed for bodies not necessarily marked as disabled. Like a face lift, a voice lift might be optional, something "regular" people do. In his study of voice lifts, Vallee argues that the conditions for which voice lifts might be prescribed are all treated by physicians as indices of "weakness." Considered as part of the beauty industry, the voice lift both performs a "disclosure" of the relationship between interior and exterior and conceals it, in the sense of compensating for or hiding conditions considered to be weak: "If the voice is affectively material, it is so in a continuous variation of bodies that are considered well and bodies that are considered unwell."[53] The aesthetics of the voice cross—and in sounding announce—the divide between impaired and not impaired, whether by age, disability, or some other imagined cause, and this imagination of cause feeds back into the voice as an imaginary organ.

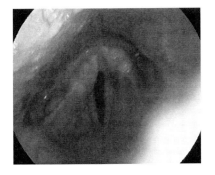 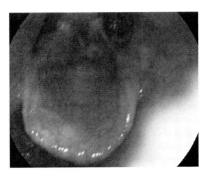

[8] Jonathan Sterne

*Author's Vocal Cords Open and
Closed, from a Video Taken on
April 27, 2016, at Montreal General
Hospital.*

Color print, on paper, poster paste,
2020.

Dimensions: 90 × 90 cm.

AUDIODESCRIPTION: Two
circular photographs of larynxes
are hung on the wall. Both are
enclosed by a rectangular frame.
Within that frame, the camera
looks down a person's throat.
Pinkish folds of flesh are visible,
with the vocal cords facing you,
like two drumskins. The shape
is somewhat cervical in appearance. In the first image, there is a
vertical, ovular gap in the middle.
In the second, the gap has closed
in on itself.

Since September 2011, I have had a voice lift about every eighteen
months, and it helps me talk, swallow, and (inexplicably) breathe.[54] My
first vocal surgery—my first surgery after the thyroid surgeries in 2009 and
2010—was not without bumps in the road.

SEPTEMBER 24, 2011

Well, I don't really recommend the operation for a good time
(graphic details below the line for the curious) but it certainly
has had an effect on my voice. It sounds different and it's easier
to talk. I would definitely do it again. My friend Derek says that
before my voice sounded like my old voice but with a cold; now
my voice sounds like I have a different kind of cold. It's still a little

gravelly—possibly because I'm sore—since the laryngologist had to poke my vocal cord several times. But I can raise it a little and it takes a lot less effort to talk. I don't feel light headed as easily. I still needed the speech amp at the Dirty Beaches show last night, but I didn't have to work as hard. If I strained, it tickled, rather than felt like my breath was rushing out of me. This should be good for about three months. They're hoping to get new goo from the US to inject next time that will last for six. I don't think either the doctor or I would relish doing the operation more than once.

. . .

Okay, so this is what happens when you get an injection medialization laryngoplasty, or at least when I did. This all happened in the ENT wing of Montreal General in a normal doctor-meets-patient ENT room.

I sit in the patient chair. The doctor makes it recline and has me stretch out my neck (with a towel behind me for support). Some of the usual stuff happens. They spray anaesthetic up my nose (this always happens) and then follow it up with a fiber-optic camera (called "scoping") which goes up my nose and down my throat so my vocal cords are on a big screen. Before the camera goes in, they spray stuff down my throat to numb it. This is especially difficult because I have a serious gag reflex, it turns out. It takes a few tries, and to everyone's surprise at one point I puke a little bit. Don't worry, that never happens, except to me! If you're worried, have them put a towel over you or bring a change of shirt (I was able to cover up so *nobody knew* afterward). Anyway, there's lots of injecting and freezing.

Once everything is numb, they insert the scope (the resident handled that part) and the doctor goes in with the needle through the front of my neck. There's a tiny needle hole but I can't get a good picture to show you (I tried) and it's going to heal quickly. Anyway, at this point there is a lot of poking around, as the doctor watches what he's doing on the screen and tries to hit the right parts of my vocal cord. It's hard. The shit hurts. It also just doesn't feel right. But I'm committed. I'm trying just to breathe through my nose and not think about what's going on, and especially not to swallow, which is difficult because apart from the poking it also tickles. The needle gets bent. He gets some in and we take a break. Then everyone goes in again. I need some extra "freezing" as one part of my nose is getting more sensitive. The second time seems easier for all involved.

I can immediately feel it is easier to talk, though my voice sounds silly and hoarse. I rest for 15 minutes (I brought a tenure file to read through—don't worry, it wasn't yours!) and then head to the bathroom, clean up and walk to the metro. I have been instructed to talk a lot, and so I change my plans for the day to do stuff that involves talking with people.

So now I understand a little bit of what some women go through for their idea of beauty (not mine, but whatever). All I can say is that if you're really committed, it seems 100% worth it.[55]

Since that first injection, I've gone from a relatively difficult patient to an easy one. I lost some weight, I got used to the procedure, and the doctor figured out how to work on me. I still bring an extra shirt anyway. For the first few days after the injection, I feel like a stoner talking, having inhaled a hit and trying to speak without releasing the precious hallucinogenic smoke. Eventually, the Radiesse settles, and my voice feels more or less like my voice, if "my voice" refers to a voice that is constantly changing. Just as the dork-o-phone is prosthetic, so too is the Radiesse, and both render my voice ambiguous. And I, like Vivian Sobchack, want to pass enough to get on with the business of vocalizing as well as to not pass, to reveal the artifice by which my voice works. Or to follow Vallee's scenario of prosthetic voice as disclosure, it is to seek a doubled disclosure: a voice as a disclosure of something else, and a voice as a disclosure of the artifice upon which it depends.

Taking the larynx as the referent for the voice, rather than the mouth, and treating the voice as a system for sound synthesis, can have a variety of implications. To learn more about laryngeal representation, hit [*]. Or continue on to Erin Gee's *Larynx Series*.

[*] LARYNX STUDIES 101

Medical and endoscopic representations of voice tend to focus on the throat and the larynx, looking in through the entrance to the throat. Taking the larynx as the referent for the voice, rather than the mouth, and treating the voice as a system for sound synthesis can have a variety of implications. This is a very different embodied referent for vocality than the mouth. To change the object of vocality from the mouth or the interiority of the subject to a larynx, for instance, is to seek out different kinds of effects in the world.[56] As it exists in my world, anyway, laryngeal vocality also begins with representation, in this case, the visual representation of the larynx, but it renders vocalization as a process made up of many elements and components. The laryngeal voice is more like an instrument, less like magic or a soul.

The desire to see the larynx begins as a tale straight from the annals of the history of Enlightenment sciences. As with other organs, physiologists, physicians, anatomists, and others sought to devise ways to see into living bodies such that they could apprehend organs in action, the larynx simply being one of many. But the larynx story has its own twists and turns. In 1854 Manuel García devised a mirror and light system to observe the workings of the larynx for speaking and singing in a living person, and hired a surgical instrument maker to produce his tool. He described it thus in an 1855 article announcing his technique: "The voice is formed in one unique manner — *by the compressions and the expansions of the air, or the successive and regular explosions which it produces in passing through the glottis.*"[57] For García, this was confirmation that the voice worked something like a reed instrument, and it provided a basis for a vocal pedagogy for opera singers that he developed. Although images of the working larynx in a living person would not appear until the twentieth century, this approach to the voice as an air column working in tandem with the modulated closures of an aperture would dominate subsequent technical representations. García is thus often credited with inventing the laryngoscope, but there are predecessors. In 1807 Philipp von Bozzini described a "light conductor" made of two parallel tubes with mirrors and a candle for a light source: one tube shined a light down the throat of a cadaver; the other was for visualization. The tubes were thick, the apparatus was not accepted by other medical researchers, and his work appeared not to have been used for research or diagnostic purposes. In 1829 Benjamin Guy Babington devised a similar device, which he called a "glottiscope" and which used a tongue depressor and a system of mirrors to visualize the larynx, using the sun for light.[58]

The humanist histories of laryngoscope favor García because of his connection to opera, over medicine or science. García's laryngoscope is a case where music and singing set the frame for the analysis of speech and language in nineteenth-century science rather than the other way around. It goes further: the entire history of laryngeal knowledge has been a history of multiple knowledges. In her wonderfully titled essay "Whose Larynx Is It?," Viktoria Tkaczyk explains how theories of the larynx moved across humanities and science disciplines: the musicologist Carl Stumpf's theory that the larynxes of singers contained "inner imitations" of their actions animated debates in music, medicine, and phonology; phonetician Eduard Sievers collaborated with others to record readers' laryngeal vibrations as they declaimed Friedrich Schiller's ballad "Rudolf of Hapsburg" to see if their larynxes moved in the same way; and theater scholar Max Herrmann built on Stumpf's ideas to posit a "secret re-experiencing" of theatrical performances among audiences that could be registered in laryngeal movements, like Stumpf's "inner imitations."[59] In all these studies, larynxes were imagined not as the *source* of vocal agency but rather as highly individuated modalities through which auditors could react to cultural experience: voice was an instrument. In musicologist Gustav Becking's estimation, musical experiences would vary with the auditor's knowledge of the music, but "such humanities knowledge was bound to inscribe itself into the unconscious motions accompanying listening."[60] The *whose larynx* question thus does double duty: multiple disciplines and regimes of knowledge claimed access to, if not ownership of, the larynx in the late nineteenth and early twentieth centuries—a situation that still obtains today. But the specificities of embodied larynxes also mean that a universal theory of culture cannot be derived from observing the motions of a body—we would have to ask *whose larynx* is being represented, and whether that subject's history might have something to do with its movements.

Nina Sun Eidsheim uses the phrase *the acousmatic question*, "Who is this?" to describe listeners'—and apparently scientists'—desires to link voices to bodies: "We ask the question because voice and vocal identity are *not* situated at a unified locus that can be unilaterally identified. . . . We can know them only in their multidimensional, always unfolding processes and practice, indeed in their multiplicities."[61] Eidsheim's analysis of Jimmy Scott, a successful Black male singer born with Kallman syndrome (a hormonal condition that prevents the onset of puberty), nicely highlights the intersections of gender, race, and disability in the reception of vocal timbre. Scott's voice was heard differently because his larynx was different. Although Scott's Black male contemporaries often hit the same pitches as Scott, they did so in a falsetto, producing "timbral scare quotes" around their performances. Scott was therefore heard as having a "high" voice, ambiguously gendered by hearings of his vocal timbre, shaped by bodily difference, but determined more by protocols of hearing and singing Black masculinity as Scott's lived experience of hormonal difference—a difference that in no way diminished his self-identification as a man.[62]

Crip voice—and the temporarily impaired voice—is still a vastly undertheorized area. And like all medical models, a mechanical model of voice has an ambiguous meaning for people with vocal disabilities: at once, folding a social relationship into and inside the speaker's body, as if it were an individual problem, and at the same time, offering real and desirable possibilities for the person. I want the vocal surgery (in fact, I want it right now as I write—I am overdue for a re-up); and I also simultaneously appreciate and laugh at the GPS voice that navigates me through strange routes in new places. But even that is problematic. QuietBob97, an alaryngeal speaker whose vocal cords were removed in 1997 because of a tumor, produced YouTube videos where he uses a series of prosthetic voices. His point is to challenge the centrality of laryngeal speech to listeners' conceptions of the human. As Caitlin Marshall writes of QuietBob97, "To describe QuietBob's speech as 'crippled' is importantly not to label it as disabled, but to emphasize that his speech *is heard as* disabled. . . . Crippled speech is thus brought into being by the disabling environment created by normative hearing. To cripple speech is a technology of power that, when applied, marks vocal difference, whether that difference is perceived as racialized timbre, queered inflection, deaf accent, or dystonic slurring. The term 'crippled speech' describes both the norm of a discriminatory mode of listening and hearing, and the markedness of non-normative utterances."[63] In other words, there is an ableism in the way I hear my own nonnormate speech and feel my cripped larynx.

[9] Erin Gee: *Larynx Series*

Erin Gee's *Larynx Series* stages the many mechanisms at work in laryngeal vocality, in part through the transductions she performs in the piece, converting a laryngoscopic image into a vocal performance. During an installation of the *Larynx Series* at the Dunlop Art Gallery in Regina, Saskatchewan, she premiered the four pieces with three other vocalists [9a]. The kind of matter and energy that a larynx *is* is converted in each stage of the work. Gee began with four simple digital photographs of four larynxes taken with endoscopes (one each), not that different from my larynx shown earlier. She converted the pixelated images to vector graphics, which allowed for infinite scalability, but through a level of abstraction:

[9a] Choral performance for four human voices.

Larynx3, 2014.

Epson UltraChrome K3 ink, on acid-free paper.

Edition of 5.

86 × 112 cm.

Collection of Saskatchewan Arts.

AUDIODESCRIPTION: Eight images are spaced from left to right around the three walls of the room. The first image depicts what you might see if the piece were being performed live as you moved through the room. It is a photograph of four light-skinned women dressed in black, standing in a semicircle, singing. In the foreground is a microphone. In their hands are binders containing sheet music. On the back wall is a series of other images—those images hang on the walls of the Larynx Room. Moving from left to right: the next image is a large rectangular picture with a tangle of circular pinkish lines running all over a canvas. On closer inspection, it is possible to see outlines of a larynx at the center that look a little like the first picture of Jonathan's throat. Horizontal lines run along the edges like musical staves. The second image takes the patterns running along the edges of the first and lays them out horizontally, and in series, each above the next, rendered in gray and white. In the bottom corner is a small reproduction of the first image. The third image takes the four lines from the second image and superimposes musical staves and notes over them, using the original images as a guide for where to place the notes. The four lines are labeled first vocal, second vocal, third vocal, fourth vocal. The fourth image is a piece of sheet music paper with the title Larynx1—Voice One. It begins with the treble clef sign and a note that it is in the key of C (there are no sharps or flats). The first eight lines are filled out with musical notes and rests.

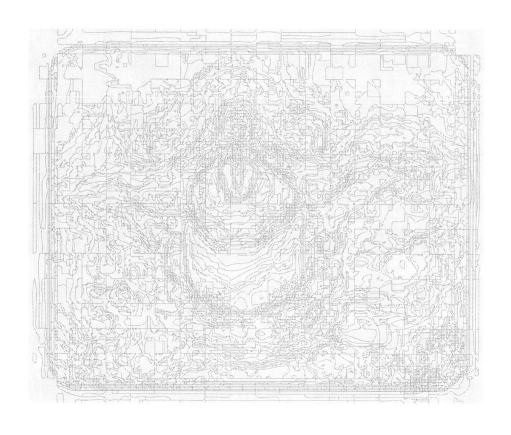

[9b] Artist study of *Larynx3* (2014).

Laser print on archival paper.

29.7 × 42 cm.

Courtesy of the artist.

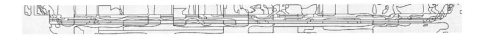

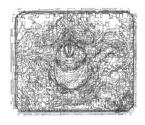

[9c] Artist study of *Larynx3* (laying out
the vector graphics in a line, 2014).

Laser print on archival paper.

29.7 × 42 cm.

Courtesy of the artist.

Larynx 1: first vocal

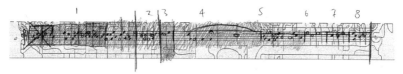

Larynx 1: second vocal

Larynx 1: third vocal

Larynx 1: fourth vocal

[9d–9g] Artist study for *Larynx Series*
(converting vector graphics to
notes on staves, 2014).

4 images, pencil and ink on
laser print.

21.59 × 27.94 cm.

Courtesy of the artist.

[9h] Sheet Music for _Larynx Series_

Pencil and ink on laser print.

21.59 × 27.94 cm.

Courtesy of the artist.

the conversion processes "eliminated the fleshy details of the original larynx: the image now emphasized architectural structures of the larynx as precise lines, which now more closely resembled a topographical map, or circuit board."[64] In essence, by converting pixels to vectors, Gee took a perspectival photograph and unspooled it, rendering an image originally structured to represent three dimensions as representing two, as if a larynx were laid out flat on a piece of paper and then abstracted to a series of lines [9b]. The center still shows the fleshy outlines of the larynx and the folds of the vocal cords—one can even still imagine them in three dimensions—but the edges of the photograph now appear as straight lines in two dimensions. Gee saw the very outer lines as reminiscent of Western musical notation: bars, staves, and notes. In a series of sketches, she laid out the four edges of the vector graphic horizontally [9c], conceived them as four separate vocal parts, and then converted the vector graphics into Western staff notation for a four-part vocal piece [9d–9g]. She then did this for the three other vector images derived from larynx photographs and produced four complete vocal parts [9h].[65]

Gee's unspooling of the larynx can also be read as a mediatic unspooling of vocalization. A computer program reads the pixels in the original photograph as instructions for reconstructing an image of a larynx. Then Gee takes over, morphing and modulating the pixels, and then changing the rules for reconstruction by asking the program to render the image as vectors. From here, she interprets as a composer and vocalist. She could have read the lines through the history of avant-garde music and interpreted them as graphic scores, but instead she mapped them onto traditional staff notation. Not only that: as the sheet music for *Larynx1—Voice One* shows, the piece is rendered in the key of C—the most fundamental key in Western notation: no notes are interpreted as sharp or flat, which means that, for instance, a pianist could play in C without ever playing the black keys on their piano. There are also no accidentals in the piece, only glissandos—slides between notes. Gee's hermeneutic doubles the process of pixelization: Western notation gives her a set of reduced possibilities for what the lines in the vectorized larynx could mean, and then the key of C further pixelates the range of potential sonic representations onto a grid. Listening to the performance in the gallery space, I hear the opposite effect. Galleries are notoriously reverberant. They are large spaces with high ceilings: "For many, the art museum is a quiet space, created for the hushed contemplation of masterpieces. . . . Yet we would be hard pressed to think of the enclosed architecture of a gallery space as being anything like silent."[66] Galleries amplify the quietest sounds, enforcing a kind of quietude in some settings like the display of famous paintings, and enforcing cacophony in others, like an art opening. In the recorded performance, the vocalists all perform in a legato style: note envelopes slope in and out of silence, and the reverberant architecture extends and commingles the sounds of the voices so that the harmonics of some notes produce their own chords and harmonies. If Gee's hermeneutic to produce the piece through Western notation was itself a kind of pixelization, the gallery performance is not so much vectorization as a kind of vocal smearing, as when watercolors run together.

I can't help but hear the a cappella vocal music resounding in the gallery as partaking an aesthetic of purity, as if it were *just* voices rising up in song. The gallery is a white cube, after all—or in our case, a pinkish cube—and all the notes are on the white keys of the piano. But that hearing, while invoked, is also impossible. For the piece sets up a chain of interpretants that returns not only to laryngoscopy—the science that dreamed it could improve singers—but also to the multiple interplays of human bodies and technologies for imaging that at once announce and deny their artifice: pixels, vectors, sheet music. This is as impure as it gets.

Once it is possible to represent vocal function as a series of sound synthesis and modulation techniques, it is also possible to take the voice outside the body, and to create voices that are entirely synthetic. This is the principle behind speech synthesis in toys and digital assistants (and in the next room) as well as a suite of contemporary audio software applications from Auto-Tune to Vocaloid.[67] The political problematic—the idea of a nonhuman or posthuman technological voice—is a familiar strand of posthumanism. Yet it is wrong to think of these technologies simply as superseding a humanist vocal subject. They enable the possibility of reframing it for "those who have no simple access to its Western, post-Enlightenment formulation, suggesting subjectivities embodied and disembodied."[68] In other words, the larynx in the *Larynx Series* at once invokes somebody's larynx and nobody's larynx. Whose larynx is it?[69]

THE SIGNALS ROOM

Exit the Larynx room to the left of where you entered. As you pass the threshold to the Signals room, the sounds change. Instead of vocal music, you hear someone or something saying "yes" in many different inflections.

Six chairs facing a white wall are arranged in a row. Some people sit and seem to manipulate the voices. Others watch. From your right wafts the smell of popcorn, and you spot two popcorn machines, one of which has clearly spent some time on fire, the other of which is making popcorn. If you walk toward it, a smiling person, who looks oddly like you — if you worked in a gallery — will offer you popcorn in a dish. A computer voice speaking nonsense emanates from the working popcorn machine, but occasionally words and phrases emerge from the babble. Its unending discourse merges with the chairs' unending affirmations: "Qocreteti neiihf hemtleexra." "Yes!" "Ca sa cfii fause." "Yeeeessss?" (and so on). On the opposite wall from where you entered, there is a video screen, with a pair of headphones on it. If you put on the headphones, you will only hear the hiss of an absent soundtrack. To your right, at the back of the gallery, is the entrance to a small alcove with black walls, with moving images projected on two walls and appearing on a flat screen that is rotated in a portrait orientation. There are some posh-looking benches to sit on. Welcome to the Signals room. From the standpoint of beholding a voice, from audition, voice is only voice insofar as it has some characteristic as a signal, a sign. This room considers what kinds of signs can make voices.

[10] Nina Katchadourian, *Talking Popcorn*

Nina Katchadourian's *Talking Popcorn* is an apparatus for speech with no subject behind it at all. *Talking Popcorn* is a sound sculpture built around a popcorn machine, a microphone, an audio interface, a computer running a custom Max/MSP patch, and speakers that take the sound of popcorn popping, digitize it, and translate it into Morse code, which is then translated into speech by the Max/MSP patch and spoken by a speech synthesizer in the gallery. For as long as there is corn to pop, it produces a continual series of speech fragments, sometimes nonsense words, sometimes intelligible speech. It offers an "audio Rorschach blot; you project meaning onto what you hear. . . . You think you hear it say all kinds of stuff."[70] The computer keeps a record of everything it says, which makes it possible for Katchadourian to go back and pick out specific words or phrases.[71] The first version of *Talking Popcorn* self-immolated on December 21, 2008, in Houston, Texas. Katchadourian built another version that began operation in January 2012.

Talking Popcorn reworks the voice synthesis paradigm, presenting a device built around an artificial larynx that is precisely nobody's: the pop-

[10] Nina Katchadourian

Talking Popcorn, 2001.

Popcorn machine, black pedestal, red
vinyl base, microphone, laptop with
custom-written Morse code program,
printed paper bags, popcorn.

228 × 228 × 182 cm.

YouTube, August 22, 2012, https://
youtu.be/YTMkzYofShc. Screenshot
by author. Courtesy of the artist.

AUDIODESCRIPTION: Two
popcorn machines stand side
by side. One has clearly been on
fire and has a series of nonsense
words emblazoned on the front.
The other is lit up and popping
away. A smiling person who looks
surprisingly like you is on call to
serve popcorn.

corn produces meaning according to a code (in this case, Morse code), and according to convention. The microphones in *Talking Popcorn* appear to vary, but they all appear to be microphones designed to pick up voices. I was particularly struck by the use of the Shure SM-57, perhaps the most common vocal microphone in the world due to its relative cheapness and legendary ability to withstand abuse—perfect for bars full of drunken patrons, speeches in inclement weather . . . or the hot interior of a popcorn popper. In *Talking Popcorn*, voice is not localized in a single source; it is distributed. The speech synthesizer is only heard as speaking when it is not speaking nonsense, and attribution of voice—nonsense or sense—falls squarely on the shoulders of auditors. Katchadourian claims that the first word spoken by *Talking Popcorn* was "we" (she later bronzed the kernels), but of course that is what she heard, not what *Talking Popcorn* intended. When *Talking Popcorn* self-immolated, she commissioned a series of expert listeners to analyze its last words: Jamieson Webster, a psychoanalyst, heard it speaking in French—"that's it, it's a game." Vanessa Price, an attorney, noted that *Talking Popcorn* self-immolated in Texas, where there is still capital punishment, and that the state's request to a subject for last words was essentially a mechanism by which subjects are called to speak their own death sentences. Christoph Cox, philosopher of sound, drew a sharp line between human and machine, and mused on Ludwig Wittgenstein's thesis that "there is no such thing as a private language" because languages require systems of rules. Cryptoanalyst Matthew Frank noted that when fed any random signal, Morse code produces a lot of *E*s and *T*s because of how it interprets individual dots and dashes, which gives an impression of "Englishness" for the apparatus' speech; he mused on what it would take to decrypt its last words if they were part of an intercepted message. Katchadourian also interviewed an astrologer, a linguist and astrobiologist, an anthropologist, a poet, and a death doula.

What a very Hegelian exercise! In this case, the subject that speaks—the popping corn—is entirely separate from the mechanism by which speech is produced. Or rather, the signifying chain's connective tissue is rendered as palpably arbitrary at every stage of sound and meaning creation. Ultimately, *Talking Popcorn*'s vocality is both technical and inherently inter- and multisubjective. The contrived nature of the apparatus suggests an underlying technicity in all voices, machine or otherwise. But *Talking Popcorn* also offers a vocality that can only be retroactively imagined: the scenario recalls the unresolvability of Eidsheim's acousmatic question—"Who is this speaking?" The demand to resolve it into an intending subject, in command of its own faculties, is one of the fundamental operations of the ideology of vocal ability. *Talking Popcorn's* playful imagination of voice is a deeply serious suggestion (or am I just speaking through it?): it demonstrates the contrived dimension of all voices — that there is no voice except through attribution, through some form of reception.

[11] Graham Pullin and Andrew Cook, *Six Speaking Chairs*

All sorts of assumptions about what is important about speech are built into augmentative and alternative communication (AAC) technologies. Traditionally, those technologies have focused on vocabulary and intelligibility at the expense of variation of expression, producing a flat-sounding affect for speakers who use them. Graham Pullin and Andrew Cook's project *Six Speaking Chairs (Not Directly) for People Who Cannot Speak* stages this problem. Rather than focusing on vocabulary and intelligibility, they built six chairs that each focus on a different aspect of tone of voice achieved through a different set of interfaces. The user can select from just a couple of preset tones of voice (Chair 1) to control of intona-

[11] **Graham Pullin and Andrew Cook**

    Six Speaking Chairs (Not Directly) for People Who Cannot Speak, 2010.

    Mixed media.

    Dimensions variable.

    Courtesy of the artists.

AUDIODESCRIPTION: Six chairs are placed in a line before you. Each has a different mechanism for generating speech. You are welcome to sit in them and experiment with the apparatuses to explore how each chair works and what it can do.

tion through drawing a waveform (Chair 4) to an array of doorbells (Chair 6). This work built on Pullin's explorations of the word *yes*—a particularly evocative one in British everyday speech—and the degrees of meaning available simply from intonation. *Six Speaking Chairs* shows that even when the voice is entirely delegated from human enunciation to device-based enunciation, parameters of control are deeply tied to experiences of intentionality and agency, both for speaking subjects (delegated and otherwise) and for those who hear them.[72]

When the technology speaks for someone who does not speak, then its political character—the managed nature of the speech possibilities and the everyday uses to which it is put—have much to say about the politics of voice and ability more generally. As Meryl Alper has shown in her study of nonverbal children and their families, AAC technologies are highly mediated. The iOS program Proloqo2Go produces a range of voices for its user, but this is still a negotiated voice, between software, speaker, and auditor. Especially for children in her study, who did not speak orally or did so with difficulty, parents can be important passage points for negotiating voice and agency. And the power of "voice" afforded by the assemblies of technology and practice she studies was strongly shaped by factors like race and class.[73] Synthetic voices and crip voices are just as raced, gendered, classed, and sexed as normate voices.

[12] Darrin Martin, *Listening In . . .*

Part of the problem with the idea behind synthetic speech, or speech in general, is that it connects expression—or, worse, expressiveness—to a single modality. Darrin Martin's project *Listening In . . . a Portrait of Charles Graser* directly considers the problem of voice reception. It is a multimedia installation built around the work of Charles Graser, who was an important early deaf test subject for cochlear implants. Martin's installation is projected across three video screens and out a set of speakers. Sound comes on and off, mixing noise, music, and speech. Sometimes there is video of Graser speaking, sometimes there is Martin's friend Daniel Sonnenfeld signing, sometimes there is writing that scrolls across a screen from left to right, sometimes someone who is not Graser reads his notes aloud.[74] Images are juxtaposed with one another: occasionally a speech waveform appears. Video noise and distortion is used to signify audio distortion and noise.

[12] Darrin Martin

Still from *Listening In . . . a Portrait of Charles Graser*, 2017.

3-channel synchronized video installation with sound.

18 minutes.

Courtesy of the artist.

AUDIODESCRIPTION: In this darkened room-within-a-room, two giant screens line the walls, showing a series of four images. The first is a ruler with some different parts of a device showing their small size. The second is a picture of an older light-skinned man, with strange colorization that makes his hair green. The third and fourth images show photographs of a light-skinned man's head from behind and the right. In the first, his hair is pulled back to reveal a small circular device installed behind his ear. In the second photo, cables extend from the ear into his shirt. A woman can be seen facing him in the distance. A screen on the right features a light-skinned man in a pink shirt, signing.

Graser's notes on a test of the cochlear implant focus a lot on qualities of voice as a signal to be perceived (or not) rather than interiority: "When talking, my voice is too loud and other voices are too quiet." "When singing in a group, I can't hear my own voice even though the person next to me can." He also treats a piano in the same fashion: "The distinctiveness and range of the piano keyboard is greater." While the politics of the cochlear implant are complicated—users and critics have discussed the emphasis on speech over music, for instance in the design of its signal processing routines, and its use as a challenge to Deaf culture and sign language—voice operates here as a *kind* of signal to be perceived, as in many of the examples already presented.[75]

Listening In . . . operates multimodally, across a d/Deaf-hearing spectrum. It is a work about a deaf man's experiments with devices for hearing. But the piece's expansion, fragmentation, and distribution of voice—especially but not only Graser's voice—suggest that non-ableist renderings of vocality must begin from understanding voice as multimodal. Whether speech, song, or other vocalizations, voice is something that can always be transduced into something else. The use of sign language in *Listening In . . .* is particularly important. In culturally Deaf contexts, signing takes up much of the agential space usually assigned to vocal speech, performing it in the visual and tactile domain (the latter especially in deaf-blind contexts). For Deaf speakers, signing can serve as a basis of sociality and intersubjectivity, potentially the foundation for political organizing as well as utopic and poetic imagination, humor and critique. The status of sign as a language is itself politically contested. Signing was for a long time excluded from language by academic linguists precisely because it did not have an oral component—an ideology of vocal ability used as the criterion for language itself. And as Karen Nakamura has shown, Japanese signers have at different times and for different political reasons argued that sign language was a different mode from spoken Japanese rather than a different language from spoken Japanese, as is common for American Sign Language (ASL) or Quebec Sign Language (LSQ). A number of North American Indigenous sign languages, also likely developed by groups of deaf people, served as lingua franca for trade and communication among geographically dispersed communities who did not share a single oral language; they were also useful for hunting and other situations where oral speech was not possible and may have been used semaphorically for long-distance communication.[76]

That *Listening In . . .* contains sign language as well as a discussion of cochlear implant history suggests a possible coexistence for these modalities of experiencing voice both within Deaf culture and without. Michele Ilana Friedner tells of suspicion of cochlear implants in Deaf communities because of their connection to oralism, a eugenic philosophy that sought to eradicate Deaf culture, even though an increasing number of culturally Deaf people want to use cochlear implants. But in *Listening In . . .* the history of the cochlear implant coexists with signing, not as a challenge to it but as one of a range of possible modes for vocality.[77] *Listening In . . .* offers a possible frame for multiple modalities of voice to coexist—speech, sound, hands, writing, and other possibilities. It does not privilege a single kind of voice that comes out of an individual's body.

[13] Hodan Youssouf, "Masques"

Hodan Youssouf's video "Masques" is part of *Our Vibrating Hands*, a project by Véro Leduc, Pamela Witcher, Daz Saunders, and Youssouf. It challenges one-way paths of musical accessibility. While strategies like sign language interpretation of lyrics and translation of sound into vibratory experience have been hallmarks of attempts to make aural music accessible to deaf audiences, they are "unidirectional; they aim to make hearing music

[13] Hodan Youssouf

Still from "Masques," 2018.

Video.

1 minute, 11 seconds.

Courtesy of the artist.

AUDIODESCRIPTION: A dark-skinned woman in a black outfit signs dramatically, moving her face behind her right hand and then bringing her face out from behind it, like putting on and removing a mask. Her body and fingertips move rhythmically. Five copies of her appear like a chorus in the background, first standing, then moving in time, until finally the image explodes into fantastic rhythmic undulations, where foreground and background become distorted through movement.

accessible to deaf people—individuals deemed to be living in a 'world of silence.' *Our Vibrating Hands* aims to deconstruct the concept of accessibility: what if hearing people had access to signed music? You don't know sign language? You can still enjoy this creation by allowing the vibrations to bewitch you!"[78]

Youssouf's "Masques" video is a particularly powerful example of the practice, combining sign language poetry with dance, visualized rhythm, and the conventions of music video. Youssouf's body announces a rhythm onto which an audience can entrain; her gestural performance moves between signing and dance; and static-expressioned copies of herself observe, shudder, and move in and out of the frame at her command, all culminating in a crescendo where the entire image bends forward and back.[79] This performance "chews and twists language," working out the contours of a tactile, bodily performance that is not audible but may well be seen as voiced.[80]

Our Vibrating Hands performs a born-Deaf form of music video, which inverts the usual accessibility narratives or building audist art to which deaf people have partial access; it suggests a new audiovisual frame for d/Deaf musicking.[81] It's not clear if anything in Youssouf's music video is actually best understood as voice, but the link to sign language poetry suggests that the possibility at least must be considered—as a fully and fundamentally nonsonic variety of vocality. Or alternatively, it could be a sign of how much of vocality can be absorbed into nonsonic or multimodal forms of expression. Like other exhibits, "Masques" also issues a political demand for voice theory: consider that there could be a voice there rather than assuming a limited set of mechanisms by which voice might be attributed. Or: consider the putative effects of voice in the world; now imagine that they can be effected with no voice at all.

EXIT THROUGH THE GIFT SHOP

Thank you for visiting "In Search of New Vocalities." The gift shop is currently closed, but feel free to stop for a rest or a bathroom break before leaving, and don't forget your stuff on the way out. Upon departure, I recommend sitting down with a friend and reflecting on your experience here and what you might do with it in the future. A guestbook is available by the door should you wish to sign or comment.

This imaginary exhibition has decentered the oral voice. The oral voice still exists in the world; it is still meaningful to people. But there are many other ways to represent, imagine, and enact voice. To that end, I have assembled groups of alternative vocal figurations to oral voice, the agential voice, and the ideology of vocal ability. Larynxes suggest an alternative point of origin for voices. Though they are just as arbitrary as the mouth as an ultimate origin for the voice, and their status as a source can be just as violently enforced and medicalized, they also open out into thinking about voices as instruments, and they are perhaps even more open to interpretation when compared to the mouth. Visual representations of the voice as an event or effect in the world unspool it as they render it in two dimensions, but they also present, in stark visual and sometimes diagrammatic terms, the tender tether between a voicing subject and a voice as an operation, one that exists in three-dimensional space, in between and among, not just from within. They also suggest one set of possibilities for nonsonic or postsonic voices. Vocal signals also starkly demonstrate the arbitrariness of the link between voice and sound—and therefore also any *particular source, kind, or quality of sound*. Perhaps this is the most difficult thing to digest aesthetically or politically, but it is also the most essential for challenging the ideology of vocal ability: voice has no necessary bodily or sonic dimension.

Voices are many things, but sometimes they are also nothing. They exist in between people; they are conditioned by their reception and circulation as much as their production. The challenge of other vocalities is, first, to imagine voices differently, and then to write and represent voice differently. It is my hope that this collection of histories, objects, and practices might inspire you, dear visitor, to imagine and represent vocal variety in new ways. If they do not, perhaps you can find other options that will work better for you. At the very least, consider returning the mouth to its place as one point source among many, consider easing up on the ideology of vocal ability, and try to imagine all the different ways in which voice, an eminently three-dimensional phenomenon, might be unspooled in still other dimensionalities.

04
—

Audile Scarification

ON NORMAL IMPAIRMENTS

In 1952, as the U.S. Navy was starting to use more powerful engines on its fighter planes and jets, it quickly discovered a problem: noise levels on aircraft carrier flight decks would be unbearable for navy personnel. In search of a solution, it commissioned the BENOX (Biological Effects of Noise, Exploratory) Report, a systematic attempt at the study of loudness and its effects on personnel. The idea was to develop a holistic account of the effects of loudness on a scientifically measurable person to discover which aspects of aircraft noise would be unbearable and find ways to mitigate those effects. The BENOX Report covered psychology, the central nervous system, communication, spatial orientation, hearing loss, and pain. Today, it is still cited for one particular measurement it helped to codify: the threshold of pain.

In hearing science, the threshold of pain is measured in decibels. A decibel (dB) is a measure of perceived loudness based on an idea of how human ears work: a single decibel change is supposed to mark a just-perceptible change in loudness.[1] In 1932, Robert L. Wegel at AT&T Bell Labs located the difference between auditory "feeling" and "pain" at different decibel levels depending on the frequency of a sound. But he considered the phenomenon only as "a matter of passing interest." In 1947 the otologist S. R. Silverman complained about the "relatively vague conception of the qualitative nature of" terms used to describe sound intolerance and chose pain as the most easily measurable quality. Silverman estimated that the threshold of pain was somewhere between 133 and 140 dB.[2] The 1953 BENOX study built on these earlier investigations and further formalized the terms of feeling and pain, becoming a standard reference on thresholds of auditory pain.

While Bell Labs and Silverman conducted their studies in laboratory conditions, BENOX asked what would happen to hearing in the open air or—perhaps more to the point—on the deck of an aircraft carrier. The BENOX researchers also clarified their terms by isolating pain from discomfort ("it is too loud") and touch ("it tickles" or "I feel something in the ear"). The study subjected five volunteer men, including three of the authors, to a series of acoustic torments: a plastic tube that exerted constant pressure directly into the ear canal that was then connected to a mercury manometer or a pistonphone; a 300-watt loudspeaker transmitting sounds at 50, 100, and 2,000 hertz (Hz); a "powerful" siren inside an anechoic chamber; and a jet engine, with afterburner, outdoors on a runway, which they approached from the side (standing behind a firing jet engine might be louder, but it is also highly inadvisable). Each subject used the same ear for all tests—left or right. For the in-ear tests, they were allowed to control the volume themselves "until the report of pain was made." For the siren and jet engine, test subjects wore calibrated microphones over one ear (to measure sound level) and then walked slowly toward the sound source with their fingers in their ears. At regular intervals, they would remove a finger and determine if they felt pain.[3] That is how they determined 140 dB was the threshold of pain. Today, other, lower measures have become important markers of industrial safety, temporary or long-term danger, sonic power, or discomfort. Even though they are rendered in the anodyne language of decibel measurements, the boundaries between pleasure and pain, safety and danger, are freighted with meaning.

While decibel talk still informs much acoustic science and sound policy, in this chapter I move beyond quantitative thresholds to consider the politics and meaning of acoustic pain and loudness as a kind of experience and as a set of cultural and political thresholds. Measurements and reports of acoustic pain are intimately tied up with the politics and production of hearing impairments. Understanding this process requires a concept of *normal impairments*: a set of impairments that are coded and experienced as normal, expected, and even desirable in some settings, to the point that they are inscribed into industrial standards, architecture, design, hospitality, and new technologies. This chapter considers hearing impairments, but normal impairments exist in many domains—perception, fatigue, emotion, endurance, mobility, and beyond. Normal impairments cut a transversal across concepts like debility, disability, ability, and capacity because they are a rare case where an incapacity may be socially preferred or even advantageous in some settings.

LOSING HEARING LOSS

Thinking with loudness can illuminate the productivity of hearing impairments. To do so, one must dispense with fixed ideas of loudness and hearing loss: that loudness is always "bad for you" and that hearing loss is always undesired and undesirable. People put themselves in extremely loud situations all the time, sometimes for practical purposes, sometimes for pleasure. Endurance of loudness can be seen as a kind of subjective self-assertion. In this way, the BENOX experiment can also be read as a spectacle of masculine stoicism. In his discussion of responses to loud sound in American military culture, Martin Daughtry writes that "the ability to display hypermasculine comfort in the face of painfully loud and invasive violent acts remains a badge of honor among service members."[4] This type of stoicism is not a rare thing. Some professions, like artillery soldiers, professional athletes, and construction or oil rig workers, carry their tolerance for loud sound as a mark of accomplishment in their fields. Although this chapter is not really about my own experience, I will confess to having performed endurance feats not so different from those of the BENOX researchers: not for the love of science but for the love of music.

What if there were a demonstrable cultural preference for not only loud sound but also a little hardness of hearing in some settings? What if hearing loss is not necessarily a loss? This chapter develops an account of *audile scarification* as a framework for thinking about culturally produced auditory impairments. I define audile scarification as *the consensual transformation of the capacity to hear*. In the next section, I specify why I have chosen scarification as a metaphor and the specific meaning of *consent* that I am using. But first, I confront the limits of the term *hearing loss* head-on.

The majority of medical and scientific writing about hearing loss simply takes as axiomatic that it is better to be fully hearing than hard of hearing and that it is better to be hard of hearing than deaf, but the medical preference for hearing over hardness of hearing or deafness is not as easy a matter as it might first appear. *Hearing, hearing loss,* and *hearing impairment* are highly medicalized terms; this much is obvious. Some of the bias for hearing might be the medical model of disability that individualizes it, and some of this bias might be attributed to the ideology of ability, since the unstated and assumed preference for ability over disability is most ideologically powerful when it is presented as obvious.[5] Either way, there is no value-neutral or culture-free space from which medicine can describe human incapacity or capacity.

The medical writing on hearing loss is shaped by a striking and fundamental contradiction: hearing loss is treated as both preventable and inevitable, sometimes in the very same text. *Presbycusis,* or age-related hearing impairment (ARHI), names "the inevitable deterioration in hearing ability that occurs with age," to quote a recent *Lancet* article, while age-related hearing impairment also includes genetic and environmental variation. Presbycusis has a long history of clinical and epidemiological study: though probably understood from ancient times, it was first clinically described in English in 1899. Recent research on presbycusis has focused on cost, quality of life for those affected, and lost productivity for employers, among other things. All these measures are at best schematic. Many jobs could probably be done without hearing anything at all; quality of life depends on factors that may have nothing to do with hearing; and cost would vary depending on access to health care. Traditionally, different paths to hearing loss have been attributed to gender, occupation, and social class. More recently, voluntary exposure to loud sound through headphone use and concert attendance has entered the epidemiological literature.[6] If most people hear in a certain way, why call that diminished or damaged? Other than a receding limit, a fantastic statistical regularity, what could undamaged hearing be?

Hearing loss is also a rather poor umbrella term to describe the variety of hearing impairments, even though it is still widely used. It is a metaphor. Just as the Earth is not actually shaped like a sphere, not everyone who acquires a hearing impairment has the same experience; some do not lose any hearing at all. Sometimes people acquire new sensitivities to sound, called *hyperacusis,* or *tinnitus,* where phantom sound comes to plague them. Deaf activists and scholars in Deaf studies have long criticized notions of hearing loss or hearing damage, and the framing of deafness as an impairment or disability is itself highly contested.[7] Some writers have proposed *Deaf Gain* as an inversion of the term *hearing loss*, as a way of centering d/Deaf people and Deaf culture. Deaf Gain is meant to mark the movement from one cultural sphere to another, highlighting capital-D Deafness as something other than the negative of hearing, and challenging the persistent misconception among the hearing that deafness produces social isolation. While the critique of hearing loss in the Deaf Gain concept is valuable, the experience of tolerating loud music clearly isn't Deaf Gain. Even if it were modified to something like "hard-of-hearing-gain," the Deaf Gain concept is still insufficient to the situation. M. Remi Yergeau has pointed out that Deaf Gain relies on ableist logics like mental fitness and visual acuity, and Michele Friedner has argued that the Deaf Gain model fits too easily into a human capital–oriented perspective where deaf people are considered in terms of "added value" to an industry or a nation.[8] A proper analysis requires moving beyond a model of impairments as nothing more than undesirable deficits.

AUDILE SCARIFICATION: A WORKING DEFINITION

The majority of acquired auditory impairments are best understood as a kind of mass body-modification project. True, some come from the decreased acuity that happens with aging or from illness. But in industrialized contexts, most auditory impairments develop as ears are touched—repeatedly, over time—by loud sounds. Those touches gradually affect listeners, who may gain the capacity to tolerate certain kinds of loudness or may become more sensitive to certain kinds of sounds. They may become less able to hear certain kinds of sounds or distinguish foreground from background in loud situations. On the skin, this kind of body transformation has been considered as *scarification*, so I will name this phenomenon *audile scarification*: the cultural tendency to transform people's capacity to hear.

Audile scarification is a metaphor, and like all metaphors it is evocative: ambiguous in some ways and precise in others. (Remember, dear reader, that the term *hearing loss* is also metaphoric.) Scarification is not a medically or mechanically accurate term for what happens to ears that are repeatedly exposed to loud sound. Perhaps ossification or calcification or hardening might be better, but *hard* or *ossified* or *calcified* evoke an inflexibility in a subject, where I want to consider how, in some circumstances, impairments can afford increased access and mobility. As a category, hardness of hearing also has its own rich cultural history. I considered *cloudy hearing* as another possible metaphor, but clouds are semantically overburdened right now, at least in media studies and in the tech business.[9]

Drawing from its usage in fields like anthropology, performance studies, art history, and Indigenous studies, I use *scarification* to describe large-scale, consensual, culturally coded modification of bodies. Usually considered alongside other forms of body art, like tattooing and branding, voluntary scarification has been understood cross-culturally as a way of writing an autobiography onto one's skin, claiming possession of history; of managing the relationship between past and present, self and other, as well as self and collective. Consensual scarification can be an assertion of agency and subjecthood. Understood this way, scarification is not necessarily ugly, violent, or an act of defacement, though those associations are common in polite, bourgeois, and white academic worlds. Audile scarification writes auditory history into the body and provides access to spaces and communities unavailable to the nonscarified.

In a particularly provocative article, David Le Breton calls adolescent self-cutting a kind of "symbolic homeopathy," a way of "hurting oneself to feel less pain. A part of the body must be sacrificed in order to save a part of the self." He found that self-cutting among the distressed adolescents he studied was an assertion of self-worth, of personal value. While intentional exposure to loud sound is not at all the same thing as self-cutting—for one thing, it has no necessary connection with distress—the connection between the aesthetic and anaesthetic that Le Breton identifies certainly plays a role in how audile scarification works. Intentional body transformations, even those that can result in impairments, are intimately connected to self-formation.[10] Audile scarification also differs from other kinds of scarification because it happens in the middle and inner ear: audile scarification is inscription *in* the body, not *on* the body. It is not immediately visible on the skin, though it might be visible by the presence of a body. For instance: when one person sees another at a loud concert, no earplugs in their ears, no visible pain on their face, no reaction of perceptible torment. Or: two workers walk through a construction site without hearing protection, treating the cacophony as background rather than an assault on the senses. Is the first case aestheticism and the second asceticism? They are, in fact, related.

Not all scarification means the same thing: it has no preordained political or cultural valence. Nonvoluntary scarification has often been a tool of surveillance and a way of materializing power on bodies, most notably those of enslaved and colonized peoples.[11] When scholars have considered something like audile scarification, it has generally been in nonvoluntary conditions and generally more in settings of violence and conflict: explosions in war, police attacking protesters with sonic weapons like long-range acoustic devices (LRADs), and "no touch" acoustic torture techniques employed by the U.S. military. Other authors have examined the politics of this kind of acoustic pain with the sophistication and nuance it requires.[12] This chapter takes the question of pain in another direction entirely: toward everyday life. Acoustic torture is sound directed against people. Audile scarification is tied to spaces designed for people to inhabit.

In everyday life, tolerance for high-volume sound becomes a kind of rite of certain institutions or an obligatory passage point to enter certain kinds of spaces: concerts, restaurants, factories, sporting events, blockbuster movies, bathrooms, airplanes, fitness classes, political rallies, even some stores. As a kind of body modification, audile scarification comes from participating in the everyday urban life of many societies; it can also come from participating in specific subcultures. It can be the result of intentionally exposing oneself to loud sound, a result of work experience, or simply being in places where loudness is part of the price of admission.

To participate in a loud music performance, to subject oneself to the roar of an airplane engine or high-powered bathroom hand dryer, to work in a loud factory: all these practices ask something of bodies. They mark them. To submit oneself to these situations is to *consent* to a certain potential (or requirement) for audile scarification, in Antonio Gramsci's sense of the term. To twist his words around a bit, audile scarification is consensual inasmuch as it involves *consent to the general direction given sonic life by the dominant group in a situation.*[13] Consent exists on a continuum with coercion, and it may be closer to "saying uncle" than offering enthusiastic, affirmative assent. It is precisely not the kind of affirmative consent currently promoted by anti–sexual violence education. It is not the informed consent of someone signing a research ethics board agreement, though legally it might be the kind of informed consent one gives when signing a contract acknowledging the dangers of a job before agreeing to do it.[14] It is consent in the sense that people are going along with the scene rather than rebelling or exiting. If the sound levels on the airplane are too loud, it's not like passengers can complain or get up and leave. If the machinery in a shop is too loud, workers are unlikely to just quit. Norms of gender and sexuality do more to discourage people from using shared public bathrooms than high-powered hand dryers placed in resonant, tiled spaces that effectively amplify them.[15] As Gramsci's concept of consent illustrates, neither population is coerced, but neither population has given affirmative, enthusiastic consent to the general direction of the situation. Consensual impairment is a much more widespread phenomenon than usually considered—either by disability scholars or in the medical literature. Where impairment is discussed as desirable, it is usually considered in terms of desire to belong to a particular disability community or as a form of malingering, in order to claim a disability benefit. The consensual impairment in audile scarification is something different: it does not come with a personal or bureaucratic identification.

If scarification anthropologizes the problem, and consent socializes it, the term *audile* raises the question of technology and technique. It connotes "hearing and listening as developed and specialized practices, rather than inherent capacities."[16] Historically, it is attached to technique and practice: physicians, telegraphers, radio operators, and eventually early users of phonographs, telephones, radios, microphones, and other sound technologies, all developed *audile techniques*. *Audile* can also be thought of as "audible minus one": an idea of hearing without a coherent, transhistorical, self-same subject at its base. To talk of audile technique is to subtract a unified subject from hearing and listening and instead treat those faculties as ensembles of techniques, practices, capabilities, tendencies, and institutions. To talk of audile scarification is to talk of bodies, spaces, and histories rather than ideals, individuals, and declining abilities.

Audile scarification is at once a physical, physiological, and cultural process. In considering audile scarification as a problem somewhere between phenomenology, culture, and technology, acquired hearing impairments indicate something more—and less—than another attack on an otherwise undamaged, fully integral listening body. Saying that some situations actively produce audile scarification is a very different claim from saying that "noise is bad for you" or that widespread use of earbuds and headphones is causing, to quote several recent studies, an "epidemic of hearing loss," or to assume that altered hearing is an object of "aversion and fear."[17] A theory of audile scarification also holds in critical suspension the claims about the radical, disruptive potential of noise.[18]

Consider a setting rarely mentioned in the writings on noise: public bathrooms. Bathrooms have been a central concern in recent queer and trans politics as sites where gender and sexual conformity are enforced or transgressed, at least in the developed world. They have also been a central site of disability organizing. Public bathrooms, especially shared bathrooms, also have a sound politics to them, from the presupposition of quiet and isolation of stalls from one another, to the conditions under which people address one another, to the noises visitors are expected or not expected to make. In situ, high-powered hand dryers like the Dyson Airblade can reach "the sound level of a road drill, and are exceptionally loud considering the sensitivity of the context." In essence, the architectural features of a standard-issue public bathroom work like an amplifier for a hand dryer: parallel walls; hard, reflective surfaces; low ceilings; lack of ventilation and access to the outdoors—all these features amplify an already loud sound. The issue here is not that the dryer causes audile scarification for users, though it certainly could over time. The issue is that the dryer installations presuppose users who are a little hard of hearing, or who do not experience these sound pressure levels as painful. The point at which a sound is painful varies widely for people by age, personal history, medical condition, even mood and time of day. Young children, or people with hyperacusis or other hearing sensitivities, may find the sound painful or even unbearable. Others may simply find it to be very loud.[19]

A bathroom sound space that requires a little hearing impairment to tolerate represents something of an inversion of the ways in which impairment and disability are normally written about. And it is not a unique situation: the same can be said for restaurants or movie theaters in many cities.[20] Robert McRuer's oft-cited term *compulsory able-bodiedness* captures the relationship between ability and disability that is legislated in countless contexts and institutions. But audile scarification is a normal impairment that functions politically *as if it were* a form of able-bodiedness—it is the preferred bodily state. Because hearing impairment is built into norms of hearing, hand dryers in bathrooms can be loud like club techno.[21] This produces a bizarre situation where one is hearing impaired if one cannot hear conversation well enough, but one is normal if one is impaired enough to survive a public bathroom with a certain kind of appliance. And because hearing impairment is built into concepts of normal hearing, loud spaces can exist without much comment, while hearing science can write about hearing loss as both preventable and inevitable.

Hearing impairment is normal hearing both in the old structural linguistic sense of something being defined by that which it is not and as a general condition. Engineers, noise abatement specialists, audiologists, and epidemiologists all know very well that normal hearing is a construct, but just the same, they act with and from a working model of normal hearing. Impairment is a product of the interaction between ears and media, between ears and technologies, ears and environments; and, as discussed in chapter 1, the concept of impairment is itself also a media concept. The contemporary concept of normal hearing emerged out of the idea of communication impairments and from a very specific time and place. For instance, the claim that normal human hearing operates between the frequencies of 20 hertz and 20 kilohertz (kHz) is the result of an alliance between the New York League of the Hard of Hearing and AT&T Bell Labs in the 1920s.[22] Today, the 20 Hz–20 kHz range can be found everywhere, from university textbooks to technical standards to the boxes of consumer electronics. And yet very few if any adults can hear to 20 kHz. By this definition, almost every normal adult (the more provocative term used in hearing research is *ontologically normal*) has hearing that infracts the norm. As Georges Canguilhem writes, norms come from "an illusion of retroactivity": "In anthropological experience, a norm cannot be original."[23] As it is now understood, normal hearing was invented after the ideas of hardness of hearing and deafness already existed.

Just as audile scarification challenges existing understandings of compulsory able-bodiedness, it also expands—perhaps uncomfortably—on Julie Livingston's notion of debility, introduced in chapter 1. Livingston connects debility to what she calls the Tswana moral imagination: one part imagination of misfortune, one part popular memory. Audile scarification is memory inscribed inside the body, somewhere between the middle ear, the inner ear, and the brain. It is a "normal and expected" form of impairment, one that has no necessary relationship to disability—sometimes it may come to be experienced as disability; sometimes it may not. As Livingston and, more recently, Jasbir Puar have both argued, the expectation that some bodies will become impaired is itself political, and stratified according to whose life and abilities are considered valuable, and in what way.[24] Audile scarification is an embodied form of memory that shapes the experience of present and future. It is a materialization of Alison Winter's claim in *Memory* that "who we are is intimately tied to our past experiences and actions."[25]

EXPECTING SCARIFICATION

In 2012 I was in Silicon Valley doing ethnographic research on signal processing technologies for sound. My interest in models of hearing built into audio technologies—an extension of my prior work on the shadows of a hearing subject encoded into MP3s—led me to a research office of DTS (Dedicated to Sound, but nobody calls it that), which produces both consumer and industrial audio technologies. In a nondescript office building somewhere near the wonderfully named city of Los Gatos, California, I met Martin Walsh, an engineer, who had been given a broad brief by the marketing department: design a "better" button for audio technologies. This was not the first better button to be introduced in consumer audio. "Loudness" buttons on midcentury home stereo systems simulated the effects of loud sound at low volumes by boosting low and high frequencies. The "bass boost" button on portable audio technologies also falls under this category. And of course, listeners have long had access to basic equalization options to boost or cut highs, midrange, and lows to their individual preferences. In essence, Walsh was being asked to make a *better* better button.

Walsh and his colleagues came up with a different approach to the problem. Instead of adjusting a static set of frequencies, why not customize the response for the person and the music in real time? This would align with the general trend of mass customization in consumer media technologies. But they went a step further. Reasoning that most people's musical taste is fixed when they are young, and building on knowledge of age-related hearing loss, they decided to design a technology that would make music sound like it did when the listener was young. To accomplish this, the designers would have to assume a certain level of impairment on the part of end users that could then be incorporated into the technology's design.

When I visited, they had a working prototype program to do just this. Each listener would take a hearing test. The software would compare its analysis of the user's hearing against its analysis of the changing frequency spectrum of the music playing through it. Then, the sound of the music would be transformed in real time according to the comparison. We discussed the implications: theoretically, this would make music sound better, but it would also, perhaps, remind the listener of what listening to music was like when they were younger, giving them ears to hear music anew, and perhaps opening them up to new kinds of musical experience as well as a renewed appreciation for music in general. To someone who loves music, this seemed like a laudable goal. I asked to try it. I will try to describe the experience (drawn from my notes at the end of the day):

> I sit down and put on a set of headphones. I take a variant of a standard hearing test. The computer plays tones, I click a mouse every

time I hear something. It registers the result and constructs a profile of me, a forty-one-year-old hearer.

I should know better, but it feels like I have aced the test. It feels like I heard everything.

The next thing I hear is the beginning of a Red Hot Chili Peppers ballad. This is not music I am inclined to love: though I purchased a couple of RHCP CDs in the early 1990s, I never thought of the band as built for ballads. I hear some guitar strums and Anthony Kiedis, their lead singer, doing his best to sound soulful.

Martin asks me if I am ready. I say yes. He clicks the mouse to switch the playback over to the processed version of the song.

In reality, it is a small gesture of a single finger, transduced into electricity and then zeros and ones, toggling between two sets of if/then options.

In my attempt to describe what happened next, I can only resort to similes:

It was like he threw a giant, weighty lever or pressed a massive, red button that was normally kept under a glass cover.

It felt like an ice pick has entered my ear.

It was as if I had been in the deepest of sleeps, in the darkest of nights, and someone pried my eyes open and shined in a halogen headlight.

It was like someone served me a meal made entirely out of monosodium glutamate.

I seek out intensity in musical experience, but this music was all out of whack. It was too *high*, too *sharp*, too *intense* in all the wrong ways.

From the look on my face, Martin could tell I didn't like it.

"We're still working on it," he said.

This is one of the interesting features of the phenomenology of apperception: one cannot hear oneself not hearing, though one may hear oneself not hearing well.[26] So I must first question my hearing, since I was the subject of this listening test. I did actually know better than to believe I had aced the test. In 2009 lightning and thunder struck in the alley behind my home office on a day when I was writing and had the window open. I lost hearing in one ear for a day or two. Shortly thereafter, an audiologist assured me my hearing was fine, even good, "for a former rock musician of my age."

Even as it brought me a certain amount of musical displeasure, auditioning DTS's technology brought me a certain intellectual pleasure: here is a technology that scripts audile scarification into its basic operation, and even its justification for existence. And my own negative reaction to it should not be taken as a critique. As in many other media fields, from sound mixing to color balance, subtle rather than total application of a signal processing approach may produce more aesthetically satisfying results, and I was experiencing a technology in its early development stages.[27] Or, to continue the seasoning analogy, this may simply be a case of "a little goes a long way."[28] As of this writing, DTS used a version of the process in a product called Headphone: X, but the technology has not otherwise been widely applied. Regardless of its final form or level of financial success, as an intellectual endeavor, the project still has a lot to tell us as a theory of the relationship between pleasure and hearing loss.

Because of the range of hearing from person to person, the software's first assumption is actually good: test the hearing; don't assume something from the positionality of the subject. It was designed to somehow overcome aesthetically what I could not overcome physically—one cannot hear through one's own hearing gaps (though the ring of tinnitus might be a reminder of scarification). And I all too willingly complied by imagining my own hearing as completely functional, even though I knew that not to be the case. So: assume audile scarification rather than uniform hearing. At least from an engineering standpoint, it is an attempt to account for aural diversity, however incomplete that gesture may be. A look at the signal-flow chart for Walsh's technology shows how hearing and the contingency of sound is written into the code (figure 4.1). The software essentially measures the changing dynamic balance of the music playing through it in real time, separating the audio into sixty-four separate bands, then compares that with a measurement of the listener's ability to hear in each of those bands, and then adjusts the sound of the music to compensate. Their accounting for the limits of human hearing as part of the schema for signal processing puts it in a long line of audio technologies from the Bell system on down. At another level, it is remarkable because even though it requires a single ideal model of an undamaged listener, it also develops an individualized profile of a listener as well as a profile of each piece of music. On one side, there is the model of all possible audible musical sound and a fully hearing listener. On the other, there are the changes in the sound of music from moment to moment, also accounting for loudness in the setting of playback, set against the affordances of one individual listener. While earlier technologies like telephone systems and MP3s operationalized the limits, gaps, and absences of hearing in an idealized human subject, Walsh's system tries to deliver more pleasure by accounting for audile scarification and tuning (in) to it. The sound it makes is shaped on the basis of the intended loudness of playback, the output capabilities of a particular device, and the "unique hearing characteristics of a listener."[29]

Walsh and his collaborators make this point explicitly in their patent application by referring to ISO Standard 7029 (2000) as prior art. Titled "statistical distribution of hearing thresholds related to age and gender," ISO Standard 7029 outlines a set of expected norms with respect to decreasing hearing sensitivity over time. The DTS patent adapts a graph that shows age twenty as a baseline for hearing, with each decade of life representing decreased auditory acuity (figure 4.2). Based on a series of papers published in the 1970s, the standard is meant to provide a method of determining what "normal" is for the analysis of hearing acuity. In other words, the International Organization for Standardization (ISO) has a specified standard for how people *should* lose their ability to hear over time. Definitionally, it is a standard for *normal impairment*. The standard itself has been subject to intense debate and criticism within the hearing research community, and it was replaced in 2017. Even the patent application takes the trouble to put scare quotes around "average" hearing difference; the averages—or, more accurately, medians—are used as baselines for comparison.[30] Audiology produces the subject of normal hearing and governs a proliferation of disabilities that radiate from that norm.[31] So too do the algorithms engineered into everyday media technologies.

Both ISO 7029 (2000) and the DTS technology are built around an idea of a normally impaired auditor. The subjects who live inside this ideological frame—and here I am the perfect example at the moment I believe I have aced the hearing test—know very well that the standard of ontologically normal hearing is unattainable and use it anyway. From this contradiction between the will to believe and the obvious falsity of a perfect auditor, the normally impaired subject emerges: a subject that is supposed to acquire impairments, in this case a subject that loses their hearing as they age. This construct can then be operationalized in all sorts of ways: from industrial standards and consumer technologies, to medicine, to urban and domestic design, to artistic practices, to gatekeeping scenes and venues.[32]

Sometimes it might be better to be a little hard of hearing; some settings actively work against an ideological preference for unimpaired hearing: factories, brass sections, galleries, public bathrooms, fitness clubs, and

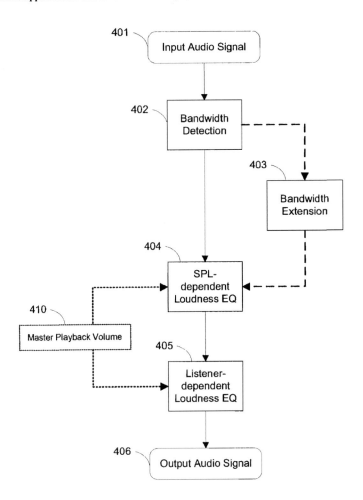

4.1 Signal processing scheme for Walsh's "Better Button." Martin Walsh, Edward Stein, and Jean-Marc Jot, "Dynamic Compensation of Audio Signal for Improved Perceived Spectral Imbalances," U.S. Patent No. U.S. 2012/0063616 (March 15, 2012), 5.

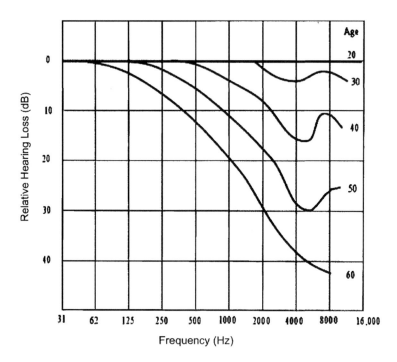

4.2   Graphic of Age-Related Hearing Loss from ISO Standard 7029 (2000), labeled as "prior art" in the patent application. Martin Walsh, Edward Stein, and Jean-Marc Jot, "Dynamic Compensation of Audio Signal for Improved Perceived Spectral Imbalances," U.S. Patent No. U.S. 2012/0063616 (March 15, 2012), 9.

sporting events are all spaces that are easier to tolerate with a little hearing impairment. Audile scarification makes these loud spaces more tolerable, even potentially pleasurable. Michele Friedner and Stefan Helmreich have argued that "experience rarely fits into ideal types such as 'seeing,' 'hearing,' 'signing,' or 'vibrating.'" They rightly argue against a "clean division" between experiences of hearing and deafness, when in fact there are many points of potential articulation.[33] Just as deafness is a construct of culture and biology, so too is hearingness.[34] Putatively normal hearing experience might have more in common with deafness than it normally lets on.[35] Echoing Du Bois's famous concept of the color line, Christopher Krentz has proposed an idea of a "hearing line" (signed HEAR LINE) to describe an analogous phenomenon that draws on "both biological and cultural notions of difference" but which nevertheless divides and hides a "wide assortment" of relationships to sound and the self, since many deaf people have residual hearing.[36] The norm of the able-eared hearing person does not have the same wide range of identifications around that faculty. In fact, the adjective *hearing* when applied to a person also papers over a wide range of fine gradations in experience, orientation, and sensibility concealed via ableism.

Recent trends in research on hearing acquisition also seem to suggest the need to broaden definitions and understandings of hearing as a set of capacities. In a forthcoming study of cochlear implants (CIs), researchers Stephanie Lloyd and Alexandre Tremblay argue that the contemporary conception of hearing is distributed across many domains of signals—auditory, environmental, biological, linguistic, visual—all with their own cadres of experts and specialists. Research on hearing acquisition has largely moved past "unisensory" approaches to hearing and speech development, and now attends to "the embodiment of disparate signals" as well as "social, economic, political, and intimate factors that are believed to shape the qualities" of sound as it is experienced. Contrast this multimodal and cross-sensory approach with the summary of hearing loss given in a recent textbook on the subject. After considering environmental noise, ototoxicity, conductive hearing loss in infancy, vestibular schwannoma (a kind of noncancerous tumor in the ear), Ménière's disease, and diabetes, Jos J. Eggermont concludes that "the dominant causes of acquired hearing loss are occupational and recreational noise exposure and being treated with ototoxic drugs." While the causes listed are contextual—occupational and recreational (a point expanded upon in his discussion of epidemiology)—Eggermont attributes the determinant cause of hearing loss to material force, either as "noise" or one or another biochemical force. This results in a fascinating split. While CI research suggests the possibility of "a range of expressions of 'hearing,'" no such possibility appears to exist in the hearing loss literature. The hearing loss literature thus reads like a funhouse mirror of the discourse on the sublime, where noise as an inherent force overrides the capacities of a sensing subject.[37]

To take audile scarification seriously is to acknowledge that most hearing people also have some residual deafness, which manifests in many different ways. Audilely scarred people might well experience themselves as "in" a certain kind of cultural scene or immune to certain kinds of auditory pain. In other settings, they might also experience that scarification as a kind of *loss*. While hearing loss is an ableist metaphor, it is also one that shapes the experience of a subset of the audilely scarred.[38] Hearing loss implies a unity of hearing from which people diverge. Audile scarification points to the essential plurality of hearingness. It also points to its own cultural utility.

SEEKING SCARIFICATION:
IS 120 DB THE NUMBER OF THE SUBLIME?

In a 2009 essay, "The Seductive (yet Destructive) Appeal of Very Loud Music," Barry Blesser searched for an explanation for why people who surely know better would expose themselves to very loud sounds when a pair of earplugs was sitting right in front of them. Ignorance? False consciousness? Cruel optimism? Residual evolutionary baggage? Drug-like endorphin release? A tendency to ignore delayed consequences? "Several years ago, I attended the awards banquet of a professional sound engineering society, which was sponsored by a company that manufacturers inexpensive ear protectors. A sample gift was placed on each plate. When the music entertainment began, at deafening intensities well over 120 dB, I was the only person in a room of 300 professional audio engineers who inserted the ear protectors."[39] When Blesser says that the music playing at his reception was over 120 dB, that was not an actual measurement. It was a feeling of "so loud as to be dangerous" or perhaps a comparison to his other experiences, or to his memories of other sonic experiences. As shown in figure 4.3, 120 dB is well above the loudness threshold where short-term exposure, without hearing protection, has the potential to produce permanent hearing impairments.

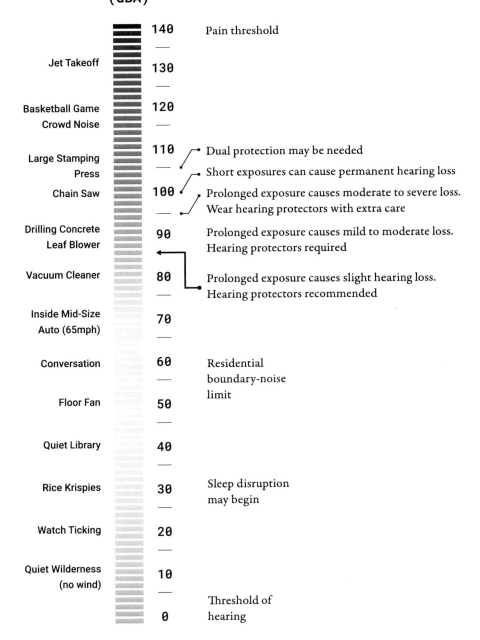

Typical Sound Levels
(dBA)

Sound	dBA	Effect
	140	Pain threshold
Jet Takeoff	130	
Basketball Game Crowd Noise	120	
Large Stamping Press	110	Dual protection may be needed
		Short exposures can cause permanent hearing loss
Chain Saw	100	Prolonged exposure causes moderate to severe loss. Wear hearing protectors with extra care
Drilling Concrete Leaf Blower	90	Prolonged exposure causes mild to moderate loss. Hearing protectors required
Vacuum Cleaner	80	Prolonged exposure causes slight hearing loss. Hearing protectors recommended
Inside Mid-Size Auto (65mph)	70	
Conversation	60	Residential boundary-noise limit
Floor Fan	50	
Quiet Library	40	
Rice Krispies	30	Sleep disruption may begin
Watch Ticking	20	
Quiet Wilderness (no wind)	10	
	0	Threshold of hearing

4.3 A decibel scale listing different everyday sounds.

In other words, Blesser is describing the point at which sound becomes too powerful, too dangerous, too painful, or otherwise too much. As with the threshold of pain, numbers stand in for much wider swaths of aesthetic experience. In philosophy and aesthetics, the breakdown of the senses is the point at which writers start to talk about the sublime. Edmund Burke used loudness explicitly to make his description of the sublime: "Excessive loudness alone is sufficient to overpower the soul, to suspend its action, and to fill it with terror. The noise of vast cataracts, raging storms, thunder, or artillery, awakes a great and awful sensation in the mind, though we can observe no nicety or artifice in those sorts of music."[40] This is a fascinating passage because it at once suggests that excessive loudness has a power all its own to overwhelm the senses, and then connects that putatively independent power to phenomena that all threaten bodies in a much more multisensory (and in some cases holistic) fashion—war and weather, as well as sounds of unknown origin. Immanuel Kant agreed with this commingling of pleasure and pain but divided the sublime into the mathematical sublime—the experience of great quantity—and the dynamic sublime, which produces an experience of fear. Kant's notion of the sublime can be linked with "an experience of inner freedom based on some kind of cognitive failure" but also through the displacement of materiality— it is the attempt at contemplation that produces sublimity.[41] The concept of sublimity is debatable in itself. Critics of the term like Ashon Crawley and Judy Lochhead have linked it to white supremacy and binary conceptions of gender.[42] Yet one finds it, or something like it, everywhere in discussions of loudness.

Much writing on loud sound tends to invoke the sublime without naming it. Loudness regularly appears in writings on modern amplified music. Olivia Lucas's description of her experience of a Sunn O))) concert provides a good sense of one reason listeners seek out loudness: "The sound envelops my body, cutting me off from other sensations, making me safe. Closing my eyes, I sway slowly from side to side to the slow beat of the vibrational pulses. I am touching sound." This is not a genre-specific phenomenon. In his ethnography of Japanese noise music, David Novak quotes from a conversation with a friend: "'The volume just sucks all the air out of the room,' leaving the listener suspended in sound."[43] Both of these experiences are meant to be extraordinary—to facilitate a different relationship to one's own body.

This kind of experience of loudness can operate as a form of consensual desubjectification (again thinking consent with Gramsci).[44] It becomes increasingly difficult to do anything other than be present; one cannot talk or be heard. One cannot do anything other than pay attention. Alongside music, this kind of description of experience also arises in relation to sporting events, protests, some religious rituals, and other events defined by their use of loudness in combination with some sort of collectivity. For instance, Pedro Marra considers sound pressure level in Brazilian football stadiums as an affective force: fans slam the bases of their chairs into the concrete below to generate extremely loud soundscapes in order to try to influence action on the field; the space explodes with levels approaching 120 dB when a goal is scored. American football journalism regularly reports on decibel levels reached in stadiums, with loudness being considered an aspect of home field advantage, and sometimes the NFL sanctions teams for juicing it, as when the Atlanta Falcons pumped amplified, recorded crowd noise into their stadium to artificially increase the volume in 2014. During the 2020 COVID pandemic, different professional sports experimented with adding crowd noise to broadcasts of contests held without fans present and even with pumping crowd sound into otherwise empty arenas to simulate the experience for players.[45]

Consensual desubjectification is also a desired result in some corners of the hospitality industry. Restaurants and bars in some countries are designed to be loud to give a sense of buzz or excitement. For instance, American hospitality scholars have attempted to correlate decibel levels and revenue. In 2010 a review of 157 papers concluded that loud music increased the time people spent in retail and hospitality spaces. *Psychology Today* announced the result with the headline "It's So Loud, I Can't Hear My Budget."[46] There seems to be a widespread belief in the U.S. hospitality industry that loudness increases pleasure, but the experimental evidence for this claim is relatively limited: few people have actually done studies that could prove or disprove the hypothesis that loudness itself is a source of pleasure. The belief itself suggests something about the cultural work that loudness—and ideas of loudness—can do.

That loudness produces pleasure and interest of its own accord is also an axiom in music production and radio broadcasting, where perceived loudness is assumed to be linked to excitement and interest.[47] Meanwhile, as Trevor Pinch and Karin Bijsterveld note, loudness seems to be part of a national culture: Swedish kindergartens use decibel meters to keep kids quiet, and even a "British" pub in Stockholm remains relatively quiet as the night rolls on.[48] This stands in stark contrast to the penchant for hard surfaces, lack of absorptive material, and pumped-in music in mid- to upscale restaurants in cities like Montreal and New York.[49] In restaurants, loudness might be a side effect of visual design aesthetics, like bare walls, high ceilings, and no tablecloths (or carpets, or acoustic tiles), or it could be understood as an intended design effect to create a sense of energy and excitement. Loudness is thus a social phenomenon, whether or not it was guided directly by intent.

Consensual desubjectification can also be a coping strategy. In Ben Hamper's *Rivethead*, noise appears as a metaphor for violence that the factory environment and assembly-line work wreak on workers' bodies. Hamper worked in an area the workers called "The Jungle": "Lifers had told me that on a scale from one to ten—with one representing midtown Pompeii and ten being then GM chairman Roger Smith's summer home—the jungle rates about a minus six. . . . The noise level was deafening. It was like some hideous unrelenting tape loop of trains having sex."[50] But over time, they got used to the noise, and they produced their own, rigging up elaborate music systems that could be heard over the din: "As for the popularity of Dead Rock Stars on the Rivet Line, I've settled upon this private theory. The music of the Dead Rock Stars is redundant and completely predictable. We've heard their songs a million times over. In this way, the music of the Dead Rock Stars infinitely mirrors the drudgery of our assembly jobs."[51] In all these cases, loudness is linked to exceptional states, dissolution of the self, and a sonic version of Kant's mathematical sublime—an aesthetic of grandiosity.

Throughout this vast literature, one finds a strange persistence of the 120 dB number. It is as if audiologists had a secret meeting to assign a number to sublimity. Imagine it as a syllogism: thunder produces sublimity, 120 dB is as loud as thunder; therefore, 120 dB sounds are sublime. Or: sublimity is that which overwhelms or destroys the senses, 120 dB is well past the threshold where sound can produce impairments in hearers; therefore, 120 dB sounds are sublime. Sound scholars have followed suit, using 120 dB as a numeric marker for an overwhelming phenomenology of loudness. Lucas also uses 120 dB as a stand-in for the physical power of Sunn O)))'s music: "Feeling Sunn O)))'s music is not a metaphor—it is an inescapable physical reality."[52] Perhaps hearing is not a purely acoustic phenomenon that touches only the auditor's ears, just as the voice is not purely a sonic phenomenon that emanates from the speaker's body.

It seems that sound and touch merge long before the threshold of pain. Artist Marco Fusinato specifies 120 dB noise in his 2015 work, *Constellations* (figures 4.4 and 4.5), in which "a 40-metre wall with a 1.5-metre gap at

4.4 Marco Fusinato, *Constellations* (speaker assembly), 2015.
Reproduced with the permission of the artist.

4.5 Marco Fusinato, *Constellations* (baseball bat technique), 2015.
Reproduced with the permission of the artist.

each end is built to bisect the gallery. Hidden inside the wall are a series of microphones connected to a PA system. The entrance side of the gallery is empty. On the other side of the gallery, coming out from the bisecting wall a baseball bat is attached to a steel chain. The audience is invited to strike the wall. Their action is amplified at 120db."[53]

As in the very definition of the sublime, almost no auditory experience at high volume is purely or even separately sonic. Fusinato's works have visual, tactile, and proprioceptive dimensions. Caleb Kelly notes that such high sound levels involve the work exceeding the gallery space and moving into neighboring spaces, inserting itself into the lives of gallery employees, a "critique of the development of art entertainment via the use of entertainment tools themselves."[54] Kelly reads the piece as transgressive—but also pleasurable for visitors, many of whom returned—while acknowledging that the experience of gallery workers may have been considerably worse, since the exhibit may well have interfered with their abilities to do their jobs.

Sometimes the 120 dB measurement can also do ideological work simply through its invocation; here, it is not the fact of loudness but the *imagination of loudness* that is important. Annie Goh writes of the right-wing #120db social media campaign, "It presents itself as a direct action campaign fighting for women's rights in the era of #MeToo. As the campaigners explain, 120db is the volume of a pocket alarm carried by many 'European women' today who fear for their personal safety. It has the dressings of a grass-roots women-led and social media-savvy movement, yet the #120db campaign has its roots in Germany's anti-immigrant far-right political party Alternative Für Deutschland (AfD), who entered German parliament in 2017. . . . The campaign cites the failure of the German state to protect its women."[55] One does not actually hear a pocket alarm as part of the campaign, and more to the point, as of this writing, there is no extant pocket alarm that could physically produce a sound as loud as 120 dB. Here, the use of the measure of 120 dB is the opposite of transgressive; it is regressive. Here, 120 dB marks a threshold and once again uses a putative measure and imagined sonic experience to describe a social experience. It conjures a mixture of right-wing rage and a desire for the state to assert its patriarchal power, a transcendence of the self into a corporal polity: a police sublime.[56]

Loudness and the sonic force behind it thus have no necessary political meanings. The experience of loudness may speak to a materiality of sound, but that materiality is always made accessible positionally, and through interpretation.[57] Collected together, the examples of high-powered hand dryers, noisy neighborhoods, construction equipment, the roar of subway trains or airplanes, stereos blasting from nearby, and right-wing appropriations of high-tech rape whistles suggest a different set of meanings and contexts for high-volume sound. Michael Birenbaum Quintero has made a similar point with respect to excess in Buenaventura, Colombia, arguing that "the loudness of the neighborhood . . . does not mean excess," because this idea of excess presupposes a split between public and private. Instead, residents and visitors "are expected not only to deliberately immerse themselves in the shared sound environments, but also to actively project their own sonority out into it."[58] This is the fundamental contradiction of loudness-as-sublimity: even the mere fact of overwhelmed senses is itself always meaningful, as David Suisman shows in his frightening study of experiments with sonic booms over Oklahoma City in 1964. While the U.S. Air Force and Federal Aviation Administration distributed pamphlets to Americans describing sonic booms as "the sound of freedom," they were also exploring the possibility of using sonic booms as sonic weapons, something not lost on the thousands of letter writers who protested them as cruel and disruptive to everyday life in Oklahoma City.[59]

From tiled bathrooms to football stadiums to concerts to assembly lines to bathrooms, audile scarification and the fact of loudness undermine a central premise of contemporary media culture: that the form and content of a message are separable. This is an axiom of information theory and modern communication engineering, the epistemic basis of the separation between carrier and content that undergirds modern internet regulation (or the lack thereof), and has become a fashionable position in some corners of media theory itself.[60] If the sound of sound changes with sound pressure level and if the experience of sound changes over time as a result of exposure to sound pressure levels, then the phenomenon of audile scarification suggests that sound culture is in part defined by the lack of separation between carrier and message. Normal impairments are not necessarily the end of hearing but direct the faculty of hearing "toward new ends, meanings and emotions."[61] Those might be the euphoria of self-overcoming as music immerses listeners, or they might be compensation for people on a loud and dangerous assembly line, or they might be a sonic assault on gallery employees. The point is not that loudness produces any particular experience or response; the point is that the experience, the phenomenon, or the feeling of sound are inseparable from the means to experience it. The meaning of something cannot be separated from its means of conveyance. The fact of loudness is unavailable to analysis without interpretation.[62]

The need for interpretation of something that can—and does—exceed the senses is the ultimate, unresolvable contradiction behind any idea of sonic sublimity. Some sonic sublimes are imagined precisely because of their sheer magnitude. Robert Fink writes of 50 Hz sound waves, which are roughly thirty feet long, as a kind of "safe" sublime, allowing people to "contemplate the vibratory energies of the bass register in comfort." In the seismological world, sublimity has been tied to earthquakes for almost the entirety of their modern history. Douglas Kahn provocatively writes that through seismology, radio was felt before it was heard, as the earth transmitted the ultralow frequencies of sound waves. Thinkers from Gerhard Richter to Friedrich Kittler reflected on the sublimity of earthquake sounds, and one of the tools used to study them, the piezoelectric transducer, became an important means for amplifying musical instruments—first violins and cellos in the 1930s and 1940s—and a few decades later *any* potential sounds for high-volume noise musics.[63] Sonic sublimity is thus in the ear of the beholder—and also always just beyond it.

Impaired hearing may be just as much a form of openness to experience and alterity as unimpaired hearing. In this scenario, loudness becomes an obligatory passage point, a ticket in or a barrier to keep people out. Audile scarification thus enables forms of participation and belongingness through and against loudness. It also assists in the production of loudness as a form of exclusion, alterity, difference, and power. In other words, and contra Jean-Luc Nancy's romantic account of listening as the basis of intersubjectivity, not hearing can be a form of openness to the world, and the foundation for connecting to others.[64] Yet even here, not all impairments are the same, nor do they work the same way: the abilities—through impairment—to tolerate loud sound in a factory, an art gallery, a public bathroom, and a concert are all, socially speaking, different abilities even if they have one shared origin in the history of an individual person. The decibel level in Hamper's factory was certainly similar to the decibel levels at Marra's football match. The decibel levels on a battlefield and at a noise concert may be similar. But their meanings, and the kinds of experiences that they produce, are not simply determined by the sheer force of the sound, or the state of a person's hearing impairments.

Impaired hearing, or not hearing, as a form of openness to the world offers an important occasion for reconsidering what it means to close one's ears. Despite the cliché that people do not have earlids, they routinely put things in their ears. And while there is a large literature on earbuds and hearing aids, there is considerably less writing about earplugs. Traditionally, earplugs, like earphones, headphones, and earbuds, have been understood as a modality of turning away from one's immediate environment, a refusal of intersubjectivity, and a closing down of the self to others—an audist fabulation based, perhaps, on the visual metonymy of closing up holes in one's head as a way of shutting off access to the world, or perhaps stereotypes of deaf people as antisocial.[65] But even though earplugs might appear to be individualizing, that does not necessarily mean that they always individualize, separate, and isolate their users. They may also be tokens or modalities of participation.

Anthropologies and histories of earplugs are just beginning to be written; they certainly deserve more attention. Earplugs have a long, shared history with hearing aids because of their intervention in the faculty of hearing and because hands originally could be used for both (by cupping or plugging).[66] They also share some iconographic history with headphones and earbuds. If you believe pervasive high-volume sound is a threat to public health, mass adoption of earplugs would seem to be a form of progress, where people learn that loud sound is bad for them and begin to protect themselves. From one perspective, this is exactly what has happened: from wax earplugs, to foam, to modern synthetic materials, as people became sensitive to high-volume sound (usually characterized as noise), they invented stuff to put in their ears.

Although a variety of earplugs were patented throughout the 1800s, the first major commercial success was Ohropax (ear peace!) earplugs, developed by Maximilian Negwer around 1907. They were made of a mixture of cotton and moldable wax, were built on other nineteenth-century innovations that also used moldable wax, and were Franz Kafka's preferred brand.[67] In his wonderful study of Ohropax, John Goodyear hypothesizes that the long-term success of the earplugs—especially when compared with urban antinoise crusades—had to do both with Ohropax's understanding of noise and their understanding of class. The antinoise crusade he studied "spoke predominantly to the intellectual class. . . . But this theorization would not have spoken to the working classes, many of whom worked to and depended on the rhythms of the loud drone of machines in factories on a daily basis. . . . Negwer's caricaturization of noisy situations satirized noise and skillfully employed symbolic visual imagery that spoke to a range of thoughts and emotions of his customers, irrespective of class."[68] This framing is central for understanding what happens next with hearing protection. Antinoise crusaders repeatedly sought and failed to eliminate the causes of high sound pressure levels, but they often did so by criminalizing sets of sounds and the people who make them in the process. Earplugs, meanwhile, were marketed in terms of their pragmatic and activity-specific use.

By the end of World War I, hearing loss had been understood as a symptom of modern life, not just a particular profession: during the war, a Dr. T. Ritchie Rodger concluded that "all men in any jeopardy of hearing loss, whether shipyard riveters or shipboard gunners, should be using earplugs." Hillel Schwartz also tells of a Scottish laryngologist, Dan McKenzie, who became an antinoise crusader, linking up all the noises of modern life—warfare, but also cars, railroads, ships, sirens, shutters, and music.[69] This definition of noise has more or less persisted throughout the history of writing on hearing damage: noise is a mix of unwanted sound and excessively loud sound. In this context, earplugs are used prophylactically in particular environments and to soften certain kinds of sounds. And earplugs are not panaceas, since they amplify the interior noises of the body—breathing sounds, speaking voices, footfalls, and tinnitus.[70]

Earplug technology progressed slowly over the course of the twentieth century and was rarely pitched for aesthetic purposes; the main promoters were military and industrial organizations. General use earplugs followed the cotton-and-wax models until the development of moldable, waterproof silicon earplugs in 1962, followed shortly by the development of moldable foam earplugs that contained sound-absorbing resins and could better maintain their shape within the ear, branded as E-A-R (Energy Absorption Resin). First marketed in 1972, E-A-Rs became widely available in the early 1970s and remained more or less stable for the rest of the twentieth century; these kinds of earplugs are still in wide use today.[71]

While foam earplugs potentially provided very high levels of volume reduction (depending on construction and use), they did not do so in a balanced way, reducing the high frequencies much more than lower frequencies (stuffing facial tissues in one's ears also has a muffling effect but is much less effective at hearing protection). While they did find some usage among musicians and music audiences, they were mostly rejected for dulling the sound too much; this is still musicians' and audience members' most common complaint about earplugs.[72] When my audiologist pinned my audile scarification to being a "former rock musician" of a certain age, she was playing on this stereotype. But in fact, the high-/low-culture binary often works in reverse when it comes to hearing protection, or fails altogether to capture it. There is much more widespread use of hearing protection among rock musicians and fans, and in genres like electronic dance music (EDM), than, for instance, in symphony orchestras.[73] Bars routinely stock cheap foam earplugs for patrons; in my experience, symphony halls never do. A musician sitting in front of the piccolo flute section of the orchestra every day will have their hearing transformed over time, and possibly considerably more than an electric guitarist who uses earplugs. Orchestral musicians do not have as developed a culture of hearing protection as musicians in other genres.

The class analysis gets more interesting when applied to examples of loud activities outside music. For instance, in American gun culture, hearing protection is standard equipment at shooting ranges; it is advertised in gun magazines, and it is considered a regular part of the "gear" one needs for hobby shooting. On a 2019 visit to an indoor shooting range in my home state of Minnesota, I found that the actual shooting was acoustically isolated from the guns-and-gun-paraphernalia shop, and that hearing protection was required as a price of entry. The shooting range itself had considerable acoustic damping installed, double-pane windows, and an airlock-like two-door system for entry and exit. As figure 4.6 illustrates, the range was divided into lanes that had some acoustic isolation from one another. The walls and ceilings were treated, and the back wall had some kind of rubber or plastic fill that both caught the bullets and dampened the sound of their impacts.

A variety of options for hearing protection were available for loan or sale, from foam earplugs on up to high-tech noise-canceling headphones that reduced the overall sound level but allowed for conversation. Hearing protection was marketed with all the paraphernalia of gun culture: camouflage, people depicted outdoors, and references to other contemporary-sounding technologies like Bluetooth (figures 4.7 and 4.8). All this sound isolation and hearing protection is bound up with the safety discourse that surrounds the promotion of gun ownership and use in the United States. This is parallel to the pattern Jeremy Packer identified for American automobility: like cars, guns are wrapped up in a discourse of freedom; and like cars, safety talk and practices may work in tandem with the

4.6 Inside the shooting range, Carrie Rentschler takes aim; Louis Rentschler looks on. Side panels divide the lanes for shooting, and the damping covers most of the ceiling and the rear of the space. Photo by the author.

4.7 Razor Slim Electronic Muffs with "protect it or lose it" tag line and camouflage styling. Photo by the author.

4.8 Razor xv Ear Buds touting Bluetooth and adjustable settings. Photo by the author.

discourse of freedom, legitimating and even domesticating it, even as both guns and cars kill far too many people every year.[74] In some cultural milieus, hearing protection is an institutionally sanctioned and even popular practice; in other "high" cultural milieus, it is not. There is no single aesthetic, classed, or raced pattern or position with regard to hearing ability, hearing impairment, or hearing protection use. It seems more situational, even subcultural.

While an uptake of hearing protection among gun hobbyists in the United States seems to be tied to safety discourses, its history with musicians is tied much more to aesthetic discussions and stigma. In the late 1980s, Elmer Carlson developed an earplug that he claimed "has response characteristics which are comparable with that of the anatomical structures of the human ear." His earplugs had a small, resonating diaphragm in them that restored some of the lost higher frequencies. Earplugs using Carlson's method consisted of a custom mold of the wearer's ear canals, with interchangeable diaphragms that provided different amounts of attenuation. Mead C. Killion and his company Etymotic manufactured earplugs in this way, alongside their businesses in hearing measurement, hearing aids, headphones, and other specialized acoustic technologies.

Killion later found a way to improve on Carlson's approach by using a flanged design, which would allow for a truly mass-produced earplug that did not excessively attenuate certain frequencies over others (figure 4.9). Remarkably, the patent also references design aesthetics as a barrier to use: "A further limitation . . . was its appearance, which was judged by some to be cosmetically unattractive for sale at 'rock' music concerts and the like, one of its important potential applications."[75] The new earplug was made out of thermoplastic elastomers, which allowed for relatively balanced sound, cheap manufacture, and ease of use. Killion also believed that most earplugs provided too much attenuation, leading people to remove them, modify them, or stop using them, even as corporate purchasing departments generally preferred to buy earplugs with higher attenuation levels, on the assumption that "more is better." Released in 1990, the Etymotic ER-20 earplug based on this design provided the first mass-produced and inexpensive "hi-fi" earplug.

While Killion and his colleagues researched new kinds of earplugs, another group worked to change attitudes about hearing impairments among musicians. In 1984 Kathy Peck, a bass player with the Contractions, developed a hearing impairment that made it difficult for her to understand conversation after they opened for Duran Duran at the Oakland Coli-

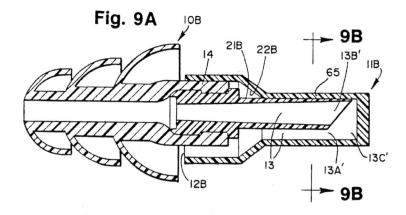

Fig. 9A

4.9 Mead Killion's Flanged Tip Earplug, from the 1992 patent.

seum. Her producer said to her, "Don't talk about it, you won't work in the business."[76] She was assigned a social worker—"in those days, they believed you needed to 'fix' deaf people"—whom she took along to a gig opening for Santana in order to try to explain what she did for a living. Finding little understanding of hearing impairments among musicians and little understanding of musicians among social workers, she cofounded Hearing Education and Awareness for Rockers (HEAR) with Flash Gordon (his real name), a doctor at the Haight-Ashbury Free Clinic. They promoted hearing protection for musicians and challenging stigma around hearing impairments. Their first benefit, in September 1988 at a local bowling alley, attracted attention from national publications like *People*, *Time*, the *New York Times*, and PBS because it broke a taboo: hearing impairments among musicians simply weren't supposed to be discussed.[77]

The following year, Who guitarist Pete Townshend became the first musician at his level of fame to publicly admit to having hearing impairments in a *Rolling Stone* interview, which further destigmatized it. Thanks to private funding from Townshend, alongside support from Deaf organizations, the National Science Foundation, and collaboration with other musicians, HEAR built a massive media catalog of materials, placing ads in music periodicals and on the radio, producing brochures, running a twenty-four-hour hotline, and eventually producing an educational film sent to forty thousand schools in the United States. HEAR also produced its own earplugs, which were custom-fit to the ear canal of each user, and worked with commercial earplug companies like Etymotic. In many ways, HEAR exemplifies the contradictions built into audile scarification and the culture of loudness. It aims to fight the stigma around hearing impairments and has worked with organizations for the Deaf and hard of hearing—to the point that Peck co-led a class action lawsuit that led to wheelchair access and assisted listening devices at movie theaters across the United States. At the same time, HEAR's educational materials very much trade in the ideology of ability: that it is better to hear than not to hear, that hearing is precious and something to be protected.

In 1989, the same year that Townshend talked to *Rolling Stone*, the Chicago Symphony Orchestra (CSO) performed Louis-Hector Berlioz's *Damnation of Faust* with 283 musicians crowded onto the stage. One of the violists, Bob Swan, wound up sitting directly in front of the massive brass section and lost his hearing by the end of the concert. This led to the musicians forming a sound level committee and to Killion being invited to work with several prominent orchestras. They conducted a hearing study of the Chicago Symphony, and then developed and marketed specialty musicians' earplugs, the ER-9, ER-15, and ER-25. There was also a stigma around hearing protection among symphony musicians. Killion would later recall a story by the CSO's contrabassoonist, Burl Lane, who said he was once dressed down in front of the whole orchestra by the conductor—Claudio Abbado—simply because he put in earplugs before a loud passage. Afterward, he had to produce a letter from his otorhinolaryngologist to justify their use.[78] Etymotic and HEAR would collaborate soon on a several projects to promote hearing protection.

With cheaper earplugs and decades of promotional efforts, earplugs are now in much wider use in musical settings. Following the expiration of Killion's 1992 patent, a newer generation of consumer-grade earplugs has begun to compete with Etymotic. Their product names are mostly bad puns: EarPeace, Eargasm, Hearprotek, Surfears, Savears, Decibullz, Loop, Vibes, and Untz Untz (my personal favorite for a name). The companies that provide origin stories mimic Etymotic's: founders who love music expose themselves to loud sound, regret it, then design earplugs to help others. The exceptions are Decibullz, where the founder is an "extreme athlete and nerd for tech," and Surfears, where the founder was a surfer with an ear infection. Design-wise, most of them follow the original Killion patents.[79] They are generally marketed for hearing protection but with an aesthetic sensibility: some are themselves design objects, coming in multiple colors and special cases, and each promises to deliver the full sonic experience while protecting wearers from music that might otherwise have a short- or long-term effect on their hearing.

This is a new phenomenon. Killion's mention of aesthetics as a concern for users in his 1992 patent was extremely unusual at the time. As recently as 2003, the Royal National Institute for Deaf People (RNID) in the United Kingdom ran a campaign to create stylized hearing prosthetics—*hearwear*—that included noise-cancellation devices and earplugs, hearing aids, and other assistive devices. Building on this project, the RNID concluded that the problem with earplug uptake was "desirability," which it promoted as a design goal for future work in the area, alongside universal access. This aligns with my discussion of vocal prosthetics in chapter 2, and fashion has certainly been taken up by post-2010 designs. Yet desirability and fashion may or may not be the primary concerns for users who actually take up earplugs, especially the young users who were the focus of the RNID study. A 2011 study of twenty-four "experienced clubbers" suggested fashion was not a factor in any of their decisions to wear hearing protection; rather, it is love of music and lack of concern about others' opinions: "I look like a dork anyway, so I'm not really too worried about looking like a dork" by wearing earplugs, as one interviewee explained. Though companies like Soundproofist go out of their way to claim that "earplugs are cool," uptake may or may not have anything to do with fashion.[80]

In an article on night modes, blue blockers, and screen media, Dylan Mulvin uses the term *media prophylaxis* to describe the "arrangement and orientation of bodies and technologies according to the avoidance, presentation, and mitigation of harm from the form of content of media."[81] Harm here is a complicated construct: on the one hand, prophylactics are made and used on the basis of an assumed harm associated with an activity that people are likely to continue doing. On the other hand, the nature of the harm or risk related to the activity may or may not be provable in any meaningful way. Prophylaxis can be imagined as a way to rebalance the relationship between chance and harm: there is no guarantee that any particular exposure to loud sound or music will cause harm, but given enough exposures, there is a likelihood that a person will lose some hearing.[82] It would seem from this perspective that earplugs fit the harm-reduction model.

Yet there are at least two limits to harm reduction as a framework for understanding earplugs and other forms of hearing protection. Because the earplugs are marketed as hi-fi and aesthetic, they are generally used in more aestheticized situations like concerts. To my knowledge, there is not widespread earplug use in bathrooms with high-powered hand dry-ers, or in loud restaurants, or even in movie theaters, for example. Even noise-canceling headphone use, which could be about loudness, has been conceived and marketed more in terms of blocking out the noise of other people than the loudness of an ambient environment.[83] Further, as Mulvin points out, prophylactics individualize and atomize the problem by "trans-ferring the duty of care to individuals and away from institutions." In so doing, they also leave aside the deeper cultural and institutional forces that might have something to do with the quest for loud sound, on the one hand, and the demand for passive consent to loud sound, on the other.[84]

Musicians' earplugs—whether worn by musicians or by audience mem-bers—suggest that not all loud sound is equal: there is continuum from sought sound to accepted sound. The latter marks the kind of consent op-erative in noisy urban environments like restaurants, bathrooms, factories, and mass transit. The former is more like loud sound for music, where pro-found aesthetic experiences may well be tied to the experience of loudness, as suggested by a wide swath of music and sound scholarship. On one level, this seems obvious: one is more likely to encounter the sublime at a concert or in an art context than while drying one's hands in the bathroom, and a sporting event, fitness class, or meal might be somewhere in-between (phe-nomenological confession: this is just my axis—someone else might set this up differently). But obviousness conceals a more profound fact: all of these experiences are or can be interconnected. As Hamper showed, loud music went with loud work.

The use of musicians' earplugs and hi-fi earplugs suggests that they might be understood as a means to copresence, participation, togetherness —the opposite of individualizing experience. A situation that may be too loud for a person to endure without earplugs may be pleasurable with ear-plugs; a situation that would be cumulatively risky becomes less so with earplugs. The history of condom usage provides a useful point of compar-ison, both because of the idea of a barrier as means to otherwise dangerous enjoyment or labor (in the case of sex workers who have sex with their cli-ents, or adult film performers who have sex in performance), and in terms of their connection to public health initiatives brought from both within and without a community, in a harm-reduction framework.[85] It also gets at some of the ways in which loudness and its management are tied up with masculinity and its management. A sarcastic editorial in the journal *Noise and Vibration* plays on this connection, suggesting that condoms could be used to protect microphones, and that since some American Navy commanders buy condoms out of budgets for earplugs, what is really needed is a "dual purpose device." Funny, yes, but also notable for the presumptive maleness of a gender-integrated U.S. Navy in 2005.[86]

The most shocking thing about hearing protection is how little is known about earplugs' effectiveness for any particular group of users, whether in the short or long term. As with condoms, a high proportion of earplug failures may be attributed to users not using them as intended: for instance, not getting a good seal between earplug and ear canal, or not inserting them all the way, or taking them out for part of the time they are in use. At least as of 2016, there was no conclusive evidence that earplug use led to significant hearing protection. At the same time, the studies do not document whether the earplugs were used as intended, and whether long-term changes in hearing thresholds might be different than short-term changes.[87] This is especially striking again, when compared with research on condoms and sexually transmitted disease (STD) prevention, where evidence is considerably more definitive. The history and politics of condom use are fraught and contested, and remain a controversial topic in queer theory, but the parallels between campaigns for musicians to use earplugs, like HEAR, and safer-sex campaigns, as well as the parallels in the medical discourse around risk and exposure, are hard to ignore.[88] As Cindy Patton wrote of "How to Have Sex in an Epidemic," a safe-sex manual published in 1983 just as the AIDS epidemic was taking form in the United States, "while it was born in opposition to a flat-footed homophobia that saw AIDS as punishment, the idea of safe sex failed to overcome the idea that queer sex was intrinsically dangerous."[89] The same issues may obtain for hearing protection: if part of the cultural meaning of loudness is that it is dangerous, that can easily be folded into aesthetics of transgression or authenticity. For both condoms and earplugs, protection, pleasure, transgression, and risk are bound together. An anonymous sound engineer explains that "this is something that really scares me. I have not confirmed it through real examination; but it is something that does scare me; losing my ears. . . . But then, you always have this thing and this aspect . . . yes, it is less sexy to use earplugs because it deteriorates the sound and . . . It is somewhat like condoms, you see? It's something like that."[90] Here, the connection between loudness and sexuality is explicit.

Sound may also be a prophylactic against sound. Mack Hagood writes of *orphic* media technologies like noise generators, noise-canceling headphones, tone-generating hearing aids, apps, and recordings—all of which fight unwanted sound with sound. In many cases, orphic sound may be preferable to hearing protection. For instance, noise-generating hearing aids have been developed for tinnitus sufferers. As with pleasure from sound, tinnitus is defined more by an affective relationship to sound than a particular decibel threshold: people who suffer from tinnitus do not necessarily have louder ringing in their ears than people who do not; they are simply more distressed by the ringing. That suffering is real, as all emotional pain is. It also demonstrates the limits beyond which it is not possible to represent one's own perceptions, or the perceptions of another.[91]

Misophonia (fear of sound) is another case where sound becomes a prophylactic for sound, to the point where the prophylaxis may produce its own audile scarification. Misophonia is a condition where everyday sounds that might otherwise be considered subtle or quiet—such as mouth sounds, coughing, typing, or tapping—produce powerful negative feelings in the hearer. Some people with misophonia also complain of similar reactions to loud sounds like others' music. Along with tinnitus and hyperacusis, Hagood calls misophonia one of the "signature infirmities of our time, representing most acutely how the desire for freedom from the maladies of the body and world can actually exacerbate them—turning our listening into aversion, fear, anger, and suffering."[92] I had the good fortune to interview a person with misophonia while working on this chapter. She described it as both "hating" and "loving" sound, as something that makes her "happiest" but also "most panicky." One response to misophonia is to seek out loud masking sounds—music, white noise, podcasts that hide a triggering sound in an environment by covering it over with another sound. My interviewee found masking sounds helpful, which led her to wear headphones in public, even with nothing playing in them, but with recordings at the ready for when a triggering sound might be heard. "Most of the time when I am panicking about noise, I listen to hard rock, heavy metal, or electronica—especially repetitive sounds," or music she knows very well. When she tells me, "I always have it at the highest volume," I ask to hear an example, assuring her I can tolerate whatever sound pressure level her music player can produce in her headphones. She hands them to me with Led Zeppelin's "Heartbreaker" at maximum volume, commenting, "I especially like John Bonham's drumming." I put them on and am immediately surprised that the music isn't even louder, forgetting phenomenologically what I know intellectually: it is loud; I can just tolerate it. I ask, "It doesn't go any louder than that?" She replies: "It can't; I wish it did." For some types of misophonic experience, loudness and its masking power is a potential balm, a barrier, but also a modality through which a person can be with others in a space that might otherwise be intolerable. At least in the misophonic world, loud sounds, the very phenomenon for which earplugs serve as a prophylactic, may have their own prophylactic dimensions.[93]

IMPAIRMENT AND INTERPRETATION

More than a century ago, Franz Boas showed that anthropologists routinely mistranscribed the languages of the people they studied because they lacked the ears to hear them. They would confuse the same sound as an alternating sound, and vice versa.[94] But this phenomenon goes beyond language. Ears—yours, mine, scholars', everyday people's, ears of the hearing, ears of the hard of hearing, ears of the d/Deaf—are not transparent vessels into the head, the subject, or the soul. They are situated; they have histories. What would it mean to build an understanding of hearing and audibility—and by extension, all perception—as always already fractured and differential; as always at a distance from an imagined ideal of normal? While historians, anthropologists, and philosophers of sound have imagined pluralities of hearing and listening and have endlessly troubled those categories, with a few important exceptions, they have rarely incorporated impairment and disability into understandings of what normal hearing is. Even more rarely do they question their own hearing when they describe the sonic worlds around them.

Normal impairment is thus a necessary addition to the lexicons of ability, capacity, disability, and debility.[95] Just as there is compulsory able-bodiedness, there are situations that demand, expect, or produce normal impairments. Attending to them requires a different approach to senses, bodies, subjects, and knowledge. Dylan Robinson argues, "Critical listening positionality . . . engages how perception is acquired over time."[96] Impairment theory puts a fine point on the formulation "perception is acquired over time" because perception is also altered over time: the very faculties necessary to apprehend one's positionality are themselves potentially impaired. Environmental alteration is a fundamental condition of human bodies, and as with all environmental conditions, there is also a human factor. Beyond any existentialist reflections on humans' shared mortality, impairment is simply a condition for most bodies at least some of the time in one way or another. It can be a disabling condition, but it can also be an enabling condition.

While this book deals with only two normal impairments, audile scarification and (in the next chapter) fatigue, there are many more. To name a few: the sought-after temporary impairments of inebriation, which may sometimes turn into long-term or permanent impairments; normal impairments of vision; normal impairments of recall and memory; normal impairments of judgment (insofar as these are understood as abilities or capacities rather than something else); normal impairments of emotions like grief or ecstasy; normal impairments of mobility, coordination, motility, or spatial senses. To find normal impairments, consider how a context sorts bodies for capacities, look for impairment where it is not normally noticed, and then challenge any explanation that begins with an ideology of ability. My approach to audile scarification in this chapter began from the strange contradiction in the medical discourse that hearing loss was both tragic and expected and then unraveled the thread of auditory ableism by examining the range of environments and situations designed for normally impaired hearing.

When something like audile scarification is thought of at all, it is usually considered a product of coercion; a result of the violence of capitalism, colonialism, patriarchy, heterosexism, ableism, militarism; or an unwanted extension of an unwanted urbanism. But this chapter shows how audile scarification—considered as a normal impairment—can also be a condition for people who live in those systems, a window of opportunity, an affordance. So here is another claim for impairment theory as an offshoot of disability theory: it is a demand to incorporate impairment as a theoretical axis into discussions of power and subjectivity. But it is not just another factor or axis: impairment theory also disputes the idea of the able, self-knowing subject as the baseline for philosophies, histories, anthropologies, and phenomenologies of subjectivity, even as a baseline against which to push back.[97] It is unclear what it would mean for the human sciences to suddenly be filled with interpretive claims that doubt the certainties of the authors' senses. I tried to perform something like that in my accounts of my own voice in the first two chapters, and my experience of hearing in this chapter. Such a maneuver is difficult to carry out. We scholars know very well to doubt others' senses, but we rarely doubt our own, and we have to get better at it. Impairment phenomenology takes the "I can't" and "I don't know" of protention as seriously as the "I can," but it also questions the easy parsing of those two terms. The human sciences have been built up on third-person effects for far too long.[98] Whatever suspicions scholars apply to the faculties and experiences of other people in the world, we should also apply to the phenomena of our own worlds as presented to our own imperfect senses.

There Are Never Enough Spoons

Fatigue is an unpleasant experience that has entered into the
life of everyone. / S. HOWARD BARTLEY & ELOISE CHUTE /
Fatigue and Impairment in Man

Sleep is an absurdity, a bad habit. / THOMAS EDISON /
quoted in *New York Times*, October 11, 1914

"Your reader is a little bit drunk," begins an "Ask Dr. Editor" advice column in *University Affairs*, the newspaper of Canadian higher education.
Addressed to academics writing job applications, tenure dossiers, grant applications, and other "high stakes" writing, the main advice is to use a clear
font and not to cut font size. "Of course, I speak metaphorically," writes the
author, Letitia Henville. "The overwhelming majority of peer reviewers
are not literally intoxicated when they read your documents (one hopes).
It's likely, however, that they're not getting enough sleep. . . . A tired reader
isn't just less likely to be patient with an author: they're also more easily
distracted and less able to process information in their active, working
memory." The article goes on to quote various medical and psychological

sources on the cognitive effects of sleep deprivation, and then finishes with its font recommendations.[1]

This is not a chapter about the diminished faculties of diminished university faculties. But consider the joke in this remarkable little column. It offers, as a normal working proposition, that readers of applications for all the stereotypically and financially important academic-professional milestones—employment, permanent employment, money or time off for research—are fundamentally impaired, or should be addressed as if they are. These readers are (presumably) university professors, who are supposed to be in full command of their intellects, experts in their fields, and alert to the subtleties of language, qualifications, and accomplishments. Of course, anyone who works in a university setting knows that this is not always the case. Plenty of research on academic labor has shown increased expectation of overwork at all levels of the university, painting a picture that is tiring to even comprehend. The figure of the so-tired-they-are-intoxicated professor, here played for laughs but also for sound application-writing advice, is based on a prior assumption of the existence of a culture of overwork, structured by a depleted and casualized labor force, that pushes beyond what a normate person can be expected to handle.[2] And there is nothing special about university staff in this respect: similar stories are told about truck drivers, pilots, office staff, warehouse workers, assembly line workers, or any number of other jobs for large, logistically oriented organizations.

I start with the academic case simply because it should be a familiar story to my academic readers, and because the article actually goes beyond noting fatigue as the depletion of energy to describing it as a phenomenological state—in this case, likened to drunkenness—which gives it a consistency and character all its own as a kind of impairment. It is surprising how rare it is to find reflections on what fatigue is and does. The word *fatigue* actually conceals as much as it reveals, collapsing a set of conditions that may or may not be related, even if they are semantically related by dint of sharing the term. *There is not one kind of fatigue.* Professors' fatigue is not the fatigue experienced by those who have been exposed to external beam radiation. It is also not the fatigue experienced by long-term activists, or athletes in the heat of extended competition, or assembly line workers, or employees of Amazon fulfillment centers, or people living in constant pain, or people who are under constant economic stress, or people living in camps surrounded by barbed wire.

Even in the world of disability theory and activism, fatigue is not as well understood as one might expect. As Wendell writes, "The fatigue of illness is different in three critical respects from the ordinary fatigue experienced by healthy people: it is more debilitating, it lasts longer, and it is less predictable." She goes on to explain how the fatigue that attends something like a severe flu, where it is impossible to even carry on a conversation, is more like the fatigue of illness than the fatigue a healthy person feels at the end of a long workday. The fatigue of disabling chronic illness "resists control. . . . It is one of the most challenging impairments to accommodate." Like pain, it can be classified, but its many forms—physical, emotional, spiritual, financial, social—seep into one another, whether for the person experiencing it or someone judging the fatigue of another.[3] Fatigue is normal in many pockets of modern life, and celebrated in some, but it is not always the same thing. When its existence is noted at all, it is most often as a kind of depletion rather than a quality or state of being.

In this chapter, I consider fatigue as a political phenomenon and an often-absent phenomenology. Elena Gorfinkel calls fatigue "a baseline symptom of survival, the constitutive condition of early twenty-first-century modernity."[4] A similar point was made at the beginning of the twentieth century by Georg Simmel with his concept of the *blasé attitude*, which he used to describe the dominant affect of urban social life.[5] Fatigue is a condition that remains poorly understood and subject to twisting and intersecting histories, including its metaphoric expansion in recent decades to describe qualities of eroded empathy alongside other eroded faculties: as in the rise of "compassion fatigue" to describe diminishing interest in journalism and advocacy that addresses violence, hunger, catastrophe, and other human misfortunes.[6] (The sad irony of compassion fatigue is that it suggests a moral obligation to heal the subject experiencing too much compassion rather than the subject experiencing the misery.) As a concept, fatigue has a hazy history, at once material and subjective. In people, it describes an impairment that is sometimes physical, sometimes mental, and sometimes both. It reaches outward and inward, marking a relation with others and a relation with one's self. Fatigue also plays a role in stories of masculine heroism and endurance, whether in everyday sports journalism; in fables of colonization and adventure, as male (and putatively white) explorers battled through their fatigue in the process of conquering lands, peoples, or nature itself; or in tales of enduring war either as a civilian or a combatant. Here fatigue can lead to legitimacy or legitimation, but it can also be the source of profound and hidden suffering. Fatigue is often listed as a symptom or effect of other impairments, but as in the "your reader is a bit drunk" example, it can also be the source and explanation of impairments, especially those involving care, judgment, support of others, or the ability to properly complete a task—particularly within an employer's time frame. On one level, a critique of fatigue ought to be a critique of the extractive powers of capitalism, and its assault on bodies, sleep, and the life chances and choices of the majority of the world's population.[7] But that is already to accept a certain political definition of fatigue, rooted in an energetic subject and its depletion. The belief in an energetic subject is a powerful mechanism for making sense of the world, and for empathizing with others, but it also has its own trade-offs, obfuscations, and occlusions.

It is the great contradiction of this chapter that it is at once the most personal for me, and the most scholastic in delivery. As I assembled the first coherent draft of this chapter in fall 2019, I started to experience the onset of fatigue from a drug I am now taking for the metastatic thyroid cancer cells still hanging out in my lungs, a tyrosine kinase inhibitor (TKI). The goal of the TKI is to keep them hanging out and not doing much by blocking their protein intake: preventing them from taking in energy and getting bigger, leaving them in stasis. Fall 2019 was my first semester teaching while on TKIS.[8] The TKI fatigue comes and goes; it often takes me by surprise, but I have never really been very good at understanding my own limits. I worked through the fatigue in order to write this chapter, while savoring the coincidence, perhaps performing a kind of manly wakefulness; or perhaps in an effort to produce meaning about an existence punctuated by the certainty of my future nonexistence; or perhaps just because I love a word processing window full of text that's ready to be edited. But I could not offer the fatigue itself up for analysis, despite it being a near-daily companion at one point or another. For the front end of this book, I was able to draw on many pages of personal reflection on my voice, recollections of endless experiments with how to speak, and how to speak differently depending on where and when I was speaking. This was because I was already entering into discourse by trying to use my voice. It was a small matter to keep going, to document my experience as it was happening, or shortly thereafter in notes, correspondence, conversation, and blog entries, and it was a handsome condition to reflect upon, even if I did not always enjoy negotiating my new vocal impairments.

The condition of fatigue offers no such benefits to thought. At the moment of their devastation, the fatigued do not welcome invitations to discourse or reflection, at least I sure as hell do not. But it is more than that. You will not likely encounter me when I am in the throes of fatigue; and perhaps more to the point, I am less likely to encounter me when I am in the throes of it. Even my recollection of fatigue is hazy. My specific memories may not be less accurate than those of my voice, but I am more likely to question them. Perhaps the memory of fatigue is like the memory of pain or depression, in that there's a predisposition to discount it, which also works as a kind of self-preservation. That is how I feel right now—in fall 2020, a year after the above paragraph on TKIs was written—as I type these paragraphs for what I hope is the final revision of this chapter. I am ending the second week of a vacation from my TKI pills. Since I have been adapting relatively well to the drug, and since it has been working to keep my cancer in check, my oncologist recommended a short vacation of about three weeks to allow a sore on the sole of my foot to heal—another side effect. The vacation gives me a chance to assess what the drugs, along with the drugs to deal with the side effects of the drugs, are doing to me. The absence of ambient pain in my hands and feet is a slow and repeated discovery. It is gone, but there is a pause before I notice I am not noticing it. I have to survey for its absence. One day, I can just go for a walk and there aren't electric shocks coming up through my foot; or I can cook without Kevlar gloves and no tingling sensation takes its revenge for hours afterward; or I can run my hands against the cable-like roundwound strings of my basses and guitars and there is no swelling of pins or onset of numbness. Walking, cooking, and playing all feel suddenly freer to me. In moments of instrumental action, I don't automatically notice my own ability, but I can rediscover it and thereby give an account to myself of what the pain does when it is there, and how it too contributes to fatigue.

But noticing the absence of fatigue is not enough to really grasp its impact. For that, I need a perspective beyond myself. I came off the drugs right as I returned to teaching online during a pandemic, and I'm teaching two challenging classes: a two-hundred-student introductory lecture and a cross-university graduate seminar. I have been pulling twelve- and fourteen-hour days and have fallen asleep in front of the TV more than once as I try to get in some relaxation before bedtime. And yet, while I am tired, it is not the same tired at all. For one thing, I awake the next morning ready to get back to it. Fatigue from the TKIs and from the sleepiness-inducing assistant drugs is more like being suspended in the moment of hitting a wall. I wake up tired. But even in such close proximity, I can't give you a good description.

One of the most common complaints of people with chronic fatigue and chronic pain is that they are not always believed, or that their impairments are minimized by others. I have noticed this disbelief as well, even from well-meaning friends. But even belief does not guarantee comprehension. I believe myself but remain unable to comprehend a feeling I experienced just three weeks ago. As Samuels writes, "How can I be sick on a good day? And if I can't figure it out for myself, how can I expect anyone else to understand?"[9] That's where I am stuck when I try to narrate it for you: I cannot be a fatigued subject when I am lively enough to write or think about it. And when I am a fatigued subject, I cannot outline my subjectivity for you.

That is why this chapter takes a more oblique path through theory and history, as I survey some writers who have tried to make sense of fatigue—their own, or others'. My goal is to construct an impairment phenomenology of a condition whose fundamental demand is to be let alone; to be cared for, sure, but also to be let be. To that end, I offer a triptych of slow meditations in this chapter. I begin by outlining the politics of fatigue as described by spoon theory, which is a wonderfully intersectional theory of fatigue, capitalism, and subjectivity developed, circulated, and used by people with disabilities. I situate spoon theory as the latest statement in a long conversation about fatigue that came out of materials science, labor management, and industrial psychology in the nineteenth and twentieth centuries, one critiqued by Marxists and feminists, among others. I then turn to medical models of fatigue, which mostly seek to define fatigue by exclusion of other phenomena (most notably, work and labor). Both of these approaches to fatigue treat it as a kind of depletion, where fatigue is what's left when energy is gone. I call these approaches *depletionist*. While they are certainly adequate to describe the experience of fatigue for many people, they are only one approach to thinking about fatigue. They are negative phenomenologies. My problem with depletionism is that it dismisses fatigue's relational dimensions in the service of nailing down meaning in an otherwise untethered chain of diagnostic, measurable, bodily, juridical, and organizational signs. It asserts: you are not fatigued, you're just not working efficiently enough; or you're not really fatigued, you're depressed; or worse, your reaction to the world, your very being does not matter; or your fatigue (your feelings, your body) is simply a problem to be managed away. The final section of the chapter attempts to construct the beginnings of a *nondepletionist* approach to fatigue, a positive phenomenology and an appropriate politics. My goal is to push through energetic fatigue to outline its contours, especially in terms of how energy and agency seem to be bound up in fatigue and fatigued discourses, and to provide resources to help others imagine some alternatives beyond what I can offer here.

Across the stories and histories in this chapter is a theme of the desire to overcome fatigue. Disability studies' critique of "overcoming" narratives as sources of inspiration or models for crip life course is well known at this point. Applied to a critique of fatigue, it raises a challenging question: is a subject without fatigue even possible or desirable? Isn't raging against fatigue a little like raging against death? Wouldn't it be better to accept fatigue and death as aspects of human finitude? Among its many other qualities, fatigue is a form of apperception—it requires feeling one's own feeling—often alongside the experience of resistance of the world to one's actions. Fatigue matters because there is a subject there. As I discuss at length later in this chapter, the organized efforts to overcome fatigue have largely come from managerial worlds—industrial science, psychology, sports medicine. These fields aim to manage bodies, to get more out of them, to extract labor, energy, power, time, money. For them, fatigue's existence itself is a pathology and a problem. Fatigue becomes a problem for people in different ways, for instance, where desire and ability do not line up, or where they are caught up in systems that demand more of them than they can provide. Chronic fatigue is still something else: medically defined as fatigue that cannot be explained by another condition (and it must be said that many medical explanations of fatigue are deeply unhelpful to the fatigued); it is fatigue that does not abate after six months. While industrial managers and sports scientists imagine bodies in terms of energy stores and their expenditure and replenishment, for the chronically fatigued subject, it is not an absence of energy. Fatigue is a presence.

SPOONS

Any account of fatigue in the world of disability politics today ought to begin with spoons. In a now-canonical 2002 blog post, Christine Miserandino described how chronic illness produces fatigue, and how fatigue forces choices that those who are unimpaired do not have to make. Sitting at a coffee shop, explaining to her best friend what it's like to live with lupus, Miserandino gathered up a bunch of spoons and handed them to her friend.

> I asked her to count her spoons. She asked why, and I explained that when you are healthy you expect to have a never-ending supply of "spoons." But when you have to now plan your day, you need to know

exactly how many "spoons" you are starting with. It doesn't guarantee that you might not lose some along the way, but at least it helps to know where you are starting. She counted out 12 spoons. She laughed and said she wanted more. I said no, and I knew right away that this little game would work, when she looked disappointed, and we hadn't even started yet. I've wanted more "spoons" for years and haven't found a way yet to get more, why should she? I also told her to always be conscious of how many she had, and not to drop them because she can never forget she has Lupus.[10]

She then walks her friend through a hypothetical day: getting up and out of bed costs a spoon; showering costs a spoon; skipping lunch costs a spoon. By the time she gets home in the evening, she has only one spoon left, hasn't eaten dinner, and will not be able to make *and* clean up from dinner, never mind chores or having fun. By the end of the story, Miserandino's friend understands the constant need to make choices when someone lives with a chronic illness or disability: "Once people understand the spoon theory they seem to understand me better, but I also think they live their life a little differently too. I think it isn't just good for understanding Lupus, but anyone dealing with any disability or illness. Hopefully, they don't take so much for granted or their life in general. I give a piece of myself, in every sense of the word when I do anything."[11]

In the almost two decades since its initial publication, spoon theory has become a lingua franca of disability and activist discourse. Leah Lakshmi Piepzna-Samarasinha uses spoons throughout *Care Work: Dreaming Disability Justice* to discuss the uneven distribution of energy and ability within disability communities, and the politics of caring for one another. Care work replenishes spoons for others, but it also costs spoons for those doing the work, an idea widely documented in the literature on emotional labor. The care worker can become estranged from what Arlie Hochschild calls "the margins of the soul."[12] Hochschild is talking about paid work—specifically, the flight attendant's smile—but the reasoning also works for other care work, even aspects of self-care. For instance, it is an aspect of "crip emotional intelligence": "noticing and showing respect for all the ways we push ourselves past our spoons all the time. . . . It is understanding that we are in a constant dance of negotiating how to work while disabled or sick or in pain."[13] Activity—both the daily actions of a person living in the world and any intentionally additional options (politics, art, care for others, and any number of other actions) occurs within limits. In spoon theory, and in the politics of disability and chronic illness, fatigue appears as a kind of index, signifying when a subject is approaching, and has exceeded, its limits.

Spoon theory offers a map of the path to fatigue; it posits a determinate relationship among subjects, energy, and fatigue. To even ask how energy works in spoon theory is a little unfair: Miserandino offered her essay in order to simplify a complex process in terms that are easy for people to understand, regardless of whether or not they have a chronic illness or disability, and others have followed.[14] Spoons have become a shorthand for talking about the politics of energy and disability (and ability), as evidenced by the spread of the #spoonies hashtag on Twitter, Tumblr, Instagram, and elsewhere, in part as a self-identification for people who live with chronic pain or fatigue of one sort or another: "'Spoonies' often associate this identity with isolation and epistemic dissonance in everyday life because often the way they see their illness is not how it is seen by others. Spoonies often report that people in their caring and support networks get tired of hearing about pain that does not eventually resolve, that their 'lack of spoons' to go on social activities is misunderstood as disinterest, and that people do not understand their inability to perform tasks others would not even consider taxing."[15]

A year before "The Spoon Theory" appeared, Wendell critiqued the energy demands built into feminist organizing: "Much feminist practice still assumes a consistently energetic, high-functioning body and mind, and certainly not a body and mind that are impaired by illness. . . . Commitment to a cause is usually equated to energy expended, even to pushing one's body and mind excessively, if not cruelly." When they transform energy expenditure into the tangible currency of commitment, how different are radical organizations from the institutional spaces they aim to transform or replace? If it measures value in energy expenditure, what is the moral difference between activism and the corporate time management rituals that Melissa Gregg calls "executive athleticism," or the celebrated endurance of certain performers or athletes?[16] Every time I read about the value of energy expenditure, I also can't help but think of the various environmental theories that understand resource extractivism as a problem, rather than a prior given, for cultural analysis.[17] A critique of extraction and expenditure is especially important in the wake of the ongoing climate catastrophe. If energy extraction is a problem that should be viewed critically when applied to materials, and if extractivism is among the destructive tendencies of modern capitalism, then it is also time to revisit the ways in which energy extraction is applied to people. It is profoundly necessary to understand how fatigue and energy are bound up politically, which is what spoon theory begins to do. But this exploration will also lead in directions for which spoon theory was never designed to go. Both Miserandino's and Wendell's discussions of fatigue still understand it within an energy extraction model. This is incredibly useful for outlining the contours of extractivist living, but both situate the politics of fatigue within a framework of understanding bodies through energy. So with my apologies—and gratitude—to Miserandino and Wendell, here I go.

In spoon theory, a spoon is a quantum of energy—a person's quantity of spoons is their "energy reserve." It imagines a subject made up of energy, finite and in need of renewal. This is an old idea; the conceptions of energy and fatigue operating in spoon theory are more than 150 years old. If spoon theory provides "a calculus of energy expenditure,"[18] that calculus is applied here by people to themselves rather than administratively from an industry or state. In English, the noun form of *fatigue* appeared in the eighteenth century as a synonym for tiredness or exhaustion. Very quickly, the fatigue concept was already bound up with routinized, industrial work, at least for the poor. E. P. Thompson shares a quote from the clergyman John Clayton, who in 1772 wrote that poor children should be "habituated, not to say naturalized to Labour and Fatigue," such that they will be amenable to "constant employment."[19] In the nineteenth century, the term took on its material, physiological, and psychological meanings: weariness from physical or mental exertion, weakness in metal or other substances caused by stress; loss of elasticity; and reduction in power or sensitivity of organs or cells.[20]

In nineteenth-century Europe, the term *fatigue* jumped from tired bodies to machinery and metals under the conditions of industry, and then back again. In 1837 Wilhelm August Julius Albert, a German civil servant who studied accidents and failures in mines, argued that a series of metal chain failures he had observed were not a result of overloading per se but the result of repeated use—"load cycles"—degrading the strength of the material. He developed a twisted steel cable that would be able to handle more loads. Following Albert's study, writings appeared on axles for rail cars and mail coaches (Germany, 1842; France, 1853). The first appearance of *materials fatigue* in English was in 1854 in an article by Frederick Braithwaite, where it became a general problem of industrial materials: brewery equipment, water pumps, propeller shafts, crankshafts, railway axels, levers, cranes, and ash pans, among other things. As he wrote, "Many of the appalling, and apparently unaccountable accidents on railways, and elsewhere, are to be ascribed to that progressive action which may be termed the 'fatigue of metal.' This fatigue may arise from a variety of causes, such as repeated strain, blows, concussions, jerks, torsion, or tension, &c."[21] Two other ideas emerged from nineteenth-century concepts of metal fatigue: endurance limits and changes in elasticity as a result of stress, both of which affected how industrial machinery was built and maintained.[22] While this analysis of materials effectively metaphorized a human condition, it would in turn contribute to an analysis of human beings in terms of material power. In *The Railway Journey*, Wolfgang Schivelbusch makes the connection directly: "What Taylorism did for the optimal exploitation of human labor power, material testing did for the exploitation of material labor power. . . . In both cases, the task was to find out how a given potential could be rearranged, and thus improved, to increase yield."[23]

The concept of fatigue traverses humans and nonhumans, bodies and minds, and is therefore an excellent opportunity to investigate phenomena that cut across the conceptual divide between physical and mental impairments. In his classic study of fatigue in the industry, medicine, and science of modern Germany and France, Anson Rabinbach also follows the material metaphor: "Fatigue acted as the regulator of labor power, much as a governor presents a machine from exceeding its efficient speed and rhythm."[24] This quote comes in a discussion of the search for chemical sources and vaccines against fatigue, reasoning that if it had a chemical cause, and the chemical cause could be neutralized, bodies could work more. Experiments with vaccines, and later stimulants, yielded the same result: effects of fatigue can be deferred, but breakdown of labor power was inevitable sooner or later. The governor metaphor is especially profound: governors convert variable power going into a system, like a hand turning a crank, into a constant rotary speed, as in a sewing machine. Governors were important for steam engines and other nineteenth-century industrial machinery but also mechanical media like phonographs, tape machines, cameras, and projectors, which required constant rotation speeds for recording and playback. In other words, governors were used in apparatuses that produced both physical and perceptual effects and depended on regularized and managed time.[25] The speed of a governor is set as a standard: for instance, in the seventy-eight rotations per minute of Emile Berliner's later gramophones (the earlier ones were hand-cranked but lacked governors). This takes on a more sinister shape when applied to machinery in factory work or industries shaped by logistics, where workers must adapt their movements to "uniform and unceasing" motion that is mechanically regulated, up to the point that the intensification of work exceeds what workers can physically handle or (preferably) up to the point where they organize and resist.[26]

Fatigue thus implied a consciousness of time shaped by the needs of industry and other modern institutions like schools—fatigue and its perception could be subjected to standards. E. P. Thompson viewed time-discipline as one of the founding subjective processes of industrial capitalism, produced by schools and religion in the service of capitalist industry. Elizabeth Freeman would later call this process *chrononormativity*: "the use of time to organize individual human bodies toward maximum productivity." In imagining work as an "economy of force," it replaced moral discourse about labor and expressed "a widespread fear that the energy of mind and body was dissipating under the strain of modernity," affecting workers, students, and even the emergent middle class. The rhythm of the working day, the pace of work, and its effects on a body whose fundamental capital was conceived of as energy all came together to form a science of work and motion. That science cut across materials and people and operated alongside a moral discourse of the value of work. To scientists in the last quarter of the nineteenth century, "fatigue was the source of the body's resistance to work and lack of efficiency," the opposite of the energy that powered it. Fatigue was a problem to be overcome, and a condition deserving of scrutiny and suspicion. It was an analytic that transcended a single context, appearing in literature, journalism, engineering, popular science, laboratory science, in writings on work, and even in Karl Marx's critique of political economy.[27]

Nineteenth-century concerns about fatigue still resound today, and not just in spoon theory: claims that modern life taxes a subject's energy, personal productivity, and quality of political activism are heard in many quarters.[28] But they also have extended in scope. No subject has unlimited energy or unlimited resources—and the same should be said of the planet. Here, an impairment theory opens out to a general theory of finitude. Though fatigue is no longer understood in purely industrial terms, energy has become a central category in several strands of environmental thought and politics. Energy is something more than just mechanical or human but is planetary in scale, where exhaustion of capacity can also refer to a planet's ability to support human life. Fatigue becomes a way of talking about how systems—personal as well as social, biological, planetary—get run down.

In depletionist discourse, fatigue names a kind of impairment because it is the name of depleted ability. Fatigue is a pretty strange choice for a common currency among bodies, minds, emotions, machinery, materials, industries, cultures, and ecologies. But in a world where agency and energy are imagined together, anything that can have agency can be fatigued. Spoon theory reanimates this history of fatigue from the bottom up. It considers fatigue as the absence of energy but then updates it and adapts it to an ill or disabled subject. Spoon theory names a political economy of energy and critiques it at the same time. Under conditions of inequality, there are never enough spoons; someone or something always demands more.

Or maybe there are too many forks. In 2018 the blogger Jenrose coined the term *fork theory* as an adjunct to spoon theory.

> You know the phrase, "Stick a fork in me, I'm done," right?
>
> Well, Fork Theory is that one has a Fork Limit, that is, you can probably cope okay with one fork stuck in you, maybe two or three, but at some point you will lose your shit if one more fork happens.
>
> A fork could range from being hungry or having to pee to getting a new bill or a new diagnosis of illness. There are lots of different sizes of forks, and volume vs. quantity means that the fork limit is not absolute. I might be able to deal with 20 tiny little escargot fork annoyances, such as a hangnail or slightly suboptimal pants, but not even one "you poked my trigger on purpose because you think it's fun to see me melt down" pitchfork.[29]

Fork theory is important because it connects fatigue with other conditions that cross the mind-body divide, like stress. Jenrose focuses on neurodivergence, but really any person with enough fatigue or enough stressors can become a "forkupine"—the fork equivalent of a spoonie.[30] Fork theory adds a concept of presence to fatigue. Forks are stressors and when stressors are removed, the ability to cope increases. When they are added, the ability to cope decreases. In fork theory, fatigue is still an impairment resulting from a depletion of energy, but it is an impairment from a presence, not an absence. Fork theory also challenges the idea of a universal subject who is subject to fatigue: neurodivergent people might have one set of reactions to the world; people with hormone imbalances another; people who menstruate a third; people living out a heat wave a fourth—and even those categories conceal all sorts of diversity within them, including variance over time.

If a spoon is a quantum of energy, a fork is a demand for energy expenditure, and energy is a kind of value that resides in a subject, then spoon theory and its offshoots are also theories of value. There is a political economy of spoons. In the first volume of *Capital*, Marx also lays out a theory of an energetic subject within the parameters of the working day, a quantity that can only "vary under certain limits." Physical limits to human beings restrict how much the capitalist can make them work—"during part of the day the vital force must rest, sleep; during another the man has to satisfy other physical needs, to feed, wash and clothe himself." The subject needs to replenish their spoons. Marx also writes of moral limits: "The worker needs time in which to satisfy his intellectual and social requirements, and the extent and number of these requirements is conditioned by the general level of civilization." Mapped onto spoon theory, the moral part of Marx's restoration recipe might more precisely be thought of in terms of either giving energy to others or receiving energy from them, as well as restorative activities conducted in solitude, including sleep. Throughout Marx's chapter on the working day, he depicts the conflict between capitalists and workers in terms of capitalists pushing against these natural and moral limits, and workers organizing to defend them: "In the place of the pompous catalogue of the 'inalienable rights of man' there steps the modest Magna Carta of the working day."[31]

Spoon theory updates and expands this modest Magna Carta by expanding the concept of work. Its basic insight: everything, whether waged or not, is a kind of labor, and labor is conceived here not as productive power per se, or the power to change the world, but rather the expenditure of energy quanta. It also does not assume that work or expended energy is the only source of fatigue, which is a profound insight (and I discuss it later). The spoon becomes a kind of use value of the subject to itself: a means of self-consumption.[32] And like all other things under capitalism, those spoons are not evenly divided among people. Some people have fewer spoons because of their social positions, but some people also have fewer spoons because of disabilities—they start with less labor power. If this sounds a bit like an extension of the old Marxist-feminist debate over the "second shift" of unwaged care labor, that's because it very much extends that reasoning.[33] Tithi Bhattacharya frames the problem this way: "If workers' labor produces all the wealth in society, who then produces the workers? What kinds of processes enable the worker to arrive at the doors of her place of work every day so that she can produce the wealth of society? What role did breakfast play in her work-readiness? What about a good night's sleep?"[34] In the context of disability, the concept of worker as a universal category must be troubled, since people with disabilities are disproportionately unemployed.[35] But the line of questioning works well for any social activity: What conditions allowed the person to arrive there at that moment? What resources were needed? Who produced the spoons, how, and at what cost?

Care work, the labor required to replenish one's own spoons and the spoons of others, has irreducibly physical and mental dimensions. For those giving care work, it costs spoons. For those receiving it, it may also cost spoons, especially in an institutionalized or other disability context, or in cases where a person must advocate for themselves or others because they do not have an officially recognized disability, or because of structural racism, sexism, ableism, or other forms of discrimination. This is why Piepzna-Samarasinha lists interdependence as a core value of disability justice (and it would really have to be a core value for any form of justice).[36] Studies of emotional labor clearly show that there is an irreducible bodily dimension to emotions and emoting, from the flight attendant or server's smile, to the scripts and monotones followed by 911 operators, to the psychologist's studied nonreaction to the patient's emotions.[37] The same could be said of the labor of care outside a waged relationship. The care work discussed by disability activists refuses any easy distinctions between purely ideational labor and physical work as well as waged and unwaged labor. But care work is necessary for social reproduction.

Disability and chronic illness have thus far been placed at the edges of current struggles over social reproduction and the ways in which institutions care for people.[38] Yet people with disabilities and chronic illnesses and those around them carry extra burdens, including the heavily racialized and feminized populations who make up the corps of essential workers in advanced capitalist societies. The fight for rights of the fatigued, the disabled, the impaired, and the chronically ill goes beyond the struggle for decent work. Rather, it is to reimagine the very framework within which paid work is a measure of life. By expanding spoons to energy, and treating all activity as energy depleting, spoon theory offers an account of a laboring subject that troubles the already shaky distinction between productive and reproductive labor.

Spoon theory expands the feminist critique of political economy to spheres beyond the employer-employee relation and beyond the reproduction of waged labor, to provide an analysis of people's obligations to one another. And here the argument comes full circle. The whole point of Miserandino explaining her fatigue to her friend was to explain her inability to meet her friend's expectations as well as some of her own desires and needs. Spoon theory provides a theory of value and a theory of limits—not just bodily or mental limits but also, crucially, a social theory of limits. It explains how activity saps energy from a subject, while that subject lives within a political economy of energy that is shaped by labor but also by disability, race, gender, sexuality, age, and any number of other axes of power and difference. Spoon theory's redemptive politics come from valuing the work of care and social reproduction, while also valuing the differences among subjects that disability and chronic illness can produce under the conditions of modern life. Spoon theory is a theory of inequality based on the idea that people don't all start with the same amount of energy or fatigue. It is less concerned with the causes of fatigue than fatigue as a social and phenomenological problem, a differential field; and it does not offer a critique of the concept of labor as such. For that, I will have to look elsewhere.

From each according to their spoons, to each according to their needs.

FATIGUE IS A SYMPTOM OF EVERYTHING

My search for an impairment phenomenology of fatigue that goes beyond depletion may come after spoon theory has run out of spoons. Or perhaps it is a fork too many for that project. But where else to search? Medicine is always a vexed place for disability theory to travel, but it is worth exploring precisely because of its vexatiousness. Doctors' frustrations with impairments can also be illuminating. Medical models of fatigue treat it as a problem that subjects cannot resolve on their own, as a symptom of something else. In medicine, fatigue is only a problem to be directly addressed insofar as an alternative cause or explanation cannot be found. In other words, there is not just one kind of fatigue. There are many kinds: the fatigues caused by maladies of the body and their treatments; the fatigues caused by stress; those caused by psychological maladies and their treatments; those caused by sport, or work, or other exertion; those caused by sleep deprivation; and many others. The problem here is obvious. Each fatigue is slightly different from the last, many cannot be quantified because they require subjects to self-report their experiences, and diagnostic thinking around fatigue produces a kind of stacking effect: you are fatigued because you are depressed; you are fatigued because you are sleep deprived; you are fatigued because you are on a certain kind of medication; you are fatigued because you are old; you are fatigued because you are fat. This is effectively a way of changing the topic to the person's other conditions, some of which are not strictly medical diagnoses, and away from fatigue as a problem.

One of the defining features of these diagnostic chains is that, with a few notable exceptions, they tend to exclude work as a cause or a diagnostic criterion—whether waged labor or the labor of social reproduction. This is quite striking when set against the history I've outlined, where energetic models of fatigue emerge as direct products of the capitalist process, or at least as a side effect of the quest for increased industrial efficiency and increased profitability. If they exclude work and social reproduction, diagnostic logics of fatigue mystify at the same time that they explicate: employers' extraction of surplus labor is bracketed off as a social, not a medical, problem, despite its inevitable human cost (with the exception of some radical work in fields like epidemiology). Yet wage and time theft are real political sites of struggle; and it is well known that poor and racialized people have less access to health care and institutional support in most places. A holistic view of a person's fatigue would need to account for all the causes in their lives that could lead to it, especially if fatigue is only addressed as a problem in itself after all other possible causes are considered and dismissed.

There is a historical reason for this bracketing tendency, beyond the standard disability studies claim that medical models of disability and illness abstract personal problems from social contexts. As fatigue became a site for conflict between labor and management, other interests moved into the discussion of fatigue, often for very different purposes. At the same time that fatigue research was being entrenched in the evolving disciplines and institutions of early twentieth-century Western Europe and America, unions, labor advocates, and Progressive Era reformers used fatigue research to argue for the rights of workers and limits to the working day. Josephine Goldmark, who would publish a book called *Fatigue and Efficiency: A Study in Industry* in 1912, used her research to serve as an expert witness in the U.S. Supreme Court ruling *Muller v. Oregon*, which established that states could pass laws limiting the working day for women and children. Goldmark used the methods of the industrial physiologists against the industrial managers whose favor the physiologists sought. She leveraged physiological research on workers to suggest that profits from a longer working day were essentially "illusory," and further, that they provided a "rational" authority for the government regulation of industry.

Goldmark built on an international network of reformers using fatigue research against industry, and their approach would continue to work in U.S. law and policy after World War I.[39]

Co-optation by labor advocates meant that industrial physiology became a less attractive area of study for managers. In industrial contexts, physiologists were often replaced by physicians, who were less likely to comment on working hours. Frederick Winslow Taylor, whose efficiency studies shaped managerial attitudes toward work, had no interest in worker fatigue at all, arguing instead for the careful selection of workers, a line later echoed by industrial psychologists, and which helped install ableism in industrial hiring practices. Another solution was to redefine fatigue entirely. The Harvard Fatigue Lab opened in 1927 in the Harvard Business School as a lab for industrial physiology with funds from the Rockefeller Foundation. The founder of the lab, Lawrence J. Henderson, was a chemist who applied chemistry to physiology, not a physiologist. Over the course of its existence, the Harvard Fatigue Lab helped redefine fatigue as a chemical imbalance rather than a result of energy depletion. Athletes replaced workers as "model organisms" in academic fatigue study because they were socially proximate to the researchers, they were convenient to study, they tolerated artificial lab conditions, they could reliably reproduce performances for the purposes of study, and they were easier to depoliticize than workers. This combination allowed Henderson and his colleague to focus on the long "steady state" period of exertion in the middle of an exercise session rather than its breakdown at the end. Conceived as a chemical imbalance, fatigue was a problem that could be managed in an organism instead of an absolute limit that would require rest and replenishment, as in the energy depletion model. It was defined as a personal rather than a structural problem. In the chemical model, workers' bodies gave out from chemical imbalance and boredom rather than energy depletion. The Harvard Fatigue Lab's turn to chemistry, which came a few years before the Nazis tried to produce a pill to cure fatigue for their soldiers, essentially defined fatigue as a problem "peripheral to industrial management," in Richard Gillespie's words. It was a problem of the individual, not the organization, and not the state.[40]

The association between academic fatigue research and athletics also suggested another way of understanding fatigue entirely: fatigue as a means of self-formation. A persistent subtheme in the critical literature on masculinity is defining it through fighting or overcoming fatigue, both in the service of specific achievements and in treating the body's needs—especially the need for sleep—as a kind of inefficiency. This is clear in both the self-promotional accounts of entrepreneurial male celebrities from Thomas Edison and Charles Lindbergh to Donald Trump, and in the accounts of working-class men describing their labor as truck drivers, crabbers, or loggers. This discursive frame aligns well with the turn to athletes in the physiological study of fatigue: fatigue becomes known and knowable through framed exertion, whether it is labor, business, mountain climbing (where romantic accounts of "mountain sickness" gave way to physiological, and later chemical, accounts of fatigue), bike riding, or distance running. The manly relationship to fatigue would be to overcome it, ignore it, push past it, supersede it, as when Edison called sleep "an absurdity, a bad habit." One can find this attitude even in highly rarefied contexts like modern art museums, which manifests in what Elizabeth Guffey calls "swaggering virility" in their performance of austerity and the demands they place on visitors.[41] Yet this form of fatigue can also yield a form of suffering, even stigmatized suffering, as in the World War I–era construct of "battle fatigue"—a precursor of modern post-traumatic stress disorder (PTSD).

Unexplained fatigue outside work has a long history in the Americas and Western Europe, taking a roughly modern form in the nineteenth century: reports of upper-class women who were too weak to get out of bed, and men who suffered from nervous exhaustion from the assault of modern life. Fatigue was often an explanation of some other disease that came to be defined later—for instance, mononucleosis—and physicians often had difficulty separating out physical or mental causes, a problem that persists to the present day. George Miller Beard, one of the nineteenth-century physicians to define neurasthenia, did not include fatigue as a symptom; Sigmund Freud did. Diagnoses like neurasthenia (more common for men) or hysteria (more common for women) sometimes were used to describe chronic fatigue of one sort or another but often were used for other purposes entirely. Many people who received those diagnoses did not complain of fatigue at all, and many people who complained of fatigue did not receive those diagnoses. Neurasthenia and hysteria fell out of favor in the twentieth century, but the terms that replaced them provide no more firm insight: outbreaks of fatigue were given labels like epidemic neuromyasthenia, Iceland disease, and atypical poliomyelitis.[42]

Today, medicine defines fatigue as pathological if it stems from a source other than work; definitionally, fatigue from work is normal fatigue. Medicine considers fatigue to be chronic if it lasts longer than six months. Most contemporary analyses of fatigue as a problem connect it in some way with myalgic encephalomyelitis/chronic fatigue syndrome (ME/CFS).[43] A now-standard article from 1994 defines ME/CFS as "severe disabling fatigue and a combination of symptoms that prominently features self-reported impairments in concentration and short-term memory, sleep disturbances, and musculoskeletal pain." The authors explicitly differentiate ME/CFS from fatigue caused by medical conditions that could explain the cause of fatigue, like sleep, thyroid issues, or medication side effects; unresolved infections or other conditions that have fatigue as a symptom; a group of mental illnesses like depression, dementia, anorexia, or schizophrenia; alcohol or substance abuse; or obesity. In other words, ME/CFS is fatigue that persists only when other medical explanations are unavailable, so long as it conforms to a bundle of criteria.[44] While ME/CFS shares a history with older terms related to doctors' difficulties in localizing a cause of fatigue, that does not mean it is a direct descendant. In fact, it is equally possible that the rising prevalence of ME/CFS reflects a host of environmental and cultural factors that did not exist in the nineteenth century. Nobody knows for certain, and one of the main responses in the ME/CFS literature has been to produce more analytics for different kinds of fatigue.[45]

The ambiguity of fatigue brings with it the potential for stigma: fatigue without a medically defined cause can quickly be pathologized as a psychological problem or derided as a bourgeois affliction: "the yuppie flu," a disease of the intelligentsia, a claim deserving of suspicion—as in the accusation "It's all in your head." Yet actual epidemiological work on ME/CFS in a diverse cross-section of Chicago (as opposed to just relying on patients in hospitals, which would overrepresent privileged white people) has shown the opposite: the researchers found higher levels of ME/CFS among racialized groups (primarily African American and Latinx), and people with lower levels of education or occupational status. In other words, chronic fatigue is very much a working-class condition. To anyone who understands the differential costs that capitalism extracts from people, this finding should come as no surprise.[46]

A 1992 review explained, "Most physical illnesses are associated with fatigue."[47] Things were not any better in 2018: "Fatigue is such a multifaceted construct it has sprouted specific research fields and experts in domains as different as exercise physiology, cognitive psychology, human factors and engineering, and medical practice. It lacks a consensus definition: it is an experimental concept, a symptom, a risk, a cause (e.g., of performance decrement) and a consequence (e.g., of sleep deprivation)."[48] Consider the range of causes of pathological fatigue, as listed in a 2014 review

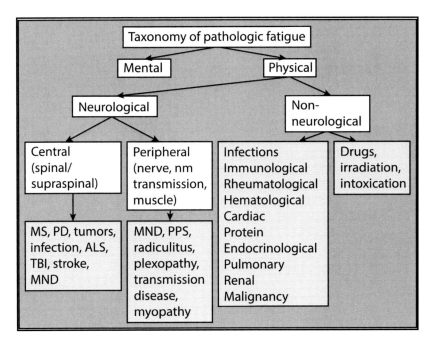

5.1 Taxonomy of pathologic fatigue. Finsterer and Zarrouk Mahjoub, "Fatigue in Healthy and Diseased Individuals," 565.

article by Josef Finsterer and Sinda Zarrouk Mahjoub (figure 5.1). The list covers an impossibly wide range of systems in the body and reserves "mental" for any cause of fatigue that cannot be explained by one of the identifiable systems, substances, or processes listed in its decision tree. This echoes what others have written about pain: any cause that cannot be explained physically is assumed to be mental in origin, which could be treated either as a form of mental illness or as an imaginary problem.[49]

The authors' taxonomy of forms of fatigue continues down the same path (see table 5.1). While there are a range of forms of fatigue that have mental dimensions—perceived difficulty, perception of effort, volition—the physiological focus of the analysis means that it is primarily conceived in relation to task completion, energy availability, and energy expenditure, often in relation to an ambiguous or personal baseline. Conceptions of fatigue formed for the purposes of increased labor efficiency return to medical schemas through the back door.

Even considering their limited scope, these physiological typologies give a sense of the incredible range of things that fall under the umbrella

TABLE 5.1 Definitions of Fatigue

GENERAL	Progressive decline in the ability to activate the muscle voluntarily
	Progressive loss of ability to generate maximal voluntary contraction during or following repeated or sustained muscle contraction
	Loss of force generation during a task
	Difficulty in initiating or sustaining voluntary activity
	Mismatch between expended effort and actual performance or exhaustion
	Reduced force production (weakness)
	Loss of exercise capacity (reduced endurance)
	Increased sense of effort or overperception of force
	Decreased power (reduced velocity of muscle contraction)
	Loss of peak force (torque) >50%
MENTAL	Perception of the feeling to be cognitively fatigued after performing demanding cognitive activities that involve concentration
CENTRAL	Motor cortex failure to recruit muscle, particularly loss of high threshold motor units
	Reduced central drive from increased inhibitory interneuron output to the cortex
	Central conduction block from demyelination of neurons
	Increased negative feedback from muscle afferents via type 3 sensor neurons
	Loss of positive feedback from muscle spindle type I sensory afferents
	Poor coordination of motor unit firing
	Delayed conduction and impairment of dynamic recruitment
	Changes in synergistic muscle contraction to net force
	Loss of coherence between central nervous system motor neurons
	Changes in joint mobility from spasticity
PERIPHERAL	Progressive decline in maximal voluntary contraction produced by a muscle
	Progressive loss of maximal voluntary contraction or decline in maximal voluntary contraction during a task
	Sense of exhaustion and lack of energy to perform repeated or sustained muscle contractions during a task
	Long-lasting reduction in the activity to contract and to exert force
	Incapacity to maintain the required or expected force
	Diminished adenosine triphosphate production due to deconditioning
	Disuse muscle atrophy secondary to inactivity
	Muscle atrophy due to loss of innervation

Source: Finsterer and Zarrouk Mahjoub, "Fatigue in Healthy and Diseased Individuals," 563.

concept of fatigue. In fact, the defining aspect of medical fatigue research appears to be the proliferation of definitions of fatigue, kinds of fatigue, qualities of fatigue experience, causes of fatigue, and timescales of fatigue. Finsterer and Zarrouk Mahjoub frame their literature review by arguing for a split between *fatigue* as a "subjective sensation (perceived fatigue)" and *fatigability* as an "objective and quantifiable change in performance."[50] Yet their turn to fatigability reinscribes a model of fatigue that separates mental and physical aspects and frames fatigue as a problem of measurable energetics above all else: it falls back on the question of asking whether workers are ready to work, and for how long.

A more promising move has been to consider fatigue as integrative and the result of many factors, for instance, in the concept of ego depletion: "Conscious acts of self-control, defined more broadly as volitional action, draw on some sort of limited resource, meaning that even seemingly different unrelated actions share a common resource pool, and thus influence one another."[51] It its original framing, ego depletion was understood as a gradual loss of willpower to resist temptation, assert control over an environment or one's own behavior, make choices, or initiate action. This notion of fatigue is quite close to the emergent, emotional, and sometimes metaphorical definition of fatigue noted at the beginning of this chapter. It is also ambiguously energetic: while it implies the depletion of resources, it does not necessarily imply the depletion of one unifying energy but rather that fatigue could come from anywhere and everywhere—so, more like forks than spoons. Even this integrative approach to fatigue leads back to category multiplication. In its currently listed draft additions, the *Oxford English Dictionary* adds "widespread apathy, boredom, or disenchantment" among a group of people—donor or audience fatigue—or in relation to a specific phenomenon, such as compassion fatigue or information fatigue. These usages arise in the second half of the twentieth century, in relation to media saturation, emotional labor and burnout among care workers, and various forms of excessive external demands placed on people: too many requests for the same thing, too many things to care about, too much news coming from too many places, too much news about the same story, too much time at the museum, too much repetition, too many microaggressions.[52] Fatigue grows, or perhaps fatigues grow, and typologies of fatigue spread. There are too many forks.

For all this momentum, there is an alternative psychological literature that critiques energetic and atomistic models of fatigue. Robert Hockey, in his 2013 textbook on the subject, lists two core failures of fatigue theory;

by "fatigue theory" he means to refer to the medical model of fatigue, but his point is equally apt for whatever rudiments of a cultural fatigue theory might exist. First, he challenges the widespread claim that fatigue "is caused by a loss of energy, caused by the activity of carrying out (too much) work," and he shows that psychological theories of drive and energy effectively remediated this industrial model of fatigue. Second, he critiques the proposition that fatigue should be interpreted as a primarily negative state: "an *unwanted* by-product of (physical and mental) work. This is a natural consequence of identifying human transactions with the environment with the work done by industrial machines, and the exhaustion of energy in the execution of that work."[53]

In opposition to these two models, Hockey proposes a theory of fatigue as adaptive, which is to say, useful for the organism. For him, fatigue is an *aversion* to an activity, or a recalibration of motivation. His central claim is that fatigue is something people do and have. It is an active state rather than a passive state of emptiness. This is a core insight for a nondepletionist understanding of fatigue, and a valuable alternative to fatigue as a negative phenomenology or energetics. One striking aspect of Hockey's work is his recovery of midcentury holistic approaches to fatigue that combine psychology and phenomenology. He quotes from a 1941 book by Raymond Cattell, "There is no fatigue as long as a purpose itself is not fatigued," which connects fatigue with something external to the subject: a motivation, a goal, an intention, a purpose. Hockey also quotes a 1943 article by S. Howard Bartley to claim that "the basis of fatigue is conflict and frustration. One of the first significant outcomes of conflict is a sense of *discomfort, danger, or failure*."[54] Again, this notion of fatigue is highly contextual—it goes beyond the subject and demands a relational analysis of fatigue as something that exists within subjects, but subjects who are positioned in a world to which they are reacting. Hockey also draws on S. Howard Bartley and Eloise Chute's 1947 *Fatigue and Impairment in Man*. On the very first page of that book, the authors call the linkage between fatigue and energy expenditure a "confused causality," one that leads to studies of impairment instead of fatigue. As this chapter has amply documented, that is because most studies of fatigue have not been undertaken from the perspective of the fatigued person. They have been undertaken from the perspective of someone who wants to "get more out of" the fatigued person—a manager, a coach, a scientist. This is why fatigue is so closely linked to impairment, studied as impairment, and defined in terms of its origins: fatigue from work, from stress, et cetera. In contrast, Bartley and Chute propose that fatigue studies need to consider fatigue as an "experience of the whole person," in other words, where psychological and physiological dimensions are inseparable, and where the experience of fatigue is cumulative rather than atomized. Fatigue is systemic, relational, attitudinal, phenomenal, and temporal. It is an orientation or a cluster of orientations in a subject. Above all else, fatigue is aversion, an "*attempt to retreat or escape from a situation.*"[55]

The midcentury literature is fascinating for its admission of philosophical and phenomenological questions into psychology—even occasionally veering into existential matters. But while it offers a promising beginning in the figure of aversion, it shies away from politics. The same is true for more contemporary critiques of depletionist models of fatigue. Hockey, for instance, justifies his analysis in problematic evolutionary terms—problematic both because he naturalizes and universalizes fatigue as a response and because he misreads Charles Darwin on adaptation.[56] A contextualist theory of fatigue would have to develop in at least two directions: it must admit politics and positionality back into the field of analysis, and it must allow for consideration of subjective states like aversion without resorting to evolutionary or universalist assumptions or justifications.

Depletionist models of fatigue have provided people, managers and labor activists, and, in modified forms, disabled and chronically ill people, with a language to discuss their understandings of human limits and the nature of the negotiations around those limits. In the case of spoon theory, second-wave feminism, and Progressive Era reform (and perhaps even in some sublimated way in the discourses of masculine wakefulness), this energetic model of fatigue has also helped challenge the ignorance of fatigue as a space of struggle—between labor and management, between women and men, between crip and non-crip, and between the fatigued subject and itself. It is this last space, the subject's reflection on itself, that brings back the question of experience and phenomenology. Critiques of medical discourses of energetic fatigue show that a nondepletionist model of fatigue is possible—and has been for a long time. But they are bound to a medical context where the goal is some kind of resolution of fatigue into something else, where fatigue is a problem to be solved. But what if it isn't? What if fatigue is conceived as a part of human existence more fully? What if it is given full admission to the human variety? What if fatigue points to a set of political problems rather than problems in subjects, energy, or efficiency?

To address fatigue as a presence, as a quality of experience, requires a language to do it. This is harder than it seems. In an essay titled "The Elephant in the Classroom," Jody Berland uses the figure of the elephant (specifically, "the elephant in the room") to acknowledge chronic fatigue as a kind of presence that can nevertheless be forgotten by others, since it operates as an invisible disability. Of the experience of writing under chronic fatigue, she says, "It's sort of like my brain starts out this big and then after an hour it shrinks and I'm working through this peephole. . . . The world sort of loses its light."[57] Here, fatigue is described as a combination of shrinking and fading; one impairment is used to describe another. Common metaphors for the feeling of fatigue in the writing on ME/CFS often involve visual occlusion—fog, shadow, twilight—or metaphors of confinement, reduction, or restriction, such as a "prison of fatigue." Part of the challenge of describing fatigue is that it includes feelings that cut across the physical and mental divide. The critique of the mind/body distinction is well established in many disciplines at this point, from disability studies and cultural studies to cognitive science. Yet that makes it no easier for a person to describe an impairment that is at once physical and mental, that exists phenomenally inside the subject but, like pain, registers no outwardly visible manifestations other than perhaps a reaction.

Because of its association with sleep and restoration, at least in the straight world, fatigue has a long-term association with time: time to exhaustion, time to rest, recovery time, sleeping time; getting old, getting busy, getting tired, slowing down, speeding up. This imagination of time can exist firmly in the Max Weber / Benjamin Franklin "time is money" world, where time is linked inexorably to labor and productivity, and the rest of life is about setting up the conditions for the productivity to occur; or within the time that Marxist and feminist theorists of social reproduction have proposed.[58] While "time as money" or "time as labor power" can be ways of experiencing fatigue and its relationship to time, there are other approaches to fatigue and time worth considering.

The philosopher most associated with fatigue is probably Emmanuel Levinas. His early writing links fatigue to the relationship between existence and time. In *Existence and Existents*, a book he began while in captivity as a Jewish prisoner of war in Germany, Levinas describes fatigue as one of a set of states that illustrate the characteristics of existence as effort. For Levinas, fatigue provided a fundamental insight into what it means to be human; it is a force within the subject rather than an absence.[59] Levinas is unusual in the philosophical tradition for considering fatigue at all, and because he gives it a phenomenological valence—as something that is there—his ideas can contribute to a nondepletionist theory of fatigue. Levinas's work is usually cited in terms of his formulation of ethics as "first philosophy": to tremendously oversimply, this is his claim that obligation to the other precedes any other philosophical concern. Against Heidegger's formulation of existence as something that precedes beings who perceive it ("being" must be understood before "beings"), Levinas takes an approach to existence that does not separate it from those who exist and their relationships to others; for him, being and beings cannot be thought apart.[60]

For Levinas, *to be* is a reflexive verb: "It is not just that one is, one is oneself [*on s'est*]."[61] Existence takes effort. If his model of existence involves a relation between a self-relating existent and its world, then states where the work of maintaining existence is a burden are of particular interest. States like fatigue, indolence, and lassitude "represent attempts to avoid the imperatives that existence imposes but cannot in any sense be said to represent judgments about existence. . . . Indeed, reflection falsifies their character as events."[62] In other words, fatigue is an existential stance, but perhaps not in the way it is usually discussed. "Existential fatigue" might sound like a kind of cosmic burnout, an absence of energy to live. But that is precisely the opposite of Levinas's idea of fatigue. For him, fatigue has substance and content, and is a modality of living where a self lags behind itself. Fatigue is "the impossible refusal" of "the ultimate obligation," which is to continue being.[63]

The substance of fatigue is the stop: effort is "made up of stops"; it is a duality of upsurge and fatigue.[64] His inclusion of fatigue within effort is what makes Levinas interesting, but also insufficient, for a crip analysis of fatigue. While the depletionists treat fatigue as the absence or subsiding of effort, a decline in efficiency of action, Levinas's approach to fatigue suggests that it is a necessary part of, or predicate to, effort itself. Imagine Levinas watching another person or animal trying to move an object; or, better, imagine watching Levinas try to move an object: rather than singling out the instant of effort, consider the "upsurge" of action in full relation to what happens before and after. To exert effort is to seize upon an activity, to try to do something, and to commit to it in an instant. But that moment of effort "lurches out of fatigue and falls back into it." Fatigue and upsurge cannot exist separately from one another. "Fatigue," he writes, "is this almost self-contradictory moment of a present that tarries behind itself." Fatigue is "an inscription in existence," a "hesitation," "the interval in which the event of the present can occur," "a delay with respect to oneself and with respect to the present."[65] Levinas's fatigue evokes the mental image of a person dawdling on the sidewalk some space behind their own existence, or at least curling up for a nap in between periods of activity.

But this idea of delay is where a crip theory of fatigue runs up against Levinas's approach. He writes that "the fundamental activity of rest, foundation, conditioning, thus appears to be the very relationship with being, the upsurge of an existent into existence," an underlying reality.[66] In his later book *Totality and Infinity*, he renders sleep as a kind of sustenance alongside ideas, soup, and air.[67] On one level, it is hard to argue with the universality of the need for sleep in animals: not only do humans require sleep, but so do squirrels, kookaburras, bearded dragons, and some sharks, in one form or another. Levinas's concept of fatigue clearly implies that it is a state that could be put in abeyance. While Levinas is not primarily concerned with a philosophy of the subject, he does seem to imagine fatigue as a condition that is resolvable, or, more precisely, not unresolvable.

But not all fatigue has a complementary relationship with sleep or sustenance. Not all fatigue resolves through restoration. An understanding of fatigue as a temporalized relation to oneself is even more powerful if it is relieved of any concept of universal or self-governed time. If fatigue involves slowing down and lingering, a way of considering that one is never fully with oneself, then it has some resonance with Samuels's description of *crip time*:

> When disabled folks talk about crip time, sometimes we just mean that we're late all the time—maybe because we need more sleep than nondisabled people, maybe because the accessible gate in the train station was locked. But other times, when we talk about crip time, we mean something more beautiful and forgiving. We mean, as my friend Margaret Price explains, we live our lives with a "flexible approach to normative time frames" like work schedules, deadlines, or even just waking and sleeping. My friend Alison Kafer says that "rather than bend disabled bodies and minds to meet the clock, crip time bends the clock to meet disabled bodies and minds." I have embraced this beautiful notion for many years, living within the embrace of a crip time that lets me define my own "normal." And yet recently I have found myself

thinking about the less appealing aspects of crip time, that are harder to see as liberatory, more challenging to find a way to celebrate.[68]

For Samuels, crip time lies in shaping the world for the subject rather than bending the subject to the world. Crip time is tragic when it is about pain and mourning—when neither the world nor the subject will bend. But a crip theory of fatigue holds promise because it marks a subject out of time with others and out of time with itself.

This suggests an existential politics to fatigue, especially crip forms of fatigue, for instance, the putatively excess fatigability of spoon or fork theory (I get fatigued faster than you do) or fatigue that does not resolve itself as it is supposed to for a normate person (I am chronic or severe in my fatigue).[69] It is existential because fatigue is an effect of being alive and continuing to live. It is political because not everyone experiences fatigue in the same way or has the same kind of fatigue, and because there are differential consequences depending on whether one's fatigue is institutionally or morally sanctioned. Crip fatigue highlights how fatigue is supposed to work under capitalism while also simultaneously highlighting the impossible expectations attached to that supposition.

Here it is useful to return to a term from the alternative psychology literature: *aversion*. If fatigue can be characterized as a temporalized aversion to something, how best to characterize it? There is not a political theory of aversion as such.[70] There is, however, a burgeoning literature on refusal and withdrawal, which is related to aversion, and which provides inspiration for a political understanding of fatigue. In studies of labor—whether organized in the form of unions, castes and peasantry, or slavery—refusal in the form of withdrawal of labor is often understood as the most fundamental act of sabotage, and one of the most powerful options available to workers: going slow, going on strike, idleness, laziness, apathy. In Black studies, this has taken the form of refusing to engage with white institutions on their own terms, or on any terms at all, against a "false image of enclosure," as Stefano Harney and Fred Moten put it. Indigenous writers have also developed an advanced theory of refusal. For Leanne Betasamosake Simpson, "refusal is always an appropriate response to oppression, and within this context it is always generative; that is, it is always the living alternative." She follows with a catalog of examples of Nishnaabeg people refusing to acknowledge white settler authority, and even deer refusing and leaving the territory when the Nishnaabeg overharvested them. From the standpoint of settlers, refusal might appear like a negative gesture because it refuses the demands of the settler state to conform to its legal, epistemological, and cosmological frameworks. By releasing its subject from white or settler frameworks, refusal affirms the institutions, spaces, and histories that Indigenous people choose to build and preserve rather than the ones demanding their inclusion. As Simpson explains, "I exist as a kwe because of the continual refusal of countless generations to disappear from the north shore of Lake Ontario."[71]

There are also other relevant histories, for instance in groups like the Socialist Patients' Collective (Sozialistisches Patientenkollektiv, SPK) and the Nap Ministry. The SPK formed in Heidelberg, Germany, in 1970 as a collective response to medicalization, with the slogan "turn illness into a weapon." The second thesis of its manifesto sounds a note of refusal: "As a result of capitalist relations of production illness in its developed form as protest of life against capitalism is the revolutionary productive power par excellence for all human beings."[72] It might seem as if all that's needed in SPK's framework would be to move from the generality of illness to the specificity of fatigue. More recently, the work of the Nap Ministry, whose slogan is "rest is resistance," might inspire even if it does hold out the promise of restoration through napping—not always a possibility for the fatigued. Founder Tricia Hersey holds workshops, events, installations, and interventions as well as maintains an active social media presence on Instagram, Twitter, and Facebook designed to "deprogram the masses from grind culture."[73] The Nap Ministry constructs a personal politics grounded in self-love, self-care, and a critique of capitalism beginning from its demands on Black female bodies while offering an inviting program for all bodies.

But wait!

This is all much too exciting for the fatigued. Fatigue that does not resolve itself suggests a refusal of, an aversion to, a configuration of the world and its time.[74] But there is a crucial difference between the politics of refusal and the refusal of fatigue: all of the refusals I have just described involve an active, self-assertive dimension. Fatigue is different because the unresolvably fatigued *already exist in a state of refusal, without willful acts of refusing to punctuate that state*. Fatigue is aversion or refusal without self-assertion; it is nonelective. Carolyn Lazard writes that resistance by way of illness sometimes "looks like leisure" or convalescence.[75] Fatigue is a problem not because the fatigued assert themselves, but because they do not.[76] Fatigue is more likely that which is to be resisted by the powerful—they may experience it as a strategy of resistance in the guise of withdrawal, rest, refusal, nonengagement—but it is rarely experienced in the first instance as a political act. In an act of self-overcoming, a person may also resist their own fatigue; and while sometimes it is as simple as deciding to stay at the party a little longer, it more often is tied up with acquiescence to a demand of power. "The Spoon Theory" is remarkable and caught on so powerfully because it is a rare self-declaration of fatigue, in language that is easy to grasp. That's not usually how it goes.

A political theory of fatigue would therefore treat it as a form of having refused, minus the initial act of refusal, *an aversion without an act of averting*. Fatigue is a modality, a potential that exists in the world. This is not how political acts are usually imagined: they are usually tied to a will-exerting, intending subject (even if that subject is not entirely rational). Cressida Heyes describes this problem as "fetishizing autonomy" or personal sovereignty; or, in Lauren Berlant's words, it is "a fantasy misrecognized as an objective state." Fatigue is precisely not a demand, but if it were to be read as a demand, it is a demand that continuing to exist has to be enough. This is a profound demand, all the more profound for its simplicity. There is no stress test for being human. Existence may require effort, but effort cannot—should not—be defined externally and applied to the existing subject. A political theory of fatigue would treat it as something that is political because of how fatigue is inherently relational: it is built on the dependency of the subject.[77] Because fatigue that does not resolve itself is also an existential phenomenon, it poses profound problems for institutions that want to put limits on the human variety and for the people caught up in relation to those institutions. Every time that just being is not enough, fatigue raises the uncomfortable question: "Why not?" Every time an institution demands self-sufficiency, fatigue suggests its impossibility.

What, then, might it mean to actively affirm fatigue? In an argument that lays out the converse to Levinas's philosophy, Gayle Salamon has argued that the capacity to withdraw into the body is a fundamental part of what it means for subjects to participate in world making. But the ability to withdraw signifies a certain measure of privilege. In her harrowing chapter on the sexual assault of unconscious women, Heyes also affirms the necessity of withdrawal while noting its connection to power: "We all need the space of anonymity—including but not limited to sleep—but for those whose waking lives are marked by the kind of hypervisibility and forced relation to a stereotyped self that typify racism and sexism today, sleep brings a special respite." Class and geography also map onto this body politics: those bodies deemed disposable are least able to withdraw. Managerial attempts to overcome fatigue and colonize sleep turn people into unwilling subjects of a stress experiment; states' profound disregard of the fatigue inflicted on whole populations can result in outright dispossession.[78]

Even within all these limits, it is still possible to imagine a liberatory politics for fatigue that is actively produced through artworks, through sport, or through religious ceremony, at least temporarily. But all those require a fatigable body as a starting point. They use fatigue as a means to produce extraordinary experience or consciousness—extraordinary because it is temporary, punctual, exceptional, possibly sublime.[79] But when not being fatigued is not a choice, the kind of liberation on offer in these scenarios is unavailable. Relations of care are another potential place to negotiate the politics of fatigue—where the fatigued depend on the non-fatigued. This is how a care web works, and it is probably part of how love works. But even there, because fatigue is also a relationship with oneself, a withdrawal inward, there is still the existential remainder, a living finitude. If the goal is not to fight, resist, eliminate, struggle—all things that are by definition beyond a fatigued subject—then perhaps a path follows from Oscar Wilde's famous solution to temptation: the only way to get rid of it is to yield to it.[80]

Recent writers on sleep have concurred. "The huge portion of our lives that we spend asleep, freed from a morass of simulated needs, subsists as one of the great human affronts to the voraciousness of contemporary capitalism. Sleep is an uncompromising interruption of the theft of time from us by capitalism," claims Jonathan Crary.[81] Note how Crary converts the productivity discourse around minimizing sleep into evidence of time theft from the subject. This inverts much of the managerial talk of fatigue as something to be overcome in paid labor and domestic life. But it also assumes the restorative (and therefore presumably uncompromised) power of sleep. As Salamon and Heyes have shown, that is an uncertainty at best for any minoritized subject, and illness and disability extend that uncertainty to a mechanical and logistical variable as well. Who gets to sleep soundly and safely? And what of people with depression and anxiety, for whom the fall of sleep is not a romantic abandonment of self-consciousness but more like a "hamster-wheel quality of an anxious brain [that] lasts a couple of minutes before the hamster simply keels over"?[82] The mechanics of a battle between wakefulness and sleep also spread as the waking world does, as the rise of blue blockers and concepts like sleep debt (to whom or what?) have shown. "Once the solution to disrupted sleep becomes a question of judiciousness, education, and self-care, it displaces the role of labor, presence creep," and "inexorable demands on attention," writes Dylan Mulvin.[83]

The right to sleep is a terrain of political struggle, just as the rights to housing, food, and health care are. In a fascinating study of a 1971 protest in Washington, DC, by Vietnam Veterans against the War (VVAW), Franny Nudelman shows how sleep is even integral to the possibility for political action itself: any multiday protest necessarily involves sleep, and any multiday occupation of a public space implies that the people occupying it will need to sleep. Yet sleep is often banned even when people have a right to be in a space. In the case of the 1971 protest, the U.S. Supreme Court ruled that the VVAW had the right to continuous presence on the Mall, which was public space, but its members did not have the right to sleep there. The VVAW protesters eventually decided to give in to the desire to sleep: "They turned sleep into a form of direct action, effectively politicizing a condition that might appear beyond the reach of radical organizing."[84] They were in refusal, without having actively refused.

If fatigue is a relationship with existence, its very relationality implies that it is something there rather than something not there. To assert fatigue as something that matters is to open up a space for alterity and unknowability, and makes them the basis of a political demand. A fatigued subject is not a subject that will necessarily exercise its will, articulate its full experience for others, or perform a deep investigation of the world as presented to its senses. These are all the usual political demands visited upon minoritized subjects, and they are exactly the ones that fatigue refuses. As evidenced by Levinas and the sleep theorists, a phenomenology of fatigue invites a descent into metaphor. One solution to this conceptual problem would be to impose a responsibility to describe fatigue in its many manifestations, in its multitudinous unfoldings: that is where the doctors keep getting stuck with their metastasizing typologies. Perhaps that is a better task for art or music or creative nonfiction. But as I suggested at the beginning of the chapter, the responsibility to describe cannot be fully met.

To assert that fatigue is something that subjects can know or feel about their relation to the world, that it is something more than epiphenomenon, is also a demand for dignity. In a political phenomenology, fatigue is a relationship that requires a letting go on the part of others, and not just on the part of fatigued subjects. If movements like sleep hygiene and time management construct one's own fatigue as a personal responsibility to be carefully managed, a political phenomenology of fatigue demands a response to others' fatigue, as an unending obligation. Fatigue should never be just a matter of self-care, even in Audre Lorde's radical sense of the term. Others' fatigue is a horizon for justice, or even new utopian fantasies and projects.[85] The observer of fatigued subjects must let the question rest; they need to be present with alterity without demanding full disclosure. In the moment of fatigue, fatigued subjects may connect their fatigue with desires to be left alone, to be relieved, to be cared for, to abandon the self, and countless other feelings.[86] That may be for the fatigued subjects to know, and not necessarily for the observer. "I am comforted, oddly, by the possibility that you cannot compare my pain to yours," writes Eula Biss. "And, for that reason, cannot prove it insignificant."[87]

I will close with a failed attempt at a phenomenology of fatigue. When I first started this paragraph in 2019, I was trying to feel my fatigue fully at the keyboard and write at the same time; and it was very difficult to do both things at once.[88] Berland was right: the fatigue is actually something in the room. But for me it is a human-sized guest that has roughly the same size and shape of those that I perceive around my body. It's not an elephant; it's just a little bigger or smaller than me. It is a presence that ebbs and flows in consciousness, making sentences like this one particularly difficult to write as I simultaneously attempt to focus on the prose emitting from my fingers and the full heaviness or juiciness running through my arms and out those same fingers, the fullness in my head. It's "not that bad."[89] I only focus on it here to describe it for you. Otherwise, I would ignore it if I were fighting through it to write. Or if I were too fatigued to write, I wouldn't write about it as it was happening. It is certainly not the most intense fatigue I have felt or could feel, since I am sitting here writing to you, dear reader, as I survey its movement through me.

The most powerful fatigue I have ever felt was radiation fatigue that came during a course of twenty-eight applications of external beam radiation to my neck over six weeks. They say you forget pain, but I still remember the mixture of pain and fatigue in my body—like a sunburn coming out from the inside of my throat—and a hot, heavy slowness. It was exquisite like no other exhaustion, and there was no full relief until weeks after my radiation treatment ended. Even so, giving in to the desire to sleep was never more total, or more joyous—especially the midday submission to fatigue after my daily treatments. On the other end, I might still wake up fatigued and/or in pain, but the onset of afternoon sleep was the most profound, delicious, exceptional relief, and often it came with our cat Ya-Ya curled up on top of me.[90] On the best days of this experience, where the cat and temperature and the covers were just right, as my consciousness faded from itself, as I allowed the force of fatigue to melt me away from waking life with no guarantee of what kind of waking experience lay on the other side, I might have felt just a touch of that upsurge into the flow of existence that Levinas was riffing on. Matthew Fuller calls this kind of fall into sleep "the luxuriance of dissolving," a phenomenon he can only describe through metaphors of rain and shimmers.[91] Or maybe it just felt good? Later, to capture that fleeting moment as I spaced out from myself and from the world, I resorted to haiku.

10

JUNE 10, 2010

Radiation sleep.
Cat rests on top, then vomits.
Sleep now, clean later.[92]

IMPAIRMENT

THEORY

——

A USER'S GUIDE

ILLUSTRATIONS BY DARSHA HEWITT

Congratulations on your acquisition of an impairment theory! You may have initially developed one through your own lived experience—and may or may not have called it an impairment theory. Or perhaps you encountered it in a book, on a digital device, on social media, or in a discussion with someone. However you came to it, thank you for taking the time to think carefully and at length about impairment. The team here at *Diminished Faculties* "contains multitudes," and we have worked hard to prepare it for you and to make it as stimulating as possible.[1] To make sure you have the latest updates before you start using impairment theory, please check your library, the internet, or whatever technology eventually replaces the internet.

WHAT IS AN IMPAIRMENT?

An impairment is a special kind of limit. It can involve a short-circuiting of intention: a transmission impairment happens when a telecommunications network doesn't behave as it is supposed to. A physical limit is experienced as an impairment when a person has a point of comparison beyond that limit. But in this way, impairment is not simply a defect or a malfunction. It is better understood as a productive distortion of an ability. The ability itself might be real or imagined. The distortion could be pleasurable or painful. The political and affective effects of impairment are never guaranteed. Impairment is not automatically good or bad. It exists in relation to something: an external norm of ability or action, a remembered embodiment or affect, an unrealized or altered intention.

Impairment is a detour. It could lead you somewhere you absolutely don't want to go; it could also lead you somewhere new and beautiful. But even the *you* here is deceptive: people can intend, but so can things. Impairment is therefore a type of orientation toward the world. It can be inefficient or indirect, but it can also forge new and powerful paths. It can direct you away from where you want to be, but it can also direct you somewhere you didn't know you wanted to be.

Because it infracts some kind of expected norm, impairment is a much bigger category than it is expected to be. It is often thought as the exception, but in surveying the world, you will find that it is in fact the rule. Nothing works as it is supposed to.

Conceptually and politically, impairment is a relative of disability, but it is not its physical substrate. Politically, impairment should be understood as one possible margin of disability — it can certainly exist outside the category of disability technically, juridically, or experientially. It can also be experienced or treated as the source of disability, as in the discussions of my paralyzed vocal cord in chapters 1 and 2, where the vocal cord was explained as the cause of some things about my speech. Just as not all things classified as disabilities are actually impairments — some simply do not conform to a norm — some impairments are not actually disabling. Disability can also be part of one's identity. But impairment is rarely thought of as an identity category; it is more typically conceived as something that can be incorporated into the self, its orientations, or the workings of an object. *Disability* has many legal, juridical, and policy implications. It is an institutional category. Impairment has a different history. Not only did AT&T Bell Labs engineers seek out impairments in their phone lines; legal thinkers in the United States and Canada have generally paired impairment with intoxication, as in the definition of driving-while-intoxicated for the purposes of criminal law. This is very different from the kinds of criminalization of disability one finds in, for example, ugly laws.

Discussions of the histories, definitions, and implications of impairment exist throughout *Diminished Faculties*, but please refer to chapter 1 for more in-depth discussion of the history of the term and its theoretical implications. Chapter 4 introduces the idea of *normal impairments*, which are impairments that are expected.

WHAT IS A THEORY?

Impairment theory draws on Stuart Hall's approach to theory. For Hall, the work of theory exists in two steps. First, it takes up things that are generally considered to be pregiven as points of departure and "shows by a critique that these are not, in fact, starting points, but points of arrival." This is the standard work of critique — showing that what is obvious is ideological and what is considered to be transcendental is actually contingent; it provides genealogies of things that appear to be given. But that alone is not enough. Theory must take a second step and produce tools to redescribe the slice of the world it considers. In other words, it must actually produce a new description of a concrete problem.[2]

Theories reconstruct context, and a good theory provides inspiration for its auditors to go out and use it to reconstruct other contexts. A theory is a portable idea that helps those who take it up describe the world in a way that was not possible before. This constructivist definition of theory has traditionally been presented as opposed to experience. But political phenomenology, along with ethnography, certain kinds of historiography, and certain kinds of criticism, provide a way back in for experience. If experience can be both apprehended and simultaneously understood as something that is constituted — in other words, if it can be described without treating it as fully given — then that description can in turn be productive for an impairment theory. At the same time, even as any theory comes from a particular standpoint and is indebted to a cluster of experiences, a theory is by definition an exercise in abstraction. Otherwise, it would not be a theory and portable from one context to another.

Liz Ellcessor suggests that a theory or conceptual framework can also work like a kit: "a modular grouping of different perspectives, methods, and interrogatories that may be picked up and deployed individually or in concert."[3] Good theory lets its auditors take away and use parts — even tiny parts — without demanding fealty to a whole. It is not an endlessly self-referential framework, or a set of terms that must be repeated endlessly. To use a standard example, good theory does not go out into the world to spot panopticons, though it might use a panopticon to seek something else out. For more on what's in the kit for *Diminished Faculties*, see the notes and bibliography.

HOW TO USE IMPAIRMENT THEORY

The first thing to know about impairment theory is that you don't have to use it the way other people use it. In fact, we recommend that you explore with it and find your own applications. But to help you get started, we offer some suggested applications and recipes. Everyone should try the first one as their first exercise in impairment theory, and the final two suggestions are also highly recommended. But it is up to you whether and how to follow any of the suggestions in this section. Perhaps you have a better idea!

01   A good starting place in working with impairment is to assume it is there. Like all epistemological shifts, the first thing to do is simply reconsider everything around you — and inside you. So much scholarship — and so many institutional protocols — take on a Panglossian best-of-all-possible-worlds attitude when describing social process, perception, interpretation, and technical operations. They assume that impairment is not there. But technologies must be constantly maintained and repaired; people must constantly repeat themselves in conversations; letters are misdelivered; great dancers trip at inopportune times; the bus runs late; VoIP is still terrible even though it's now ubiquitous in the Global North; people get sick; bodies break down; systems fuck up. The world is full of impairments.

02   Try being an unreliable narrator for a while. Impairment as a hermeneutic is also useful when turned back on the interpreter. Under what circumstances can you write as an unreliable narrator of your own experience or the experience of others? What strategies are available if you let go of the idea that your descriptions of the world are empirically accurate? What happens when you describe an event, a text, an artwork, a memory? What kind of interpreter can you be when your interpretation of something — a detail, a contour, a color, a regulation — is not guaranteed by the authority of the text?

03   If you have acquired or use an impairment, then distance yourself from it. There are all sorts of methods for distancing: writing and reflection, field notes, comparing with others' experiences, making art or music. Then try an impairment phenomenology, taking into account the contingency of the impaired experience you are describing, and always, always, supplementing the phenomenology with other methods, so that experience never pretends to transparency or sufficiency.

04   Take an impairment or an access technology to a place it hasn't gone — or is not supposed to go. Take notes afterward. For people who have impairments, this is just a fact of going out. So go out, be in the world, and when things go wrong, consider it like a bad sociology field experiment and write about it as if it were introduced into the world for the reasons of acquiring knowledge rather than just as a fact of life for you.

05   Historicize an impairment or an access technology — how has it been defined, deployed, and experienced over the years? What are the recurring tropes? What are the changing institutional sites? Collect materials from different sources such as newspapers; ads; fiction; poetry; political speech; medical and scientific writing; early users' accounts; memoirs and diaries; recollections; discussion groups; pamphlets; instruction manuals; institutional archives (and be open as to the kind of institution you choose—do not limit your search to official keepers of memory); personal collections in garages, in file cabinets, or on hard drives.

06 Break down classifications and wear down new paths through time, space, and materials. When you encounter a body of documents (in an archive, database, etc.), always start with the miscellaneous category to see what didn't fit the scheme (in archival collections, there is very often a file actually called "miscellaneous"). When you look at diagnostic documents, consider what they require and what they exclude. When you look at databases or collections of data, consider what confuses, troubles, or jumbles the categories they set up. Think and write transversally: combine things that are not supposed to go together. Always track the boundaries and comminglings between impairment and disability, impaired and unimpaired, temporary and permanent, sick and not sick.

07 Look for impairments that are normalized. For whom and in what contexts are they accepted or stigmatized? What is their function? How do they shift and move across sites? How might power work in multiple ways in each context or setting? Look for impairments around techniques of exclusion or gatekeeping, rites of passage or institutional belonging, marks of achievement, indices of cool: scars and marks (metaphoric or real), new embodiments, abilities acquired or lost (and celebrated or mourned), remnants of surgeries or procedures, boundaries set up in someone's psychic or emotional life to describe a "before" and "after" or an "in" or "out." *Diminished Faculties* did this with audile scarification by investigating sites and scenarios that either presuppose or intentionally produce impaired hearing as part of what is to be considered normal social conduct.

08 When analyzing impairment in terms of standpoint, it's good to work intersectionally, but don't try to do all the intersections at once. Pick one or two intersections as the ground for analysis and then

study how other kinds of power relations appear to operate from the vantage point you have staked out. Even in its most avant-garde forms, writing is still fairly linear, which means that complex intersections need to be broken down and explained in easier-to-render-and-understand sequences.

09   Be rigid. Adhere to a discipline to describe an aspect of impairment. Pick a form or format — essay, exhibition, song, architecture, fabrication, device — and pursue it doggedly and with the strictest possible adherence. Only improvise within the parameters you have set out in the work. This manual is an example of a formal attempt at such an approach through the use of form in writing: since I wanted to produce a didactic theory of impairment, I committed fully to the didactic form — I wrote a manual instead of the usual introduction or conclusion to a book.

10   Be undisciplined. Go the opposite way and refuse to succumb to what John Wylie calls the "methodological error" of separating practice and conceptualization.[4] Impairment will not always reveal itself simply through adherence to a disciplined research process. Practice — even the most humble and ordinary practice — could be the best point of entry for conceptual discussions. Sometimes the best ideas are built on concepts and experiences that are not supposed to go together.

11   Build an impaired version of an existing theory. The easiest way to do this is to simply find where the theory requires mastery and subtract some aspect of that mastery. Another way to work with an impaired version of a theory is to work differently with its limits. Usually, the limits of theories are considered to be their faults. An impaired version of a theory could instead treat those limits as opportunities to move or think in other ways.

12 Demedicalize impairment. Many writers (including this one) seem to think phenomenology is useful as a way out of medicalizing impairment. But that is only one possible approach. Invent an impairment materialism and practice it. Study impairment ideologies. Do impairment histories and ethnographies.

13 Bring the fight. In doing this work, you will probably meet and talk with many impaired people (either in person or through other modalities—it does not matter). Help us find common cause, locate political goals, and work together to achieve them. Work to build alliances and support movements. If you've got access to resources, find effective ways to share them and use them. Always keep justice in mind. However, this may or may not be well represented in your writing or artwork about impairment. That is OK! You can be reflexive without constantly announcing your reflexivity.

14 Maximalize. Imagine outlandish, elaborate, impractical solutions that prioritize working with impairments rather than other things. What looks impossible one day could be easy the next. Build massive installations, tell outrageous stories, follow ideas through to their logical conclusions and then just keep going. But if you build things, remember that fabulation and fabrication have roles to play but will never alone be the authors of justice itself. Any major advance in rights, justice, and access will have to come from people organizing together.

15 Minimalize. Reduce complexity, break things down to their simplest functions, look for the minimal possible complexity in social arrangements, interpersonal obligations, physical demands, time rigidity, technical know-how, energy and resource usage. Build something simple and small. Focus on a detail. Describe a tiny scenario. Write a microhistory or a one-line manifesto.

16   Please: if you are going to work on impairment, be accommodating! If you write about impairment, write something you would want to read. If you make stuff about impairment, make stuff you would like. If you are working with a community, ask them what they want and try to serve them with joy. Sometimes the work is a matter of life and death, but if we can't do it with love, how can we expect to build a world worth living in? For instance: try not to be Reviewer 2 (who, it turns out, is often Reviewer 3).[5] Read things in terms of what they seem to want, what they are trying to accomplish. Treat the world and others as something to think and work with and not against. Treat limits as opportunities.

17   Take frequent breaks and regular time off.

TROUBLESHOOTING

Existing forms of impairment theory may not fit your preferred example or application. In these cases, you have four options:

—   You may fashion additions or revisions to impairment theory through the use of other texts and schools of thought. This is considered normal usage, and the theory is working correctly.

—   You may immerse impairment theory in warm water, and then carefully mold its shape to the new case. Note that you may also have to remove some parts of impairment theory (or create others yourself) in order for it to work properly in a new context.

—   If it is not suited to your purpose at all, you may set aside impairment theory for later use on another project, or dispose of it entirely. Please refer to the instructions for disposal below.

—   In some cases, impairment theory may break when used for purposes that are contrary to those for which it was designed, such as (but not limited to) ableist scholarship, stigmatizing metaphors, mansplaining or techsplaining, and that thing that happens when writers attribute claims to texts that they did not actually read. By definition, impairment theory cannot be restored to an unimpaired state, but it will still be usable for other purposes after breakage.

LIMITED LIABILITY

Impairment theory makes no claim to universal applicability, nor to universal relevance. Impairment theory is meant to extend disability theory into areas where it has not yet been applied because those areas might or might not really qualify as disability. But some aspects of impairment theory are nonnegotiable. As with disability theory, the experiences and perspectives of people who have a particular impairment are essential to its analysis: "Nothing about us without us." Labeling someone or something as impaired is also fraught and must be done with care, lest it become an exercise of power, stigmatization, and marginalization.

Impairment theory will not adequately address all conditions related to impairment, disability, and chronic illness or experiences thereof. Due to the nature of impairment theory, it is quite likely that impairment theory has a number of defects. Some of these may be features, while others may be bugs. You will have to decide. Most bugs can be easily repaired by additional reading, which we highly recommend (see troubleshooting). We do warrant that as of this release, the accounts offered in the preceding pages are as up-to-date as possible.

This version of impairment theory also has some particular deficiencies in terms of application to impairments and disabilities acquired at or near birth as well as those that are automatically fatal. It is also geographically specific to Jonathan Sterne's world and conceptually specific to his reading habits. While future updates are planned to rectify some of these shortcomings, the limits of impairment theory actually produced it, and some may be necessary for its successful operation.

Diminished Faculties assumes no liability for cheesy, inelegant, or awkward uses of impairment theory, such as (but not limited to) shoehorning into an alphabetical literature review after "affect theory" and "crip theory" but before "media theory," strictly formalist readings of aesthetic objects, or compulsory citation without application. Your mileage may vary.

Diminished Faculties does not refer to any past, present, or future musical ensembles composed of professors or other education professionals.

INSTRUCTIONS FOR DISPOSAL

Please dispose of impairment theory while keeping in mind the extension of its usable life through modification or integration into other ideas. Please keep it separate from your regular trash. Some options for disposal include regifting it; upcycling it; modifying it into something else; decoration or use as a fish tank, terrarium, or bird/squirrel feeder; or simply forgetting that it exists and not citing it. Another convenient option for disposal is citing something else that says the same thing as impairment theory but was published more recently. Please dispose of the objects through which you encounter impairment theory—such as a printed book, digital file, or digital device—in accordance with local regulations and with maximum use-life and the environment in mind.

BACKWARD COMPATIBILITY AND FUTURE VERSIONS

While we have worked to ensure backward compatibility and long life, impairment theory may be incompatible with some prior writings on impairment, especially those that refer to hypothetical impairments or use impairments as examples of deficiencies without referring to the actual experience of people with those impairments. While we strive to be up-to-date, the currents of scholarship move in unpredictable ways. While we expect to update impairment theory, we cannot guarantee

a particular schedule of updates, and we cannot currently comment on the potential inclusion of planned features in future revisions. Happily, impairment theory is not subject to annual operating system updates from quasi monopolies that demand constant revision of basic code simply to keep things working. Impairment theory is well prepared to quietly sit on a shelf for long periods of time, and if properly stored, it should be ready for use the moment the need arises. It does not come with an expiration date.

CREDITS

The following people provided essential research assistance. They helped me find and shape the components of the book and understand the materials I wanted to talk about:

Ariel Appel

Rachel Bergmann

Ky Brooks

Zoë de Luca

Rebecca Feigelsohn

Burç Köstem

Laine McRory

John Watson

Julia Yudelman

The staff people who actually run the institutions where I work helped me find things and solve problems and do all sorts of things that make my job possible. I could not have written this book without them:

Mary Chin

Maureen Coote

Matt Dupuis

Dave Greene

Amitsu Huang

Natasha Klein-Panneton

Cynthia Leive

Susana Machado

Birgitta Mallinckrodt

Isabella Motillo

Kate Sturge

Tamar Tembeck

Sophie Toupin

The following people read (or listened to) part (or all) of the manuscript and provided critical suggestions for revision and improvement:

Neta Alexander

Michael Bérubé

Karin Bijsterveld

Sadie Couture

Zoë de Luca

Arseli Dokumaci

Bob Fink

Michele Friedner

Sumanth Gopinath

Jessica Holmes

Burç Köstem

Laura Kunreuther

Mara Mills

Dylan Mulvin

Amit Pinchevsky

Alex Rehding

Shirley Roburn

Allyson Rodgers

Mehak Sawhney

Margaret Schwartz

Luke Shirock

Andy Stuhl

Tim Taylor

Fred Turner

Mickey Vallee

Parts of this project benefited from audiences at:

Bard College

Carleton University

Concordia University

Harvard University

The Hemispheric Institute's 9th
   Encuentro

Institute for the Public Life of Arts and
   Ideas at McGill University

Johns Hopkins University

Philharmonie de Paris

Princeton University

University of Basel

University of California, Berkeley

University of California, Irvine

University of California, Los Angeles

University of Minnesota

University of Southern California

My understandings of disability theory and politics were shaped by the students in COMS 411: Disability, Technology, and Communication at McGill University (2011, 2012, 2013, 2015, 2016, 2018, 2019, 2021). I have also drawn much nourishment and inspiration from my grad students and from the visiting scholars and postdocs who make up the Culture and Technology Discussion and Working Group (CATDAWG) at McGill University.

The following people provided vital advice, or pointed me to references, materials, and ideas that shaped parts of the manuscript, or taught me something about a relevant idea that made it into the book:

Mitch Akiyama
Darin Barney
Gloria Bell
Lauren Berlant
Cornelius Borck
Li Cornfeld
Drew Davis
Patrick Feaster and David Giovannoni
    at First Sounds
Sabine von Fischer
Loretta Gaffney
Annie Goh
Catherine Gustavino
Tim Hecker
El Toby Higbie
Cecily Hilsdale
Reem Hilu
Robin James
Amelia Jones
Randolph Jordan

Nick King
Eric Lewis
Sheetal Lodhia
Ash McAskill
Alyssa Michaud
Landon Morrison
Aydost Parlak
Cindy Patton
Pamela Patton at the Index of
    Medieval Art
Lilian Radovac
Christine Ross
Vicki Simon
Jason Stanyek
Katie Stewart
Peter Szendy
Tamar Tembeck
Marie Thompson
tobias c. van Veen
Katie Zien

Parts of this book benefited mightily from answers to general queries on social media, by friends and colleagues like:

Maria Damon
Emily Dolan
Bob Fink
Aaron Fox
Mack Hagood
Robin James
Doug Kahn
Eric Lewis
Olivia Lucas

Pedro Marra
Julie Beth Napolin
Michael Nardone
David Novak
Gascia Ouzounian
Gavin Steingo
Jenny Stoever
Neil Verma
Axel Volmar

The following people said "DO THIS" when I was considering whether to actually carry out the book. Their encouragement was essential to making it happen:

Courtney Berger

Jess Holmes

Cait McKinney

Mara Mills

Ara Osterweil

Nina Eidsheim and Annette Schlichter (who got me started thinking about voice studies and that it might be worthwhile to include my voice in it)

My thanks to the artists, the designers, and the people depicted for their willingness to be included in the book and for sharing ideas and materials with me, as well as the artists who agreed to illustrate for me:

Louisa Bufardeci

L. Alexis Emelianoff

Marco Fusinato

Erin Gee

Darsha Hewitt

Lochlann Jain

Nina Katchadourian

Rafael Lozano-Hemmer

Darrin Martin

Graham Pullin

Hodan Youssouf

In addition to encouraging me, Courtney Berger at Duke University Press has helped me shape the project at every stage. I also want to thank her for the trust and encouragement to do something a little out of the ordinary and for pushing at all the right times. Thanks also to Ken Wissoker, my other editor at Duke, who also provided encouragement and advice along the way; to Ellen Goldlust for managing the production of the book; to Sheila McMahon for copyediting; to Sandra Korn for design and logistics assistance; to Laura Sell for her promotion work; and to the art department for taking an interest in a creative layout.

Inspiration of other sorts came from friends, family, and colleagues. I must begin with Carrie Rentschler, who can appear on no lists for me because she belongs in every category, and then defies them. Everything rocks more with her around, and not just because she learned the drums and recorded two records with me during the time it took to write this book. I wouldn't have had the last thirty years any other way than being with her, and (speaking purely hypothetically, of course) there is no one I would rather be locked up with during a pandemic. Carrie makes every part of my life sweeter, and often funnier—and not just because of her infectious laugh, though also not *not* because of it. I am so incredibly grateful that she is part of my life every single day. Apart from illustration and artwork, she has done every single thing for which I've credited someone else in this text. She had to live through everything with me, then consent to appearing as a figure in the book (and even appearing in a photograph), and then consent to my renderings of our experience. She was also there for every other part: we discussed the ideas over countless meals, walks, and trips. And she has read through multiple drafts of every chapter, giving me advice as I worried over arguments, phrasing, terminology, ideas, concepts, and politics. Both of us working on projects is normal, so there is no "now that this book is done." All I can say is thank you thank you thank you, Carrie. Let's keep doing it, whatever we decide we want "it" to be.

Friends and family near and far have always been a lifeline for me. Some listed here provided especially important support as I was going through these experiences; others have provided an ear or shoulder when I needed it; some have been professional confidants or cancer mentors, or given crucial life advice; still others are trusted colleagues who keep me grounded in my workplace or outside it; some have four legs; some are all of the above and some are none of the above, but loved for still other reasons:

Jonathan Abel
Amy Alt
Judy Andersen
Lisa Barg
Darin Barney
David Baumflek
Nancy Baym
Bobby Benedicto
Jade Duchesneau Bernier
Craig Bierbaum
Shannon Bierbaum
Andrea Bohlmann
Georgina Born
David Brackett
Wendy Brown
Jenny Burman
José Cláudio Castanheira
Niko Clemesac
Biella Coleman
Brian Cowan
Kate Crawford
Alex Csisar
Carlotta Darò

Marguerite Deslaureies
Manon Desrosiers
Nick Dew
Emily Dolan
Gustavo Ferreira
Lisa Friedman
Galaxie
Tarleton Gillespie
Joe Gone
Eszter Hargittai
Jayson Harsin
Iben Have
Reem Hilu
Charles Hirschkind
Alix Hui
Karine Lalechere
Christine Lamarre (may her memory be a blessing)
Tom Lamarre
Kay Larsen
Steve Lawson
Marie Leger
David Lévesque

Eric Lewis

Sheetal Lodhia

M.

Peter McMurray

Mara Mills

Nick Mirzoeff

Jeremy Morris

Negar Mottahedeh

Sue Murray

Lisa Nakamura

Derek Nystrom

Ara Osterweil

Jasmine Parsons

Laila Parsons

Simone Pereira de Sá

Nacho Gallego Pérez

Trevor Pinch

Andrew Piper

Marc Raboy

Emily Raine

Arvind Rajagopal

Anu Rao

Elena Razlogova

Dianne Rentschler

Louis Rentschler

Andrea Robbins

Tom Robbins

Kellie Robertson

Enrique Rodríguez-Allegría

Joseph Rosen

Steven Rubio

Wayne Schneider

Renaud Séguin

Carol Stabile

Abby Sterne

Adam Sterne

David Sterne

Lori Sterne

Muriel Sterne

Kyle Stine

Jeremy Stolow

Will Straw

Tako

Alanna Thain

Viktoria Tkaczyk

Fred Turner

Mrak Unger

Axel Volmar

Haidee Wasson

Nancy Whittier

Kate Wiegand

Robert Wisnovsky

Mike Witmore

Ya-Ya

I would like to thank all the doctors, nurses, and hospital staff who have tended to me and helped me out over the years, as well as the members of the online cancer and disability communities to which I belong. I am not going to name names here.

Also: fuck cancer.

This project was completed with financial support from the Social Sciences and Humanities Research Council of Canada; the Fonds de recherche—Société et culture, Quebec; the Max Planck Institute for the History of Science; the Beaverbrook Fund for Media@McGill; the Institute for the Public Life of Arts and Ideas at McGill University; the James McGill Chair in Culture and Technology; and the Arts Research Internship Award. An earlier version of chapter 2 appeared as

"Ballad of the Dork-o-Phone: Toward a Crip Vocal Technoscience," *Journal of Interdisciplinary Voice Studies* 4, no. 2 (May 2019): 179–89.

My deepest apologies—and gratitude—to anyone I inadvertently left out.

Diminished Faculties emerged as a set of sketches and ideas over a long time, and always cohabited with other projects until I took dedicated leaves in 2019 and 2020 to focus and finish. Both terms came courtesy of McGill University: a half-year sabbatical, and two course releases I was owed from teaching overloads during my time as department chair in 2007–10. The fact that I could collect on that time owed me was a privilege not available to many academics or many writers, and I am grateful for it. The fact that I could do it while going on a new drug regimen that was putting my body through all sorts of hell was a result of a stable home life, good doctors and medical care, and supportive family and friends. My effusive gratitude goes out to everyone listed above—and many others who aren't listed. It cannot be fully captured here.

Diminished Faculties would not have been possible without a world of people holding me up. May it do a little to hold you up as well.

NOTES

ONE. DEGREES OF MUTENESS

1 See, e.g., Bischoff and Rundshagen, "Awareness under General Anesthesia."

2 On July 29, 2019, I checked this story with Dr. Q. He looked at his notes and reconstructed the scenario with me. He was careful to say that his memory of the events was as subjective as mine (and he does more than three hundred surgeries per year). From his notes, he concluded that the events I describe did happen, and they probably happened on February 12. He also believes that the scenario ended with me being able to take a breath on my own before being put back under. But I am not so sure, and my partner, Carrie, also questions this because of the sequence of events. Since I was sedated and intubated for the weekend, and then given a temporary tracheostomy on February 15, it's possible that I might *not* have been sufficiently able to breathe on my own and that that was confirmed on the fifteenth. In the end, none of us will know for sure what happened on what day.

3 In other writing, I have explored these conditions technologically, materially, culturally, and historically.

4 Heyes, *Anaesthetics of Existence*, 15.

5 Husserl, "'Phenomenology'"; Heidegger, *Being and Time*; Merleau-Ponty, *Phenomenology of Perception*. If you are new to these authors and want a good introductory gloss on their positions, I recommend the relevant entries in Center for the Study of Language and Information, *Stanford Encyclopedia of Philosophy*.

6 Al-Saji, "Bodies and Sensings," 16n9.

7 Carel, *Phenomenology of Illness*, 21. For more on phenomenology, see Peirce, *Philosophical Writings of Peirce*, 76; Merleau-Ponty, *Primacy of Perception*, 12–27; Ihde, *Listening and Voice: A Phenomenology of Sound*, 25–46; Ramsey, *Long Path to Nearness*, 13; Young, "Throwing like a Girl"; Ahmed, *Queer Phenomenology*, 5–12; Abrams, "Cartesian Dualism and Disabled Phenomenology."

8   Berland, "Contradicting Media." There is also a literature in political science and political philosophy that calls itself political phenomenology but works more in the universalist tradition. I deliberately do not engage with that work.

9   For a more formal attempt to resolve the contradictions between genealogy and phenomenology, see Heyes, *Anaesthetics of Existence*, 27–51.

10 Ahmed, *Queer Phenomenology*, esp. 1–24. I discuss Ahmed in more detail later in this chapter.

11 Crosby, *Body Undone*, 20. This is a running line of argument in several canonical disability studies texts, such as Linton, *Claiming Disability*; Claire, *Exile and Pride*; Siebers, *Disability Theory*. But the intellectual and political history of the idea is difficult to trace because different terms are used, and different writers draw from feminist, Black, and queer traditions. See, e.g., Pliner, "Listening to the Learning Disabled," 52–90. A similar idea to what is found in the disability studies literature is also quite prevalent in writing that uses the medical model of disability. See, for instance, Brillhart, "Predictors of Self-Acceptance."

12 Spencer, *Metagnosis*, 7.

13 A note on nomenclature: currently, there is no consensus within Deaf studies regarding how to represent deafness typographically. Capital D–*Deaf* generally refers to people who use sign language and understand themselves as belonging to a deaf community. Lowercase d–*deaf* is generally used to refer to people who cannot hear but may not understand themselves as culturally Deaf. Even this category is difficult, since "cannot hear" is itself a cultural status: most biologically deaf people have some residual hearing. Some writers in Deaf studies have used *d/Deaf* to describe both categories, while others wish to use *deaf* as a more general, capacious category. I use *Deaf* to describe a self-conscious identity and *deaf* to describe a mixed biological and cultural phenomenon, which *may* also include the culturally Deaf.

14 Quotes are from an unpublished oral history of Southworth's work taken in summer 2013 in Berkeley by Sabine von Fischer. Many thanks to Sabine for sharing it with me. See also Southworth, "Sonic Environment of Cities"; Ihde, *Listening and Voice: Phenomenologies of Sound*, 57–71; Kleege, *More Than Meets the Eye*, 14–28; Fleet, "Accessibility, Augmented."

15 Happily, Danielle Spencer's *Metagnosis* appeared in early 2021, just soon enough that I could include this note. Its heavy focus on impaired visuality makes it an excellent companion to this book. Spencer is working in a slightly different frame—narrative medicine—but the approach is complementary.

16 Marks, *Skin of the Film*, 1.

17 It also began as a riddle. I had originally wanted *Diminished Faculties* to simply end with a cat vomiting on me as I passed out, which is how chapter 5 concludes. However, readers of the manuscript unanimously wanted a conclusion. This presented a problem: there are very few examples of "great" conclusions to scholarly books. A search through my bookshelf and queries on social media yielded little. The function of a conclusion is usually to restate a book's argument and to suggest some further implications—how it might be useful out in the world, beyond its pages. This led me

to the genre of the user manual, which didactically provides instructions for use, application, and problem solving. There are many great examples of creative user manuals. I decided to follow the genre conventions as rigorously as possible and to apply them to the scholarly approach developed as I wrote this book.

18 Diawara, "One World in Relation," 6; Du Bois, *Souls of Black Folk*, 3; Fanon, *Black Skin, White Masks*, 109–40; Gilroy, *Black Atlantic*, esp. 1–40, 111–45; Moten, *Black and Blur*.

19 The standard critique of "paranoid" reading is Sedgwick, *Touching Feeling*, 123–51. But my purpose here is not to advocate for reparative reading. Instead, it is to advocate for impaired reading. See also Poss, "Distortion Is Truth." Please note that this is not meant as a comment on the current "post-truth" and "fake news" discussions. For that, see Harsin, "Toxic White Masculinity."

20 As told on August 2, 2020. Throughout this text, there will be "as I write this sentence" notes referring to what's happening to me or to the world as I'm writing that sentence. But the sentences in the text were written out of order, so the exercise also reveals the mixed-up chronologies operating in *Diminished Faculties*: there is the time of the text, the time of my experience, the time as marked by date, and whatever temporality you enact in reading it. These temporalities do not line up, which nicely performs a version of the disjunctures that constitute impairment more broadly.

21 There was one experimental presentation, "Footnotes to a Manifesto for Diminished Voices," as part of the Hemispheric Institute's 9th Encuentro in 2014. During the "5 Minute Manifestos" project, I sat and played a video I made and then answered questions. The video is available at https://player.vimeo.com/video/108830830?app_id =122963 or https://hemisphericinstitute.org/en/enc14-5-minute-manifestos/item/2609 -enc14-5min-sterne.html. In chapter 2, I discuss presenting my voice in the context of other kinds of public speech. Buck's vocal cord paralysis was the result of misapplied anesthesia during a hair plug replacement surgery (in 2011, when it happened, he lied and attributed it to a virus). See Casselberry, "Joe Buck Admits." Adele's vocal cord problems were just the latest in a long line of singers who have had similar issues. See Warner, "Why Do Stars?"

22 "Consider the history of 'what appears' and how it is shaped by histories of work. . . . Going back to the table, we would remember that the table was made by somebody, and that there is a history to its arrival. . . . Things come to matter by taking shape through and in the labor of others." Ahmed, *Queer Phenomenology*, 43–44.

23 Young, "Throwing like a Girl," 36; Ahmed, *Queer Phenomenology*, 197n15; Merleau-Ponty, *Phenomenology of Perception,* 93, 204, 220, 221, 247, 330, 390.

24 Later in this chapter, I discuss an alternative perspective on wholeness. The choice to avoid a language of wholeness or unity is also borrowed from another source, Gilles Deleuze and Félix Guattari's injunction to "write to the nth power, to the n-1 power" (*Thousand Plateaus*, 24).

25 Wendell, "Unhealthy Disabled," 23.

26 Linton, "Disability Studies," 530. Immediately following this, she cites the "corridors at a Society for Disability Studies conference" and "the back rooms of an indepen-

dent living center" as the two examples for impairment phenomenology. While both certainly could provide phenomenological discussions of impairment, as I discuss later, we may not want to tie the concept too closely to a status as a "real substrate" to disability as a social and constructed phenomenon, both because of critiques of disability as *only* a construct and because impairment is a leaky concept that exists both inside and outside disability. However, it's worth noting that calls for a phenomenology of impairment appear very quickly after the emergence of disability studies as a field, at least in the United States and the United Kingdom.

27 Kafer, *Feminist, Queer, Crip*, 1; Bérubé, *Life as We Know It*, 14; Price, *Mad at School*, 1 (see also her helpful discussion of rhetoric and credibility, 25–57); Yergeau, *Authoring Autism*, 16, 24, 31; Siebers, *Disability Aesthetics*, 37.

28 Siebers, *Disability Theory*, 10. I discuss the ideology of ability throughout this book.

29 "Under such a construction of symptomatology, the only arguably reliable story I've offered in this introduction comes from my presumably nonautistic mother, her competing narratives of my autistic selfhood. Her words about autistic identity and shit smearing carry far more weight than my own. In many respects, this is how I feel about the world of rhetoric—it is a steaming pile of competing, ableist theories about distant Others that extend up to my neck. How to lob rhetoric at the wall? How to smear it on my face? Where is my intentionality? Must one have intentions in order to be rhetorical? Theory of whose mind?" Yergeau, *Authoring Autism*, 31.

30 Lagerkvist, "Existential Media."

31 Young, "Throwing like a Girl," 35–38.

32 Crosby, "Articulating Disability and Debility," 4–5.

33 Siebers, *Disability Theory*, 24–25.

34 Crosby, "Articulating Disability and Debility," 2.

35 If I had to guess, it probably began sometime in the early 2000s, while I lived in Pittsburgh. At least two other people in my old department at the University of Pittsburgh had been diagnosed with thyroid cancer during the time I worked there, so it is possible I was one of them and simply didn't know it until much later.

36 Derrida, *Speech and Phenomena*, 86. I am aware of the inherent contradiction in the very question of Derrida's intent. But that joke has already been told enough already.

37 Kafer, *Feminist, Queer, Crip*, chapter 1.

38 Pullin and Cook, "Six Speaking Chairs," 40. Pullin and Cook continue: "Writing and speaking are fundamentally different ways of conveying language, and yet text-to-speech treats them as if they were equivalent."

39 Sterne, "Disability Studies 101."

40 Siebers, *Disability Theory*, 10.

41 There are certainly exceptions to this history, usually where intellectuals, reading, and learning were celebrated, but loss of eyesight has always been a fraught and contested category.

42 Pullin, *Design Meets Disability*, 16–23.

43 Fanon, *Black Skin, White Masks*, 84; Rubin, "Traffic in Women"; J. Butler, *Bodies That Matter*; Du Bois, *Souls of Black Folk*; Gilroy, *Black Atlantic*.

44 Wendell, "Toward a Feminist Theory," 109–10.

45 Kafer, *Feminist, Queer, Crip*, 11–13; Wendell, "Toward a Feminist Theory"; Goffman, *Stigma*; Dolmage, *Disabled upon Arrival*; Chen, *Animacies*, esp. 157–222; Murphy, *Sick Building Syndrome*; Jain, *Malignant*.

46 Canguilhem, *Normal and the Pathological*.

47 "Convention on the Rights of Persons with Disabilities and Optional Protocol," opened for signature March 30, 2007, United Nations Treaty Series, Article 1, https:// www.un.org/disabilities/documents/convention/convoptprot-e.pdf. Interestingly, this updates the UN definitions cited in Wendell's classic 1989 article, where impairment was a loss of ability compared with a norm, disability was a lack of ability compared with a norm, and *handicap* was a disadvantage (including stigma). In that model, disability was the substrate of handicap and impairment was the temporal experience of disability; in the 2007 definition, impairment is the substrate of disability. Wendell, "Toward a Feminist Theory," 107.

48 In French, the term *impair* refers to an odd number as well as to a faux pas, which would provide another interesting reading, at least in a bilingual setting.

49 Mills, *Hearing Loss and the History of Information Theory*.

50 Noll, *Introduction to Telephones and Telephone Systems*, 89, quoted in Mills, *Hearing Loss and the History of Information Theory*, quoting: "Hence, the human factors of transmission impairments are an important consideration in the performance specifications for transmission system."

51 Mills, *Hearing Loss and the History of Information Theory*.

52 Chang, *Deconstructing Communication*; Peters, *Speaking into the Air*; Hainge, "Of Glitch and Men"; C. Kelly, *Cracked Media*; Alexander, "Rage against the Machine."

53 Mowitt, "Sound of Music"; Poss, "Distortion Is Truth"; Hilderbrand, *Inherent Vice*; Pinch and Trocco, *Analog Days*.

54 For a much deeper cultural approach to accents, see Rangan et al., *Thinking with an Accent*.

55 This is my amendment to Kafer's proposition that "drawing a hard line between impairment and disability . . . makes it difficult to explore the ways in which notions of disability and able-bodiedness affect everyone." Kafer, *Feminist, Queer, Crip*, 8.

56 Kafer, *Feminist, Queer, Crip*, 11.

57 Rose, *No Right to Be Idle*, 7.

58 Rose, *No Right to Be Idle*, 7.

59 Danziger, *Constructing the Subject*, 68–87; Quetelet, *Treatise on Man*; Schulten, *Mapping the Nation*; Bouk, "History and Political Economy," 89; Dolmage, *Disabled upon Arrival*.

60 The DALY was designed to combine data about morbidity and premature mortality, essentially converting all disability and impairment into a numerical "effect" on life expectancy. The idea was to create a universal statistic that allowed for comparative decision-making on a global scale, a measure by which organizations like the WHO could decide to target funds. Given that it is an astounding work of quantification and averaging, it has come under criticism from a variety of quarters. An ironic result

of this critique is the growing trend among epidemiological researchers to retreat to a *different* universal measure that has many of the same problems, just in a different register. Kristin Voigt and Nicholas King have argued that epidemiologists have been too quick to assume that proper or optimal funding would "align" with the GBD and that a higher relative "burden of disease" would bring more funding to a country. Just as DALY converts quality of life (itself a highly contestable term) into quantity, the GBD fails to account for *severity, communicability*, or a variety of other factors. Further, as Voigt and King argue, "misalignment" of WHO and GBD factors may also be a result of decision-making processes, which raise their own questions of legitimacy (those decisions that are made by a representative, deliberative body versus those that are made by wealthy donors). Bouk, "History and Political Economy," 96; Voigt and King, "Out of Alignment?"; Voigt and King, "Disability Weights."

61 Livingston, *Debility and the Moral Imagination*, 234. Jasbir Puar has proposed *debility* as an alternative to *disability*, which she locates as a particular condition within a field of debilities. Inasmuch as she is drawing on Livingston's coinage, she is right to parochialize the concept and experience of disability as geographic, raced, and classed. Puar is, of course, *also* correct that Anglophone disability studies is still shaped by a presumptive whiteness, a hypothesis that can be confirmed by a short look at any disability studies bibliography (and this study is unavoidably shaped by its whiteness—I can parochialize my experience at every turn, but it is still my story, even if it seems I live in a world where Jews have suddenly become *less white*). But Puar's critique of the whiteness of disability studies slides too easily into an imagined privilege for the concept of disability where there is none—a fantasy of friction-free disablement for white people. For instance, she writes, "The biopolitical management of disability entails that the visibility and social acceptability of disability rely on and engender the obfuscation and in fact deeper proliferation of debility" (*Right to Maim*, xv–xvi). While this statement is certainly the case in many instances where disability takes on a bureaucratically recognized existence, it is *also* the case that in many places—even within the most privileged spaces of the West—disability is neither visible nor socially accepted. Puar illuminates the moral and epistemic costs of the violence of states against their subjects in the cases of the Black Lives Matter movement and the struggle for Palestinian liberation; she describes the ways in which certain subjects and bodies are rendered as discountable, destructible, and disposable; but her critique of states' institutional approaches to disability cannot in any simple way be extended to the experience or politics of disability for people, *tout court*. As Liat Ben-Moshe explains in *Decarcerating Disability*, "The biopolitics of debilitation can't explain or account for what becomes of/to people on the level of activism or ontology once they are disabled/debilitated" (30). This may very well be a hard limit—or perhaps an impairment—constitutive of biopolitical analysis more generally.

62 Livingston, *Debility and the Moral Imagination*, 235–36.

63 Livingston, "Insights," 118.

64 Livingston, "Insights," 120.

65 Wendell, "Unhealthy Disabled," 23.

66 When I first wrote that sentence, I had been on a new course of treatment for expanding lung metastases for only a few weeks. Metastatic thyroid cancer in the lungs
used to be fatal because it cannot be effectively treated with surgery, external beam
radiation, radioactive iodine, or traditional chemotherapy. The drug lenvatinib is a
new kind of targeted therapy—whereas chemo attacks cell division, tyrosine kinase
inhibitors like lenvatinib attack proteins and reproduction of blood vessels in tumors.
Like all cancer drugs, it can lead to a host of iatrogenic conditions, including high
blood pressure, stomach ailments, hand and foot disease, all the way up to strokes.
(Fragments of this story continue to appear throughout the text—the chemical fatigue I describe in chapter 5 comes months after the entry given here.)

67 Herndl, "Disease versus Disability," 593.

68 Amundson, "Disability, Handicap, and the Environment," 113.

69 There is also a parallel story to be told here around the intersecting and conflicted
histories of fat studies and disability studies, though the contradictions are more on
the surface: both address bodies that move through a world not designed to accommodate them; both share political and intellectual roots in civil rights movements
and the academic response to those movements. But there are plenty of occasions in
which fat and disability theorists would rather not be associated with one another:
or, rather, where each group mobilizes (or in some cases internalizes) stigmas against
the other in the service of their own cause.

70 See also Wendell, "Unhealthy Disabled," 30.

71 Carel, *Phenomenology of Illness*, 36, 38; Toombs, *Meaning of Illness*, 20.

72 Frank, *Venus on Wheels*, 124.

73 Shakespeare, comment on Bérubé's blog entry.

74 If the cancer went too low in my neck, they would have had to do a maneuver with the
unfortunate name of "the sternal split."

75 Quebec hospital rooms have one, two, or four beds in them. I chose a private room
and had to pay out of pocket for it. My private insurance through McGill University
would have covered a semiprivate room with two beds for free. Including some meals,
taxi rides for Carrie and my mom, and a few other frills, I estimated that the total
out-of-pocket cost for my hospitalization came to approximately $1,500—totally ab-
sorbable for someone on a cushy full-time professor salary but prohibitive for someone who is poor, especially given that they would not have had access to my private
insurance. Even under socialized medicine, class can still play a role.

76 Sterne, "Cancer Crawl Feb 20th."

77 It turns out I am one of the 5 percent of people who hallucinate while on Dilaudid. I now have a much better aesthetic appreciation for bad heroin art. Also, while
I have rethought my interactions with that orderly, I have not revised my opinion of
nurse M, who did not wash his hands, and who spread some kind of nasty gastro virus
through the entire ward, to which I and everyone else succumbed (including him).
Nurse M can still fuck off.

78 Stoever, *Sonic Color Line*; Eidsheim, *Race of Sound*; Stanyek, "If There's a Place in
Your Voice."

79 See, e.g., Crosby's discussion of hospital thirst. Crosby, *Body Undone*, 25.

80 Sterne, "Cancer Crawl Feb 26th."

TWO. MEET THE DORK-O-PHONE

An earlier version of this chapter appeared as "Ballad of the Dork-o-Phone: Toward a Crip Vocal Technoscience," *Journal of Interdisciplinary Voice Studies* 4, no. 2 (2019): 179–89.

1 Hosokawa, "Walkman Effect"; Bull, *Sounding Out the City*.

2 McKay, "Speaking Up"; Emily Thompson, *Soundscape of Modernity*; Radovac, "Muting Dissent"; Tkaczyk, "Shot Is Fired Unheard"; Sterne, "Space within Space"; Michaud, "No One in the Spotlight"; Eidsheim, *Race of Sound*.

3 Maldonado, "Taking Eyeglasses Seriously"; Seagrave, *Vision Aids in America*; Mills, "Hearing Aids"; Mills, *On the Phone*.

4 "SoundBuddy Portable Speaker Kit."

5 Pullin, *Design Meets Disability*, 67–69, 93. On curb cuts, see Hamraie, *Building Access*; and on closed captioning, see Downey, *Closed Captioning*.

6 "Spokeman Personal Voice Amplifier."

7 See Hendren, *What Can a Body Do?*, 25–28. Although she doesn't mention Marshall McLuhan, her point that "a body is almost never not extended" (26) also suggests a crip critique of his ableist tropes of extension and amputation. See also Ott, *Artificial Parts, Practical Lives*, especially 21–24.

8 Much of the description in this chapter carries a heavy debt to Kleege, *Sight Unseen*.

9 Obligatory COVID-era footnote: this is not the same thing as wearing a medical mask. However, there is also a disability politics to masks for people with facial differences. See Buckley, "Covering a Facial Difference during COVID-19."

10 Labelle, *Lexicon of the Mouth*, 3. To be fair, Labelle is both ambivalent about this construct and at least in principle willing to critique some of its ableism and universalism. On the last two pages of his book, he claims a desire to extend and complicate "what a voice can be and how narrative may actually be performed—especially for those who might not have a voice, but who may certainly have a mouth," and he extends this sentiment in his brief discussions of muteness, aphasia, and stuttering, calling Christian discrimination against the deaf "problematic" and prejudices against vocal impairments "discriminations" (186–87). These ideas are not, however, worked out or developed in the rest of his book, which takes a more psychoanalytic and universalist approach to the problem of voice and mouth, as when he argues that "to lose voice is to lose agency" (143).

11 Haraway, "Situated Knowledges," 581.

12 Sounds and voices can also be perceived—and have real effects for the percipient—without a material analog, at least on this plane. See, e.g., Moreno, "Antenatal Aurality"; Hagood, *Hush*, 42. As the recent debate between Marie Thompson, Annie Goh, and Christoph Cox (as well as a recent article by Brian Kane) has demonstrated, a

claim to materialism is no guarantor of better politics of epistemology. Cox, "Beyond Representation and Signification"; Kane, "Sound Studies"; M. Thompson, "Whiteness and the Ontological Turn"; Goh, "Sounding Situated Knowledges"; Cox, "Sonic Realism and Auditory Culture." For more of my spiel on this issue in media and technology studies, see Sterne, "'What Do We Want?'" For an actual defense of immateriality as something to which scholars should attend (which is not exactly my angle here), see Peters, *Marvelous Clouds*, 10–12.

13 Ginsberg, *Passing and the Fictions of Identity*, 4; Samuels, "My Body, My Closet," 237.

14 Wendell, "Unhealthy Disabled," 21.

15 Gyenge, "Res Oralis," 2, 8, 9; Gyenge, "Laocoon's Scream." Gyenge's rereading of Gotthold Ephraim Lessing's *Laocoön: An Essay upon the Limits of Painting and Poetry* examines the difference between the visual representation of the mouth in art, in this case a "screaming" statue with a markedly placid face, and understandings of beauty and aesthetics—specifically, the unpresentability of agony. Though she does not pursue this line of questioning, Lessing's use of "deformity" as describing the state of the face in pain partakes of a particular form of disability aesthetics, where disability is that which short-circuits the possibility for critical distance necessary for the appreciation of art. See Siebers, *Disability Aesthetics*.

16 Weheliye, "'Feenin'"; Latham, "Our Jaded Tomorrows"; Guffey and Lemay, "Retrofuturism and Steampunk."

17 The third meaning of *dork* listed in the OED is "penis," which fits this account a little less well until one peruses the examples of usage and stumbles upon this nugget of ableist masculinism from 1984: "A man with one leg and a vermilion bladder, violet stomach and testicles and a scarlet dork is seen putting it into another amputee." If that is an exemplary usage for the OED editors, then *dork* definitely deserves a reclaiming for disability theory, alongside the reclaiming of *nerd* in relation to Asperger's and autism.

18 Beach, Williams, and Gilliver, "Qualitative Study of Earplug Use."

19 Pullin, *Design Meets Disability*, xxxiii, 16–17, 41, 235.

20 Mills, "Hearing Aids."

21 Virdi, *Hearing Happiness*, 73–79, quote from 75.

22 Sobchack, *Carnal Thoughts*, 214.

23 Sterne, "The Loaner." Once again ableist language—*lame*—creeps into my own attempts to understand an experience of acquiring a disability. Draw your own conclusions.

24 In negotiating ableist environments, the assertive strategies of fat and crip self-presentation have a lot in common. But that is a thread for someone else to unspool.

25 The phenomenology of fatigue is the subject of chapter 4.

26 The curiosity of acquaintances and strangers is a common experience for people with prostheses. See Hendren, *What Can a Body Do?*, 36–37; Sobchak, *Carnal Thoughts*, 220–21.

27 Chion, *Audio-Vision*, 64–94.

28 For more on feedback as an aesthetic phenomenon, see Novak, *Japanoise*.

29 Stanyek and Piekut, "Deadness," 19.

30 Eidsheim, *Sensing Sound*, 21, 156.

31 Samuels, "My Body, My Closet," 246. Samuels also writes about the suspicion that often greets declarations of invisible disability, both by nondisabled people and by people with visible disabilities. She describes it as a catch-22: fail to come out and you're passing; come out and nobody believes you. I return to this issue in chapter 5 when I consider fatigue, which is almost by definition invisible, and widely denigrated. Samuels, "My Body, My Closet," 239–40, 242; Montgomery, "Hard Look."

32 Hamraie, *Building Access*, 103.

33 Piekut, *Experimentalism Otherwise*, 19.

34 See Emelianoff's website, Lutherie Postmoderne, https://www.lutheriepostmoderne .com. See also Pullin, *Design Meets Disability*; Hamraie, *Building Access*; Williamson, *Accessible America*; Hendren, *What Can a Body Do?*

35 Mills, "Hearing Aids," 30.

36 I have no idea why the MiniBuddy plays MP3s, at least in the imagination of the designers. The manual refers to the files stored on the card or USB stick as "sound effects." One could also imagine stock phrases, like my failed flash card experiment in chapter 1.

37 However, Microsoft Teams introduces a horrific level of distortion by disabling the gain control in my interface and diming it. Someone, somewhere, should write a history of the term *disable* in engineering and software circles, especially in terms of its relation to actual disability.

38 Foucault, "Of Other Spaces," 24.

39 Meizel, *Multivocality*, 7–17, quote at 7.

40 Cavarero, *For More Than One Voice*, 12.

41 Meizel, *Multivocality*, 21.

42 For more on the ideology of ability, see chapters 1 and 3; Siebers, *Disability Theory*, 10.

43 Despite rumors that Quebec switched out the R. D. Laing in the water supply for Deleuze and Guattari sometime in the 1970s or 1980s, there are still plenty of Cartesian subjects roaming Montreal. Perhaps relatedly, Quebec still has not fluoridated its water supply, which has been bad for public health but great for denturologists— dentures being another prosthesis that await their encounter with a cultural theory of prosthetics. On the various theories of the subject enumerated here, see Descartes, *Discourse on Methods*; Brooks, *Liner Notes for the Revolution*, 31–33; Robinson, *Hungry Listening*, 37–47; Marcel Mauss, *Sociology and Psychology*; Elias, *Civilizing Process*; Bourdieu, *Logic of Practice*; Deleuze, *Foucault*; Deleuze and Guattari, *Thousand Plateaus*; J. Butler, *Gender Trouble*; Haraway, *Simians, Cyborgs and Women*; Edwards, "Body as Object"; Moten, *In the Break*; Siebers, *Disability Theory*; Norris, "Colonialism." On the social history of dentures (including their connection with speech), see Woodforde, *Strange Story of False Teeth*.

44 Eidsheim, *Race of Sound*, 3.

1   The "imaginary museum" has a long history, as do imaginary museums of imaginary things, like the Museum of Imaginary Musical Instruments (http://imaginaryinstruments.org; accessed October 19, 2020). For other imaginary exhibitions tied to theory, see S. Butler and Lehrer, *Curatorial Dreams* (which uses the term *imaginary exhibition* in terms perhaps closest to what I do here); Schmidgen, *Horn*.

2   For more on hand dryers (really), see chapter 4.

3   There are also potential disadvantages to an exhibition format, even in imaginary form. The gallery space is intimately tied to histories of colonialism and capitalist extraction, and the very format may install a white racial frame. Galleries are also highly classed. For recent work on this subject, see Igloliorte, "Curating Inuit Qaujimajatuqangit"; D'Sousa, *Whitewalling*. See also Clifford, *Predicament of Culture*, 215–51.

4   Nakamura, *Deaf in Japan*; Friedner, *Valuing Deaf Worlds*; Meizel, *Multivocality*; Kunreuther, "Earwitnesses."

5   And therefore also forever closed.

6   Tony Bennett has written that the exhibitionary complex is a "set of cultural technologies concerned to organize a voluntarily self-regulating citizenry." Since it is imaginary, my exhibition is designed not to do this. Instead, it is meant to challenge the processes of vocal subject formation and to suggest and highlight alternatives. But what better way to do that than to stage it in a vehicle historically used by states and classes as a modality of self-formation. Bennett, "Exhibitionary Complex," 76.

7   As of this writing, the question of how to audiodescribe the appearance of race and gender remains unresolved. I have chosen to use "man" and "woman" as identifiers throughout, but these are clearly judgments on my part and should be taken as such. I experimented with "male-presenting person" and "female-presenting person," but in writing it, I found the language unhelpful if the goal is to challenge cisgender identification as a default in gender description. There is also no expert consensus: there are good analytical reasons for trans people to hold strongly to the categories of man/woman and male/female, but there are also good reasons to disrupt those categories in support of nonbinary gender identification. I am not in a position to resolve that question, but I look forward to reading more about it. Similarly, there are no clear standards on the audiodescription of race (and my judgment of skin tone and its meanings may be different from yours); however, all audiodescription guides I checked indicated that if skin color is mentioned, it should be mentioned for everyone to avoid making whiteness an unnamed default. Since race tends to matter quite a lot to the visual interpretation of images of people, I have erred on the side of including it here. For some example guides, see Rai, Greening, and Petré, "Comparative Study of Audio Description Guidelines"; "All about Audio Description"; Pearson, "Described Video Best Practices."

8   See, for instance, Dolar, *Voice and Nothing More*, 15.

9   Vallee, "Technology, Embodiment, and Affect," 84.

10 Vallee, "Technology, Embodiment, and Affect," 86.

11 Stoever, *Sonic Color Line*; Kirkpatrick, "'A Voice Made for Print'"; C. Marshall, "Crippled Speech."

12 Friedner and Helmreich, "Sound Studies Meets Deaf Studies," 81.

13 As Annette Schlichter has written, "The assemblage named 'voice' merges material and ideational aspects." Schlichter, "Un/voicing the Self," 18.

14 "We don't emphasize precise analyses or carefully controlled methodologies; instead, we concentrate on aesthetic control, the cultural implications of our designs, and ways to open new spaces for design." Gaver, Dunne, and Pacenti, "Design," 24; see also Gaver et al., "Cultural Probes."

15 Pullin, *Design Meets Disability*; Hamraie, *Building Access*; Williamson, *Accessible America*; Kafer, "Crip Kin, Manifesting." In addition to the tradition of thinking with materials in disability studies, the work on art, literature, and music "-as-theory" in Black studies and sound studies are areas that do this particularly well (and I'm sure there are others as well—this is just the work I know best). Some books that do this well are Gilroy, *Black Atlantic*; Eshun, *More Brilliant Than the Sun*; Moten, *In the Break*; Brooks, *Bodies in Dissent*; Voegelin, *Sonic Possible Worlds*; Stoever, *Sonic Color Line*; Bronfman, *Isles of Noise*; McEnaney, *Acoustic Properties*; Schulze, *Sonic Fiction*; Napolin, *Fact of Resonance*.

16 Fernandez, "Others Need Not Suffer."

17 Bargu, "Silent Exception," 12, 19, 27; Rajan, "What Do Refugees Want?," 528–29, 536.

18 Rajan, "What Do Refugees Want?," 540.

19 Pugliese, "Penal Asylum."

20 Fernandez, "Others Need Not Suffer." Lip sewing has also continued to be used in the political vocabulary of migrant protest: in 2015 a group of migrants stuck on the border of Greece and Macedonia sewed their lips shut to protest a nationality-based test for entrance into Europe; in 2016 a group of migrants sewed their lips shut to protest the clearing of a camp in Calais, where many people had suffered brutality at the hands of French police. "Refugees Sew Lips Together"; Quine, "Calais Jungle Refugees."

21 Jones, "Performing the Wounded Body," 46.

22 Weidman, *Singing the Classical*, 289.

23 On modern digital surveillance as a form of listening, or suraudience, see James, "Acousmatic Surveillance"; Feldman, "'Problem of the Adjective'"; Szendy, *All Ears*.

24 Bargu, "Silent Exception," 27.

25 The transnational and transcultural extent of the ideology of vocal ability is an open question. Like all ideologies, it pops up near and far, but it is not universal in reach, even in places where it is pervasive. For instance, in her study of voice in Kathmandu, Laura Kunreuther links ideas of voice as signs of personhood and as a personal property or possession, which would suggest some aspects of this ideology can operate in postcolonial contexts. But voice is a recurring theme in ethnographic work on sound and does not follow a single cultural pattern. In some cases, like Steven Feld's work on the Kaluli or Weidman's work on Carnatic singing, it seems not to operate in the

same way at all. See, e.g., Feld, "Orality and Consciousness"; Meintjes, *Sound of Africa!*; Fox, *Real Country*; Weidman, *Singing the Classical*; Kunreuther, *Voicing Subjects*; Feld, "Acoustemology."

26 There is a large and acrimonious literature on the theory of ideology. I draw my understanding of it from two primary sources: the cultural studies tradition, which understands ideology as something lived, everyday, and negotiated rather than simplistically followed; and the critique of cynical reason, which argues that even when people are aware of or critical of ideology, they may still act in concert with it. See, e.g., Sloterdijk, *Critique of Cynical Reason*; Hall, *Cultural Studies 1983*.

27 "The suturing of lips stages the graphic disruption of the social contract as founded principally on an ethics of speech and dialogue"; the sutured lips of refugees "open up the violent disjunction between law and justice." Pugliese, "Subcutaneous Law," 31–32.

28 Pateman, *Sexual Contract*; L. Davis, *Enforcing Normalcy*; L. Davis, *End of Normal*; Simpson, *Mohawk Interruptus*.

29 Puar, *Right to Maim*; Dolmage, *Disabled upon Arrival*.

30 Brown, *Edgework*, 86. Brown is building here on Foucault's model of power in his discussion of confessionals and psychoanalysis: a subject's truth is constructed through its speech. Power sits quietly and listens as the subject unfolds itself and gives itself up. See Foucault, *History of Sexuality*, 53–73.

31 Foucault, *History of Sexuality*, 51–73.

32 Antimask protests during COVID-19 also seem to partake of the same logic, but from the right.

33 Tomlinson, *Singing of the New World*, 38–39.

34 Tomlinson, *Singing of the New World*, 40, 37; King, "Hearing the Echoes," 104–8. The same could be said for song and dance, which would also link vocalization to the activities of other bodies besides the singer's. See Monaghan, "Text in the Body," 89–90.

35 Boone, "Introduction," 19; see also Pohl, Pope, and von Nagy, "Olmec Origins."

36 Wishart, *On Sonic Art*, 300. "From the point of view of sonic analysis," he writes, "the distinction between language and paralanguage . . . is somewhat arbitrary. It is not based on a distinction between what is semantically meaningful or not, but on a distinction between what is captured in writing and what is not."

37 Camille, "Seeing and Reading," 28; see also 27 and 31. Banderoles do not necessarily need to contain speech. See Kantorowicz, *King's Two Bodies*, 61–78, 516; Somers, "Listening to the Text."

38 Camille, "Seeing and Reading," 38; Maginnis, *Painting in the Age of Giotto*, 157–63; Kerby-Fulton, introduction, xxiv; Somers, "Listening to the Text"; Kwakkel, "Medieval Speech Bubbles."

39 Flett, "Significance of Text Scrolls," 53.

40 Camille, "Seeing and Reading," 43.

41 This narrative is drawn from Feaster, "Enigmatic Proofs," 20, 30.

42 Brain, *Pulse of Modernism*; Brain, "Representation on the Line."

43 As Feaster points out in his eduction essay, the perspectival dimensions of sound are never reproduced in a sound reproduction. Rather, the reproduction imparts its own perspective, combined with the space of the room in which it resounds. This is also true for sculptural representations that use speech scrolls of any kind: the dimensionality of the sound—the space of its resonance—is not inscribed, at least not in its sonic dimensions.

44 Cavarero, *For More Than One Voice*, 173. Cavarero's ontology of vocal uniqueness maps ontologically stable voices onto ontologically stable people: every human is an incarnate "singularity" so long as "she or he manifests her- or himself vocally" (7). I am suggesting here that there is a way to attend to the uniqueness of voices—and people—without simply mapping them onto one another. If there is to be an "ontology of vocal uniqueness" (Adriana Cavarero's term), it must lie in the vocal event rather than the speaker.

45 This is usually but not always the case. Some audio codecs (protocols for encoding or decoding sound digitally) are tuned to vocal or musical sound.

46 This is one of the major revisions I would make to the argument about transduction in the section of *The Audible Past* where I discuss the phonautograph. The way it is presented there too easily allows for the possibility that transduction somehow implies a necessary circuit of reproduction, when it does not, as Scott's approach on one end, and methods of sound synthesis on the other, clearly demonstrate. In his 2019 essay, Feaster attributes to me the claim that a scientific consensus emerged in Scott's time that his tympanic approach was the best or most accurate way to reproduce sound, but I cannot find that claim in my original chapter. The tympanic principle was the basis for informal resemblance and linkages across practices, but I explicitly say it was not a matter of consensus, deep structure, or ideal type (*Audible Past*, 83–84). That the human ear became a diagram—to use a term from Foucault—for sound's reproducibility in no way implies that everyone thought about it in the same way, or that it was an unchanging deep structure. This distinction is crucial for contextualizing Scott's contribution to the history of sound reproduction more broadly. See Feaster, "Enigmatic Proofs," 18; Sterne, *Audible Past*, 31–85. On eduction, see Feaster, "What Is Eduction?"; Feaster, "What Is Paleospectrophony?" On First Sounds' eduction of the 1860 phonautogram, see http://firstsounds.org. Mitch Akiyama and I discuss it in Sterne and Akiyama, "Recording," 544–60.

47 Li and Mills, "Vocal Features," 138, 154; Mills, "Deaf Jam"; Strachan, *Sonic Technologies*, 57–80; Sterne, "Player Hater."

48 Bulut, "Case of Tactile Speech."

49 Stanyek and Piekut, "Deadness," 20.

50 Anastasia, "Voice," 263; see also Blake, "Finding My Voice"; Roy, "Remapping the Voice."

51 I am not sorry for using "scopic regime" here.

52 The connection goes deeper still. The application of laryngoscopy to endotracheal anesthesia was developed by a pair of British doctors to assist in facial reconstructive surgery for soldiers following World War I. It was believed that the soldiers would

tolerate the surgery better under general anesthesia, but the tools for general anesthesia had to be modified for surgeons to more easily work on patients' faces. In turn, that reconstructive surgery would eventually lead to techniques for cosmetic facial surgery, which in turn would provide a rhetorical frame for injection medialization laryngoplasty. Quite a chain of events! Pieters et al., "Pioneers of Laryngoscopy," 8.

53 Vallee, *Sounding Bodies*, 28. I prefer "variety" to "continuous variation" but otherwise agree with this point.

54 It appears that plastic surgery on the vocal cords—as an alternative to cutting the neck open and doing regular vocal cord surgery—came into vogue only shortly before I needed it. Mallur and Rosen, "Vocal Fold Injection."

55 Sterne, "Voice Lift Review."

56 Here I am drawing on Charles Sanders Peirce's concept of an *interpretant*: the effect or meaning of a sign, which could also be another sign. In Peirce's semiotics, signs are made up of three parts: the object, which is the thing the sign represents (which could be physical or imaginary); the sign (or *representamen*), which represents the object (words representing things, or clouds representing rain; it does not have to be arbitrary of linguistic, as it does in Saussure's semiotics); and the *interpretant*, which is the sign's ramification as a form or effect, which could be anything from a meaning like a lexical definition, or rain, to a reaction like pulling a hand away from a hot stove, *and* it could also be another sign (which is how it is possible to have a signifying chain). Peirce, *Philosophical Writings of Peirce*; Turino, "Signs of Imagination."

57 García, "Observations on the Human Voice," 189; see also Eidsheim, *Sensing Sound*, 136.

58 The account of Bozzini and Babington is taken from Pieters et al., "Pioneers of Laryngoscopy," 4–5; this article provides a nice overview of the current state of knowledge of who did what, when, in the history of laryngoscopy.

59 Tkaczyk, "Whose Larynx Is It?," 63.

60 Tkaczyk, "Whose Larynx Is It?," 66.

61 Eidsheim, *Race of Sound*, 4.

62 Eidsheim, *Race of Sound*, 91.

63 C. Marshall, "Crippled Speech."

64 Gee, *Larynx Series*.

65 Gee, *Larynx Series*.

66 C. Kelly, *Gallery Sound*, 29.

67 This story will be told more fully in a forthcoming work by Mara Mills and me, tentatively titled *Tuning Time: Histories of Sound and Speed*. In the meantime, for more on the vocoder, see Mills, "Media and Prosthesis"; Sterne, *MP3*, 106–7.

68 Weheliye, "'Feenin,'" 40.

69 As of this writing, Gee is experimenting with machine transcription instead, but the program she is using "seems to want to invent solos, insert staccatos, ignore triples" (Gee to Sterne, October 29, 2019).

70 Moren, "'Talking Popcorn.'"

71 Mills has written on the history of an actual audio Rorschach test: Mills, "Evocative Object." I will return to mishearings in the next chapter.

72 Pullin and Cook, "Six Speaking Chairs."

73 Alper, *Giving Voice*. It's worth noting, too, the amount of work normate parents do in "voicing" for their children with disabilities in one way or another, and with and without the child's consent. See Bérubé, "Disability and Citizenship."

74 "That is my friend Daniel Sonnenfeld signing. Daniel was pretty self conscious about the task as he is not a native signer. Though deaf since birth, he was taught orality and lip reading growing up in France and learned ASL later in life. Since getting cochlear implants a number of year[s] back, he has not been using sign as much and said he was fairly rusty. However, after speaking with a Deaf acquaintance about the project, I was really drawn to have a translator that fit his profile for all the complexities that cochlear implants present to ASL & Deaf culture." Darrin Martin, email message to the author, November 19, 2019.

75 See Mills, "Do Signals Have Politics?"; Friedner, *Valuing Deaf Worlds*, 23, 24, 152.

76 Friedner and Helmreich, "Sound Studies Meets Deaf Studies," 79–80; Nakamura, *Deaf in Japan*; Friedner, *Valuing Deaf Worlds*; J. Davis, *Hand Talk*.

77 Sign language has a long, conflicted, and political history in both Deaf and hearing cultural contexts. See, e.g., Mirzoeff, *Silent Poetry*; L. Davis, *Enforcing Normalcy*; Baynton, *Forbidden Signs*; Nakamura, *Deaf in Japan*; Friedner, *Valuing Deaf Worlds*.

78 "Our Vibrating Hands."

79 "Masques" is currently available at https://vimeo.com/356263985. A later iteration of the project is also available at https://nac-cna.ca/en/video/transformations-hodan -youssouf (accessed March 25, 2021). I also experienced a 2018 live screening of the video that included a vibratory component.

80 The phrase is drawn from Simon Reynolds's description of Mary J. Blige's singing, via Daphne Brooks writing about Blige's post-Katrina duet with U2's Bono. There is nothing stylistically Blige-like in Youssouf's performance, but there is the same tension with sense and language, and the same excess of meaning in performance. Brooks, "All That You Can't Leave Behind," 191.

81 "Our Vibrating Hands." Christopher Small's concept of "musicking" is meant to turn music from a noun to a verb and to highlight the potentially infinite ways that people can engage with musical practice, without presupposing a hierarchy—musicking involves musicians and audiences but also the people who stage the event or clean up after it, among others. See Small, *Musicking*.

FOUR. AUDILE SCARIFICATION

1 This is all a series of tremendous simplifications. Decibels are not the same thing as acoustic power or wattage of an amplifier. Perceived loudness doubles with every increase of 10 dB, but it can take ten times the wattage of an amplifier to double its perceived loudness. Further, *volume* and *loudness* are not preferred technical terms because they are imprecise: in auditory psychology and acoustics, writers are more likely to refer to sound pressure level, which is measurable (though the terms of mea-

surement are disputed, as I discuss later) and exists independently of perception—though this is not entirely the case—or perceived loudness, which is a perceptual measurement. Terms such as *volume* and *loudness* conflate these two phenomena, which is why they are useful for a political phenomenology: they do not assume that the important parts of experience of sound are the measurable, separable parts. For a thorough explanation of decibels, see Everest and Pohlmann, *Master Handbook of Acoustics*. For a discussion of the history of psychometric measurement and the just-noticeable difference, see Boring, *History of Experimental Psychology*, 242; Sterne, *MP3*, 102–5; Hui, *Psychophysical Ear*, 3–21. For a history of the decibel, see Mills, *Hearing Loss and the History of Information Theory*.

2   Silverman, "LVI Tolerance," 658–60; Wegel, "LVIII," 778–79.

3   Gierke et al., "Aural Pain," 30–31.

4   Daughtry, *Listening to War*, 136–37. The 1953 study used a very narrow and specific definition of pain as a certain kind of physical sensation, meaning that sounds considerably below 140 dB could be experienced as unpleasant and painful but are not defined—at least within audiology—as causing physical (and one wonders if this means "actual") pain. In the tests for the BENOX project, pain becomes a technical matter rather than a phenomenological one.

5   In the conclusion to an essay I discuss further below, Barry Blesser cites two studies to support the claim about hearing loss being a bad thing, which turns out to be very rare in the literature—it is usually taken as a given. But Blesser's cites reveal the limitations of such claims: one from 1955 that claims undiagnosed hearing loss as the main cause of mental illness in the elderly, and the other a study where the simulation of hearing loss was claimed to cause paranoia in otherwise hearing subjects. Both studies are problematic: the 1955 study no doubt has been updated; and disability simulations have been widely criticized as pedagogical or analytical tools. For alternative models to simulations, such as evaluating environments, that do not individualize disability and still allow nondisabled researchers to learn about access and disability, see, e.g., Aimi Hamraie's Mapping Access project, https://www.mapping-access.com; Kafer, *Feminist, Queer, Crip*, 4, 9, 154; Siebers, *Disability Theory*, 28–29.

6   The perspectives of people with impairments and disabilities are still remarkably absent from most medical literature on those subjects, though after a few decades of disability scholarship and activism, this too is beginning to change. Gates and Mills, "Presbycusis," 1111; Schuknecht, "Presbycusis"; Fransen et al., "Age-Related Hearing Impairment"; Eyken et al., "KCNQ4"; Eggermont, *Noise and the Brain*, 27–30, 210–39.

7   A reminder: *Deaf* is a cultural category for people who use sign language and understand themselves as belonging to a Deaf community; *deaf* refers to people who cannot hear but who may or may not be culturally Deaf. See chapter 1, n. 13.

8   Yergeau, *Authoring Autism*, 253n17; Friedner, *Valuing Deaf Worlds*, 11–12.

9   On clouds, see Morris, "Sounds in the Cloud"; Peters, *Marvelous Clouds*; Hu, *Prehistory of the Cloud*; Peters, "Cloud."

10 Le Breton, "Understanding Self-Cutting in Adolescence," 37.

11 Schildkrout, "Inscribing the Body," 338; Browne, *Dark Matters*; Benthien, *Skin*. For more on scarification and body art, see, e.g., Jones, *Body Art*; Jones, *Self/Image*; Pitts-Taylor, *In the Flesh*.

12 Goodman, *Sonic Warfare*; Akiyama, "Silent Alarm"; Cusick and Joseph, "Across an Invisible Line"; Cusick, afterword; Daughtry, *Listening to War*; English and Parker, "'People's Lives Are at Stake'"; Tahmahkera, "Becoming Sound."

13 Gramsci, *Prison Notebooks*, 145. Gramsci's original language describes this consent as "the 'spontaneous' consent given by the great masses of the population to the general direction imposed on social life by the dominant fundamental group; this consent is 'historically' caused by the prestige (and consequent confidence) which the dominant group enough because of its position and function in the world of production." He contrasts this with the coercive state power that is applied to those who do not "consent" actively or passively (all scare quotes are his).

14 Affirmative consent is still difficult to define legally and procedurally. Eve Feder Kittay comes close with this articulation: "Consent cannot be understood on the contractual model, but on a model of mutual desiring, a desiring which must be alive at each moment." Kittay, "Ah! My Foolish Heart," 158. See also Bussel, "Beyond Yes or No"; Powell, *Sex, Power, and Consent*; and Groeneveld and Rentschler, "Consent." On research ethics and consent, see Herrera, "Ethics, Deception"; Grant, *Playing the Whore*.

15 See, e.g., Halberstam, *Female Masculinity*, 20–29; Kafer, *Feminist, Queer, Crip*, 149–70; Adair, "Bathrooms and Beyond."

16 Sterne, *Audible Past*, 196.

17 Ragg, "Epidemic of Hearing Loss Predicted," 675; Bowen, "Doctor Recommends 60/60 Rule"; D. Fink, "Will Kids Face an Epidemic of Hearing Loss?"

18 Hagood, *Hush*, 41. Noise is a long-standing obsession in sound studies, but it comes with a vast array of political baggage. For some standard studies, see Attali, *Noise*; Emily Thompson, *Soundscape of Modernity*; Schwartz, *Making Noise*; Ochoa Gauthier, *Aurality*.

19 Drever, "Sanitary Soundscapes"; Drever, "Case for Auraldiversity," 6. I have noticed this phenomenon in my own workplace. After taking advantage of McGill University's free flu-shot program, I used a bathroom with a high-throughput hand dryer that was so low I had to bend down to use it, thereby bringing my ears much closer to it and effectively making it even louder.

20 For public health–oriented studies that aim to document this phenomenon, see, e.g., Warszawa and Sataloff, "Noise Exposure in Movie Theaters"; A. Kelly et al., "Occupational Noise Exposure," 148; Berkowitz, "Hand Dryer Noise in Public Restrooms." The crappy decibel meter on my iPhone registered 105 dB average levels, with a maximum of 115 dB at a preview for the movie *Dunkirk* in late 2017.

21 McRuer, *Crip Theory*, 1–32. A key part of McRuer's argument is lost in my telling here, which is that compulsory able-bodiedness is inextricably bound up with compulsory heterosexuality. His text came out before same-sex marriage was legalized in many countries, and in many U.S. states, and before mainstream attitudes in the United States toward sexual diversity had shifted some. While heterosexism still ex-

ists in many forms, including antiqueer violence, its relationship with ableism has shifted in the past fifteen years. A full accounting of that shift has yet to be written, but concepts like *homonormativity* and *homonationalism* are clearly central to the project. See Duggan, "New Homonormativity"; Muñoz, *Cruising Utopia*, 19–32; Puar, *Terrorist Assemblages*; McRuer, "Any Day Now."

22 Mills, "Deafening." See also her forthcoming book *Hearing Loss and the History of Information Theory*.

23 Canguilhem, *Normal and the Pathological*, 147. He continues: "Rule begins to be rule only in making rules and this function of correction arises from infraction itself." Normal hearing comes after hearing that is found to infract, as when deafness is constructed as an aberration or monstrosity. See also L. Davis, *Enforcing Normalcy*; Baynton, *Forbidden Signs*.

24 Livingston, "Insights," 120; Puar, *Right to Maim*.

25 Winter, *Memory*, 7.

26 This does not work out the same way for each hearing impairment (tinnitus is audible some or all of the time; impairments may be noticeable when other people are present; the absence of sound is simply an absence) and each sense, though there are some interesting comparisons to be made with vision. Chion's point that causal listening is the "most easily influenced and deceptive" form of listening is also apropos here. Chion, *Audio-Vision*, 26.

27 Zak, *Poetics of Rock*; Frith and Zagorski-Thomas, *Art of Record Production*.

28 A bigger practical question would be how one might scale up: What happens when a group of people listens together to speakers in a room, rather than individuals with headphones?

29 Walsh, Stein, and Jot, "Dynamic Compensation of Audio Signal," 1.

30 Walsh Stein, and Jot, "Dynamic Compensation of Audio Signal," 10; Stenklev and Laukli, "Presbyacusis"; Kurakata and Mizunami, "Reexamination of the Age-Related Sensitivity Decrease."

31 Hagood, "Disability and Biomediation"; Hagood, *Hush*.

32 Normal impairment is a variation on Kirkpatrick's concept of the *ideal abnormal*. In an article about U.S. radio in the 1920s, Kirkpatrick coins the term *ideal abnormal* to describe the figure of the shut-in, for whom radio provided a necessary compensatory service, and who could therefore "be subjected to management and justify the extension of state power into new realms." The shut-in also "became a necessary mechanism of biopolitics," which allowed a mechanism of compulsory able-bodiedness to guide U.S. radio policy making. Kirkpatrick, "'A Blessed Boon,'" 180, 181.

33 Emily Thompson, *Soundscape of Modernity*; Friedner and Helmreich, "Sound Studies Meets Deaf Studies," 73, 81.

34 Harmon, "Addressing Deafness"; Krentz, "Hearing Line," 423.

35 Holmes, "Expert Listening." Kristen Snoddon's approach to baby sign as a kind of deaf gain suggests this possibility as well, though of course her case involves the use of sign language, which is clearly understood by at least the parents as having a relationship to Deaf culture. Snoddon, "Baby Sign as Deaf Gain."

36 Krentz, "Hearing Line." Sound scholars will have to sort out their relationship to Du Bois's color line and its intersectional legacies: Is, for instance, the sonic color line, as outlined by Stoever, something that subtends the hearing line, or is it preconditioned by it? See Stoever, *Sonic Color Line*.

37 Lloyd and Tremblay, "No Hearing without Signals," 25, 27; Eggermont, *Hearing Loss*, 203, 209–30, 235–38.

38 The most aggressive challenges to public presentations of this project have come from medical professionals who connect hearing loss with depression, isolation, falls, and other maladies. While I am sympathetic to the misery one can experience on the occasion of a diminished faculty, what my interlocutors miss is that the unhappiness they describe is also occasioned socially and environmentally.

39 Blesser, "Seductive (yet Destructive)."

40 Burke, *Philosophical Enquiry*, 151. Despite the ubiquity of this quote in writing on sound and the sublime, there exists no thorough theoretical survey or synthesis on sound and sublimity—this is certainly a topic someone should pursue elsewhere. The closest we get are surveys of music and the sublime. Some musical writing takes sublimity as a formal maneuver, as in the music representations of storms in opera; other writing takes sublimity as a material force or power of music. The two most useful surveys I found were Lochhead, "Sublime"; Wurth, *Musically Sublime*. See also Gallope, *Deep Refrains*; McClelland, *Tempesta*.

41 Loughridge, "Technologies of the Invisible," 223; Kant, *Critique of Judgement*, 75–164; Crawley, *Blackpentecostal Breath*, 118; quote from Morton, "Sublime Objects," 217. On Burke versus Kant, see also Schwartz, *Making Noise*, 146–48.

42 Crawley, *Blackpentecostal Breath*, 140–44; Lochhead, "Sublime," 63, 64, 67; Battersby, *Sublime*. On white fears of Indigenous singing, see Rath, *How Early America Sounded*; Tomlinson, *Singing of the New World*. From a somewhat different angle, Salomé Voegelin argues that there is no sonic sublime because "there is no sound whose magnitude is external to my listening. There is no horizon, no off the map that impresses the fear and awe of my own disappearance. . . . There is no perfect distance from which the magnitude of the sublime reveals itself; there is only simultaneity and coincidence and the imperfection of formless being as doing." Her point seems to be that Kant relies on a visualist model, though other writers might disagree with her claim that all sonic magnitudes are within the field of her hearing. Voegelin, *Sonic Possible Worlds*, 117, 118.

43 Heller, "Between Silence and Pain," 45; Lucas, "Loudness, Rhythm and Environment," 50; Novak, *Japanoise*, 46.

44 Heller uses "listener collapse," which is a considerably more elegant phrase than "consensual desubjectification" but less precise for my desired usage here. Heller, "Between Silence and Pain," 44–46.

45 Marra and Trotta, "Sound, Music and Magic"; Patra, "Atlanta Falcons Lose 2016 Pick"; Hagood and Vogan, "12th Man."

46 Garlin and Owen, "Setting the Tone"; Anthes, "It's So Loud." For instance, Kellaris, Mantel, and Altsech, "Decibels, Disposition, and Duration," only studied college-age

women and argued only that louder music would affect temporal perception and enjoyment if the subject was in a "neutral" mood.

47 Devine, "Imperfect Sound Forever"; Waddell, "Considering Commercial Advertisement Loudness Mitigation"; Ludwig, "Loudness Wars."

48 Pinch and Bijsterveld, "New Keys to the World of Sound."

49 As of the date I first wrote this sentence, anyway—fashions can change, and at the moment of editing, restaurants are *very* quiet and empty.

50 Hamper, *Rivethead*, 33.

51 Hamper, *Rivethead*, xviii.

52 Lucas, "Loudness, Rhythm and Environment," 48–49.

53 Description of the artwork at http://marcofusinato.com/art/constellations/ (accessed March 15, 2021).

54 C. Kelly, *Gallery Sound*, 2, 82.

55 Goh, "On Noisy Femininities in 2018," 48–49. For more on imagined loudness, see Heller, "Between Silence and Pain," 46–48.

56 While loudness has a long history of associations with masculine power, especially in terms of musical virtuosity and sonic arts, as scholars we should be careful not to essentialize it as a gendered expression, especially at this moment where more women are gaining access to the institutions of loud music and loud art. Whiteley, "Progressive Rock and Psychedelic Coding"; Bayton, "Women and the Electric Guitar"; Waksman, "California Noise"; Carson, Lewis, and Shaw, *Girls Rock!*; Kheshti, *Modernity's Ear*; Born and Devine, "Gender, Creativity and Education"; M. Thompson, *Beyond Unwanted Sound*.

57 Kane, "Sound Studies"; Heller, "Between Silence and Pain," 49–50.

58 Quintero, "Loudness, Excess, Power," 145.

59 Suisman, "Oklahoma City Sonic Boom Experiment," 173.

60 Pierce, "Early Days of Information Theory"; Geoghegan, "From Information Theory to French Theory"; McChesney, *Telecommunications, Mass Media, and Democracy*; Kittler, *Gramophone-Film-Typewriter*; Gumbrecht, *Production of Presence*; Winthrop-Young, *Kittler and the Media*.

61 Siebers, *Disability Aesthetics*, 93.

62 Peirce, *Philosophical Writings of Peirce*.

63 Douglas Kahn, *Earth Sound Earth Signal*, 134–61; R. Fink, "Below 100hz," 95; see also Volmar, "Listening to the Cold War."

64 Nancy, *Listening*.

65 The current, best critique of this approach to hearing is James, "Affective Resonance." My early work on headphones ("Headset Culture") critiqued this idea, as have some other scholars, most notably Hosokawa, "Walkman Effect." It is also worth noting that in practice most headphones and earbuds allow for some sound from the ambient environment to reach the wearer's consciousness.

66 Bennion, *Antique Hearing Devices*.

67 Goodyear, "Escaping the Urban Din," 28.

68 Goodyear, "Escaping the Urban Din," 31.

69 Schwartz, *Making Noise*, 583–85.

70 Hagood, *Hush*, 15–16.

71 Gardner and Berger, "History and Development of the E-A-R Foam Earplug"; Berger, "History and Development of the E-A-R Foam Earplug"; Kerr et al., "Historical Review."

72 This conclusion comes from years of anecdotal evidence from attending live music performances but is also borne out in survey research and interviews. See, e.g., O'Brien and Beach, "Hearing Loss." Also of note, this is a rare study that found hearing protection more common among orchestral musicians than nonorchestral musicians. Perhaps it is a national difference since the study was conducted in Australia.

73 There are even some notable cases of artists providing audiences with earplugs, such as the band My Bloody Valentine, who are famous for their high-decibel shows.

74 Packer, *Mobility without Mayhem*; see also Furness, *One Less Car*.

75 Carlson, "Passive Ear Protector"; Killion et al., "Audibility Earplug," 3; Killion, "Parvum Bonum"; *Audiology Online*, "Interview with Mead Killion."

76 Peck, "Oral History Interview."

77 Sauter, "HEAR This"; Rosen, "Rock Fans Fighting Hearing Loss."

78 "Interview with Dr. Mead Killion."

79 Thanks to Ky Brooks for pointing this out to me. For origin stories, see "Our Story," Earpeace, https://www.earpeace.com/pages/our-story; "Earplugs Are Cool—an Interview with Ryan Parry of Eargasm Earplugs," Soundproofist, March 1, 2019, https://soundproofist.com/2019/03/01/earplugs-are-cool-an-interview-with-ryan-parry-of-eargasm-earplugs/; "Our Story," Surf Ears, https://surfears.com/our-story/; "Our Story," Untzuntz Ear Plugs, https://untzuntzearplugs.com/pages/our-story; "About," Loopear Plugs, https://www.loopearplugs.com/pages/about; Karen Gilchrist, "An Injury Landed This 29-Year-Old a Spot on 'Shark Tank'—and Millions in Sales," CNBC, July 31, 2018, https://www.cnbc.com/2018/08/01/shark-tank-vibes-earplugs -founder-jack-mann-inspired-by-injury.html. All sites accessed May 28, 2020.

80 Dong, Green, and Thomas, "Redesigning Earplugs"; Beach, Williams, and Gilliver, "Qualitative Study of Earplug Use."

81 Mulvin, "Media Prophylaxis," 176.

82 Lochlann Jain's profound writing on the fear of cancer shapes my thinking here, though cancer and audile scarification are two very different phenomena (at least in my own experience). Even though it is well established that certain environmental factors cause cancer in general, it is often impossible to prove that a particular act of pollution caused a particular case of cancer. Jain considers this problem from a legal standpoint through the rise of "fear of cancer" lawsuits in the United States. See Jain, *Malignant*, 179–201. See also Cindy Patton's discussion of risk in the context of the antigay climate of the 1980s—i.e., how does one conduct a general public health campaign while not speaking about sex to the general public? Patton, *Fatal Advice*, 24–30.

83 Blue V, "Hear What You Want"; Hagood, "Quiet Comfort"; Hagood, *Hush*, 179–219.

84 Mulvin, "Media Prophylaxis," 196–97. Hagood also noted "the belief that individuals

are responsible for protecting their own hearing from the effect of mediated sound." Hagood, *Hush*, 40.

85 In his dissertation on loudness in heavy metal, Max Chauvin notes a similar overlap and also compares exposure to loudness to other public health concerns like tobacco smoking, eating junk food, and earplugs to condoms, ski helmets, and life vests. Chauvin, "In and out of Control," 39–40.

86 Noise and Vibration Editors, "Earplugs and Condoms," 2. A confession: I can't tell if the editors are joking about the condoms coming out of the earplug budget.

87 To be clear: there is a medical consensus that prolonged exposure to high-volume sound increases risk of hearing loss, but the specifics are not widely agreed upon. Smeds and Leijon, "Loudness and Hearing Loss"; Carter et al., "Leisure-Noise Dilemma"; Kraaijenga, Ramakers, and Grolman, "Effect of Earplugs." For a review of the literature on the causes and mechanisms of hearing loss, see Eggermont, *Hearing Loss*.

88 See, e.g., "Websites," Hearsmart, https://hearsmart.org/resources/websites/; "All Ears Campaign," https://allearscampaign.com; "The Campaign," Hear for Musicians, https://www.hearformusicians.org.uk/the-campaign; "Workplace Solutions," National Institute for Occupational Safety and Health, https://www.cdc.gov/niosh/docs/wp-solutions/2015-184/pdfs/2015-184.pdf. All sites accessed October 20, 2020. On condom usage, see, e.g., Crimp, *AIDS*; Patton and O'Sullivan, "Mapping"; Treichler, *How to Have a Theory*; Lord, *Condom Nation*; Treichler, "'When Pirates Feast'"; Schieber, "Money, Morals, and Condom Use."

89 Patton, *Fatal Advice*, 97. As Patton notes, "How to Have Sex in an Epidemic" appeared in 1983, three years before the term *safe sex* (and later *safer sex*) came into common usage in the United States and Canada. During this earlier period, it was profoundly difficult to organize around risk when there was no common term.

90 Quoted in Chauvin, "In and out of Control," 169.

91 Hagood, *Hush*, 34.

92 Hagood, *Hush*, 223.

93 Interview with an anonymous person with misophonia, November 20, 2019. Hagood's discussion of misophonia is the only one I recall encountering in disability studies literature. It is a topic I hope to pursue elsewhere, especially given that it is very much the converse of the current craze for Autonomous Sensory Meridian Response (ASMR). In the meantime, scholars interested in the phenomenon should look online for first-person testimony, such as on "R/Misophonia" (accessed October 20, 2020, https://www.reddit.com/r/misophonia/) or on blogs and other personal sites. For a sample of the medical thinking around misophonia, see Brout et al., "Investigating Misophonia"; Spankovich and Hall, "Misunderstood Misophonia."

94 Boas, "On Alternating Sounds."

95 On standpoint acoustemology, see Peake, "Listening like White Nationalists."

96 Robinson, *Hungry Listening*, 10; see also Gilroy, *Black Atlantic*; Meintjes, *Sound of Africa!*; Rodgers, *Pink Noises*; Ochoa Gauthier, *Aurality*; Hoffmann and Mnyaka, "Hearing Voices in the Archive"; Goh, "Sounding Situated Knowledges"; Peake,

"Listening like White Nationalists"; McKittrick and Weheliye, "808s & Heartbreak"; Steingo and Sykes, "Introduction."

97 There have been a range of arguments advanced for beginning from a plurality of concepts of hearing subjects, though we must also be careful not to universalize single modalities of hearing as indices for whole social categories like Deaf, autistic, misophonic, hard of hearing, or aging no-longer-former rock musician. See, e.g., Straus, *Extraordinary Measures*, 150–81; Friedner and Helmreich, "Sound Studies Meets Deaf Studies"; Cheng, *Just Vibrations*; Howe et al., *Oxford Handbook of Music and Disability Studies*; Holmes, "Expert Listening beyond the Limits of Hearing," 209–14; Drever, "Case for Auraldiversity."

98 The "third-person effect" is a communication theory that claims that people tend to believe media messages have an effect on other people but not themselves. This is the one media effect that it is possible to predict with a fair amount of certainty. Davison, "Third Person Effect in Communication."

FIVE. THERE ARE NEVER ENOUGH SPOONS

1 Henville, "Your Reader Is a Little Bit Drunk." Don't forget lots of white space as well!

2 There is a large literature on the abandonment of higher education by liberal states (usually in the form of defunding—which leads to loss of jobs and higher tuition for students—and increased bureaucratization), administrative attitudes with very different priorities than faculty, the casualization of the professoriate, and the erosion of universities as sites for intellectual work. The connections between this literature and disability are only beginning to be made. See, for instance, Dolmage, *Academic Ableism*; Price, *Mad at School*. Discussions of fatigue are sprinkled elsewhere throughout this literature, though not directly connected to theories of disability and ability. They most commonly appear in the "quit-lit" genre but also in discussions of burnout and the broader labor politics of academia. For some standard American examples, see, e.g., Childress, *Adjunct Underclass*; Kezar, DePaola, and Scott, *Gig Academy*; Bousquet, *How the University Works*. While Marc Bousquet's empirical research is now dated (and focused on literary studies and the humanities—the problem also exists in the sciences but takes somewhat different forms), his declaration that "it's not a job market, it's a labor market" is still a needed wake-up call to all faculty. Meanwhile, a wave of studies has shown that recently tenured academics—who are theoretically among the most privileged—are among the most unhappy in the U.S. context. Jay Dolmage refers to this phenomenon as "boutique stress" (*Academic Ableism*, 56). Although it psychologizes the problem somewhat, an overview can be found in Wilson, "Why Are Associate Professors So Unhappy?" Studies of faculty depression in the UK have suggested something similar, though the contract-permanence balance is different. See Fazackerley, "'It's Cut-Throat.'"

3 Wendell, "Unhealthy Disabled," 25; Biss, "Pain Scale," 8.

4 Gorfinkel, "Weariness, Waiting," 342.

5 Simmel, "Metropolis and Mental Life."

6 Susan Moeller describes compassion fatigue as the phenomenon of news audiences becoming "overstimulated and bored all at once" in response to too many different stories of misfortune, or repetitive coverage of the same crisis without new information. Moeller, *Compassion Fatigue*, 10. The term also comes up in discussion of psychotherapists' experiences of their patients' problems and in other areas of care work as well. See, e.g., Figley, "Compassion Fatigue"; Reim Ifrach and Miller, "Social Action Art Therapy."

7 This is more or less Jonathan Crary's "war on sleep" thesis in *24/7*.

8 This paragraph was written in 2019; two paragraphs later we will be in 2020.

9 Samuels, "Sick and Well Time."

10 Miserandino, "Spoon Theory."

11 Miserandino, "Spoon Theory."

12 Hochschild, *Managed Heart*, 7.

13 Piepzna-Samarasinha, *Care Work*, 71. For other uses in disability studies, see, e.g., Kafer, *Feminist, Queer, Crip*, 39; Stevens, "Care Time."

14 Kafai, "Spoons, Spoons, Spoons." Hannah V. Bingham Brunner has suggested that spoon theory is a way that people with chronic illness or disability "take responsibility" for the meaning of illness in their lives, and the nature of that responsibility is storytelling. This is an interesting contradiction: it sets up spoon theory as spoon-expending activity (narration) and at the same time locates spoon epistemology in terms of the frame of the individual—hence the use of responsibility. Brunner, "Disability Theory Online."

15 Gonzalez-Polledo, "Chronic Media Worlds," 5.

16 Wendell, "Unhealthy Disabled," 24, 25; Gregg, *Counterproductive*, 53–77.

17 The critical literature on extractivism and supply chains is massive, cutting across anthropology, media studies, cultural studies, Indigenous studies, geography, and several other fields. See, for instance, Devine, *Decomposed*; Tsing, *Mushroom at the End of the World*; Szeman and Boyer, *Energy Humanities*; R. Maxwell and Miller, *Greening the Media*; Gómez-Barris, *Extractive Zone*; Mezzadra and Neilson, "On the Multiple Frontiers of Extraction"; Junka-Aikio and Cortes-Severino, "Cultural Studies of Extraction"; L. Simpson, *As We Have Always Done*; Cowen, *Deadly Life of Logistics*; Sheller, *Aluminum Dreams*; A. Simpson, *Mohawk Interruptus*; Coulthard, *Red Skin, White Masks*.

18 Conrad, "Consider the Spoons," 86.

19 E. P. Thompson, "Time, Work-Discipline, and Industrial Capitalism," 84.

20 This is not surprising given the Latin words *fatigo* and *fatigāre*, which indicate weariness and vexation, and their descendant in French (*fatigue*), which at least in Quebec is used as *tired* is in English ("je suis fatigué," I am tired), as well as Spanish, Italian, Albanian, and Catalan variants. *Oxford English Dictionary*, s.v. "fatigue"; Charlton Lewis and Charles Short, *An Elementary Latin Dictionary* (1879), accessed November 2019, http://www.perseus.tufts.edu/hopper/text?doc=Perseus:text:1999.04.0060:entry =fatigo. The English noun emerges by the seventeenth century, according to the *OED*.

The relationship of fatigue to a soldier's dress will have to await another discussion, but it too emerges in the nineteenth century.

21 Braithwaite, "On the Fatigue and Consequent Fracture of Metals," 463; Schütz, "History of Fatigue," 264–65. The term may already have been in use, as Braithwaite credits a "Mr. Field" for the idea (467).

22 Schütz, "History of Fatigue," 266–67; Timoshenko, *History of Strength of Materials*, 377.

23 Schivelbusch, *Railway Journey*, 128. As I discuss later in this chapter, Taylor was interested in efficiency but not fatigue.

24 Rabinbach, *Human Motor*, 172. Rabinbach's study is the one monographic English-language study of fatigue as a phenomenon in modernity and is cited as the standard work in almost all the critical work on fatigue since it came out.

25 Wolfgang Ernst wrote of governors that their "automation is defined precisely by the fact that 'human controls have been disabled'"—or more accurately placed at one remove, though the potential ambiguity of disability in the phrase is apt. Ernst, "From Media History to Zeitkritik," 137; see also J. Maxwell, "On Governors."

26 Marx, *Capital*, 546, 532; Cowen, *Deadly Life of Logistics*, 13, 15, see also 91–128.

27 The most famous example of these experiments was the Nazis' manufacture of antifatigue pills for their soldiers, which worked in the short term but had disastrous results later; American sources still hoped to replicate their "success," in part as a way to make commercial use of soybean crops. E. P. Thompson, "Time, Work-Discipline, and Industrial Capitalism"; Freeman, *Time Binds*, 3; Rabinbach, *Human Motor*, 5–6, 11, 133, 142–45; Wik, "Henry Ford's Science and Technology for Rural America," 255.

28 Rabinbach, *Human Motor*, 11.

29 Jenrose, "Fork Theory."

30 Jenrose also suggests a coming grand unification called the "Spork Theory."

31 Marx, *Capital*, 341, 416.

32 Contemporary discourses of time management, work process, ergonomics, and mindfulness also tend to begin from this proposition, but for very different purposes. Gregg, *Counterproductive*, 32; on mindfulness, see 103–26; Gilbreth and Gilbreth, *Fatigue Study*; Frederick, *Household Engineering*; Krenn, "From Scientific Management to Homemaking"; Graham, "Lillian Gilbreth's Psychologically Enriched Scientific Management." Betty Friedan's 1963 *Feminine Mystique* critiques many avenues of women's education (both formal, in schools, and informal, through magazines), and the advice they give seems quite directly descended from Frederick, Gilbreth, and other earlier twentieth-century writers who effectively secularized homemaking and white middle-class women's economic roles.

33 Capitalism functions by excluding as much work as possible from waged labor. Unwaged reproductive activity—care of self and others—is an example of something that is necessary for the production of labor power to be sold by workers. This has the effect of lowering the value of labor power overall, because only part of the labor expended to do the job is compensated as waged work. In an economic relationship between employee and employer, this offers the employer a tremendous advantage.

But this way of thinking spreads beyond the wage relation, to anywhere that one finds a conflation between waged labor and productive labor, as if they are the same thing. See Best, "Wages for Housework Redux"; Mezzadri, "On the Value of Social Reproduction"; Bhattacharya, "Introduction," 3. For the historical context of these debates, see Federici, *Wages against Housework*; Sargent, *Women and Revolution*; Fraser, "From Redistribution to Recognition?"; Federici, *Revolution at Point Zero*; Arruzza, *Dangerous Liaisons*.

34 Bhattacharya, "Introduction," 1.

35 Rose, *No Right to Be Idle*; Piepzna-Samarasinha, *Care Work*.

36 Piepzna-Samarasinha, *Care Work*, 27–28, 39–47.

37 For examples of the distinction between emotion and affect along ideational/embodied lines, see Hardt, "Affective Labor"; Hardt and Negri, *Multitude*; Anderson, *Encountering Affect*, 7. On emotional labor, see, e.g., Hochschild, *Managed Heart*; S. J. Tracy and K. Tracy, "Emotion Labor at 911"; Raine, "On Waiting"; Truţa, "Emotional Labor Strategies." The relation between fatigue and burnout has been considered in medical contexts but awaits a proper cultural history. See Leone et al., "Two Sides of the Same Coin?"

38 Fraser, "Crisis of Care?," 35.

39 Around World War I, several countries (including the United States and United Kingdom) established committees to study worker fatigue in an effort to boost production. Physiologists used fatigue as a way to leverage the prestige of government commissions and industrial managers to aggrandize their own expertise, thereby expanding their home discipline beyond clinical medicine. Goldmark, *Fatigue and Efficiency*, 3, 117–18, 131; Scheffler, "Fate of a Progressive Science," 49; Scheffler, "Power of Exercise," 397–98; Gillespie, "Industrial Fatigue," 237, 241, 250.

40 Scheffler, "Fate of a Progressive Science," 50–53; Scheffler, "Power of Exercise," 396, 412, 415; Johnson, "Measuring Fatigue," 294–96; Johnson, "'They Sweat for Science,'" 448–49; Gillespie, "Industrial Fatigue," 238, 255–56.

41 Felsch, "Mountains of Sublimity," 353, 355, 359–60; Fleras and Dixon, "Cutting, Driving, Digging, and Harvesting"; S. W. Tracy, "Physiology of Extremes," 650; Derickson, *Dangerously Sleepy*, 5, 11, 12, 16–17, 22–23; Guffey, "Disabling Art Museum," 66; Levy, "Digital Surveillance," 361–65.

42 A recent article in the *Atlantic* squares the circle, updating the term *nervous breakdown* for twenty-first-century use, treating it as a sort of escape hatch for when there are too many forks or not enough spoons—a way to declare "emotional bankruptcy." The piece is an interesting blend of modern psychological talk about stress and older conceptions of breakdown that did not separate bodily and mental crisis. While it relies on an assumption of access to health care and recovery and romanticizes some historical figures, it does offer an interesting critique of contemporary approaches to what is often called emotional fatigue. See Useem, "Bring Back the Nervous Breakdown."

43 The naming conventions are themselves contested. The disease has had a decidedly political history, and current practice *seems* to be to place the myalgic encephalo-

myelitis ahead of the chronic fatigue to signal its successful medicalization. But of course *medicalization* is also a fraught term in the literature. In "The Elephant in the Classroom," Jody Berland uses CFS/ME, but current usage seems to be ME/CFS. I use *chronic fatigue* to describe the experience of fatigue that does not abate.

44 Fukuda et al., "Chronic Fatigue Syndrome," 953, 955–56; see also Wall, *Encounters with the Invisible*.

45 MacMillan, "Beard's Concept of Neurasthenia"; Shorter, "Chronic Fatigue in Historical Perspective." Of course, diagnoses, especially in the nineteenth century but still often today, cannot be separated from the politics of medicine and social control. See Ehrenreich and English, *Complaints and Disorders*. On proliferating typologies, see Jason and Jessen et al., "Examining Types of Fatigue"; Jason and Evans et al., "Fatigue Scales and Chronic Fatigue Syndrome." Work on other conditions like multiple sclerosis has also moved in this direction. On suspicion, see chapter 1; Wendell, "Unhealthy Disabled," 28–29.

46 Jason and Richman et al., "Community-Based Study"; Torres-Harding and Jason, "What Is Fatigue?," 4–5, 7, 9; Berland, "Elephant in the Classroom," 700. The Torres-Harding and Jason introduction is an especially useful critical review. It is possible that men may underreport chronic fatigue symptoms as well.

47 Lewis and Wessely, "Epidemiology of Fatigue," 93. One of the authors of this study, Simon Wessely, would later become a controversial figure in chronic fatigue research because of his claims that ME/CFS was primarily a result of psychosocial factors rather than physical causes. The problem with this claim is simply that in the medical model of fatigue, *all* unexplained physical causes are assumed to be mental causes, whereas they may in fact remain unexplained physical causes. Jason, Evans, et al., "Fatigue Scales and Chronic Fatigue Syndrome."

48 Pattyn et al., "Bridging Exercise Science," 1.

49 The idea that an imagined problem isn't real to the patient is itself a problem worth interrogating, especially given that conditions like tinnitus and pain are in part defined by an affective relationship to one's own body (I discuss this, and Hagood's work on tinnitus, in chapter 3). See also Scarry, *Body in Pain*. Jennifer Brea's documentary *Unrest* does an excellent job of showing the effects of psychologization on people suffering from ME/CFS.

50 Finsterer and Zarrouk Mahjoub, "Fatigue in Healthy and Diseased Individuals," 563.

51 Pattyn et al., "Bridging Exercise Science," 2; see also Baumeister, *Self-Regulation and Self-Control*, 16–18.

52 Figley, "Compassion Fatigue"; Smith, Allen, and Danley, "'Assume the Position'"; Nordmarken, "Microaggressions," 130; Guffey, "Disabling Art Museum," 66–69. Related concepts like museum fatigue straddle the border between energetic and phenomenological theories, especially given that museum fatigue was coined as a concept in the 1910s as a physiological problem that could be solved with more chairs, and then later revised into a psychological problem.

53 Hockey, *Psychology of Fatigue*, 7, 8, 11.

54 Cattell, *General Psychology*, 624; Bartley, "Conflict, Frustration, and Fatigue," 161.

55 Bartley and Chute, *Fatigue and Impairment in Man*, 53–56, quote on 53.

56 Hockey argues that fatigue should be understood as an emotion, and one that serves specific adaptational purposes that are "advantageous to the organism; a basic solution to a very primitive problem" (104–5). This evolutionary explanation is problematic on its own terms. In Darwin's evolutionary theory, organisms do not evolve traits to adapt to environments, though environments may select for certain traits over others. A better way of understanding this relationship between organisms and environments would be through feedback and feedforward mechanisms of mutual, contingent, and contextual influence. The classic critique of adaptationism can be found in Gould and Lewontin, "Spandrels of San Marco." Stephen Jay Gould and Richard Lewontin propose a range of alternative models that would be familiar to anyone schooled in contextualist cultural theory: no one predetermined factor can in every case explain another. They even cite Darwin, who himself argues that natural selection is neither a complete nor a universal explanation. For a critique of the conservatism of adaptationist thinking in psychology, see McKinnon, *Neo-liberal Genetics*. For an alternative approach to evolution and culture, see Tomlinson, *A Million Years of Music*. He outlines his approach and major theses on pages 42–50 (this follows a less politicized critique of adaptationism).

57 Berland, "Elephant in the Classroom," 705.

58 Weber, *Protestant Ethic*.

59 Like almost all phenomenological writers in this period, Levinas is politically complicated, at once providing a philosophical position that has been useful for feminists, queer philosophers, and others; and at the same time, problematically universalist and patriarchal in how he writes. Levinas tries to write a philosophy without a universal subject and yet sometimes refers to a universal subject that turns out to be a lot like him: male, neurotypical, heterosexual. As Simone de Beauvoir writes, Levinas "deliberately takes a man's point of view." At the same time, later feminist writers have argued that Levinas's philosophy is actually useful for feminism despite these shortcomings because of its emphasis on alterity, above all other things. For instance, Gayatri Chakravorty Spivak takes up his conception of ethics as obligation to the other even as she critiques his sexism: "I can't learn anything about sexuality from such a person's lucubrations about the role of woman in the household." His patriarchal perspective is occasionally explicit in *Existence and Existents*. For instance, while he discusses birth several times, only fatherhood comes up as something prior to birth (there is no mention of motherhood), and at the end of the book he argues that "having a son" is a path to "asymmetrical intersubjectivity," which is "the locus of transcendence." Levinas, *Existence and Existents*, 96; Beauvoir, *Second Sex*, xix; Chanter, *Feminist Interpretations of Emmanuel Levinas*; Guardiola-Rivera, "Gayatri Spivak."

60 Levinas scholars do not generally view *Existence and Existents* as his "mature" work, and in many ways it differs somewhat from his later philosophy. But his ideas of fatigue are one place where his earlier writings are consonant with his later writings, as when he assumes and affirms the restorative power of sleep in *Totality and Infinity*, as I discuss later. On the place of *Existence and Existents* in Levinas's work, as under-

stood by Levinas scholars, see Vasey, "*Existence and Existents* by Emmanuel Levinas"; Bloechl, "Difficulty of Being."

61   Levinas, *Existence and Existents*, 28, brackets in the original.

62   Wyschogrod, *Emmanuel Lévinas*, 5.

63   Levinas, *Existence and Existents*, 24–25. By indolence, Levinas is referring to the simple fact of reluctance to undertake something, without implying moral judgment; it is more like an aversion to effort.

64   Levinas, *Existence and Existents*, 33.

65   Levinas, *Existence and Existents*, 31, 35; see also Copjec, "Battle Fatigue," 145.

66   Levinas, *Existence and Existents*, 36. The next sentence suggests that the quoted material is the thesis of *Existence and Existents*: "This entire essay intends only to draw out the implications of this fundamental situation." Deleuze seems to echo Levinas in a passage from *Cinema 2*: "Perhaps tiredness is the first and last attitude, because it simultaneously contains the before and after . . . , life" (189).

67   "We live from 'good soup,' air, light, spectacles, work, ideas, sleep, etc. . . . These are not objects of representations. We live from them." Levinas, *Totality and Infinity*, 110.

68   Samuels, "Six Ways of Looking at Crip Time." See also Lazard, "How to Be a Person in the Age of Autoimmunity."

69   On the concept of *severe* in disability theory, see McRuer, *Crip Theory*, 30–32.

70   For instance, Brown's *Regulating Aversion* is mostly a theory of tolerance; aversion is not the main concept in the book. Aversion also shows up in the concept of loss aversion in economics: that people are more willing to take risks to avoid a loss than to realize a gain. Aversion might also be thought in relation to aesthetics and politics in the tradition of Elias (revulsion) and Bourdieu (distinction), as in Derek Hook's analysis of aversion as a kind of bodily revulsion tied to white racism in South Africa, but that is not a path I follow here. Kahneman and Tversky, "Prospect Theory," 269; Bourdieu, *Distinction*; Elias, *Civilizing Process*; Hook, "Racism as Abjection."

71   Harney and Moten, *Undercommons*, 14; Paulsen, *Empty Labor*, 100–138; Shukaitis, "Learning Not to Labor"; Scott, *Domination and the Arts of Resistance*; L. Simpson, *As We Have Always Done*, 33–34; Ahmed, *Living a Feminist Life*, 64–88; Brudholm, *Resentment's Virtue*; Coulthard, *Red Skin, White Masks*, esp. 105–29; Barney, "Withdrawal Symptoms," 127. Piepzna-Samarasinha's care webs are another iteration of this idea of refusal by turning away from the institutions of liberal state toward other, alternative formations, describing crip institutions that provide a care network outside the spaces of institutionalized care. Piepzna-Samarasinha, *Care Work*. See also A. Simpson, *Mohawk Interruptus*; Sharma, "Manifesto for the Broken Machine"; Pinchevski, "Bartleby's Autism."

72   Socialist Patients' Collective, *Turn Illness into a Weapon*.

73   Nap Ministry, "About."

74   Melville's figure of Bartleby is also a standard point of reference in the literature on refusal and has also appeared in the literature on disability. See, e.g., Pinchevski, "Bartleby's Autism"; Pinchevski and Peters, "Autism and New Media."

75   Lazard, "How to Be a Person."

76 Harney and Moten, *Undercommons*, 53.

77 Heyes, *Anaesthetics of Existence*, 12; Berlant, *Cruel Optimism*, 96, 97; Llewelyn, *Emmanuel Levinas*, 36. Berlant's concept of slow death has some political resonances with my analysis of fatigue here, and her approach to practical agency depends on a depletionist critique of capitalism. Her use of exhaustion is quite similar to my use of fatigue when discussing labor and extraction. But her political analysis is aimed at developing a theory of "relief, not repair" tied to slow death. While I consider the connections between fatigue and death in their finitude, I make no assumptions about the teleology of fatigue itself as a human condition, following Wendell's approach to chronic illness. For other critiques of self-asserting subjects as the basis for a theory of politics, see Mahmood, *Politics of Piety*, esp. 5–21; Cvetkovich, *Depression*, esp. 1–26.

78 To be clear, Salamon herself introduces this qualification through her reading of Fanon's "Look, a Negro!" experience and his repeated assertion back: "I wanted to be a man, nothing but a man," just to exist. Salamon, "'Place Where Life Hides Away,'" 109; Heyes, *Anaesthetics of Existence*, 62; see also Puar, *Right to Maim*; Suisman, "Oklahoma City Sonic Boom Experiment."

79 In addition to the macho exertion models discussed previously, see, e.g., Hu, "Wait, Then Give Up," 350–51; M. Fink, "It Will Feel Really Bad."

80 "The only way to get rid of a temptation is to yield to it. Resist it—and your soul grows sick with longing for the things it has forbidden to itself, with desire for what its monstrous laws have made monstrous and unlawful." Wilde, *Uncensored Picture of Dorian Gray*, 74–75.

81 Crary, *24/7*, 10.

82 Fuller, *How to Sleep*, 135; Heyes, *Anaesthetics of Existence*, 118; see also Nancy, *Fall of Sleep*.

83 Mulvin, "Media Prophylaxis," 197.

84 Nudelman, *Fighting Sleep*, 120. As she writes later, it is hard to read the Supreme Court's action as anything but punitive, given the well-known effects of chronic exhaustion extending from the hypervigilance soldiers often developed while on deployment: "Controlling sleep, in legal as well as clinical contexts, is an expression of institutional power" (122).

85 Care might be imagined interpersonally, but it can also be thought collectively. A simple example is a 1932 socialist fantasy from composer Leopold Stokowski, who imagined his music in "great gardens of recreation, serving factory workers who are fatigued and society women who are equally fatigued." While gender roles remain undisturbed, there is a sense of obligation to the fatigued here. Quoted in "Stokowski Seeks True Tone Colors," 23. For more on Stokowski's technological imagination, see Ouzounian, *Stereophonica*, 70–77.

86 This is why the letting go of death is not a good model for the letting go of fatigue, even though there are resonances: the letting go of the self in death is nonnegotiable. "My death—my death is mine," writes Alphonso Lingis. "Each one of us dies alone." Yet for Lingis, to die is also a form of connectedness, to give place to others; letting go of life is a sacrifice and a gift to others. But death, too, can be a demand. Lingis, "Irrevocable Loss," 172.

87 Biss, "Pain Scale," 82.

88 This sentence has been repeatedly revised, so it now signifies a moment in time for me in a more synthetic fashion.

89 The scare quotes are essential: however bad it actually was, it was also "not that bad" in all the bad, dismissive ways of macho pushing through. I am not a reliable narrator.

90 Ya-Ya passed away at almost twenty years of age in February 2014. He was an utter failure as a cat—expressive like a dog, uncoordinated, useless as a hunter—but a wonderful companion. For readers familiar with my other writing, he would have wanted it known that he objected to the entirety of chapter 2 of *MP3*.

Ya-Ya the cat. Photo by the author.

91 Fuller, *How to Sleep*; Heyes, *Anaesthetics of Existence*.

92 Sterne, "10."

IMPAIRMENT THEORY: A USER'S GUIDE

1 Which is a way of saying it's just me, Jonathan, the authorial voice. Or it's me, Jonathan, the author function, which should also include all sorts of other people. See the Credits section for a more comprehensive list. Apologies for the Walt Whitman reference.

2 Hall, "Marx's Notes on Method"; Hall, *Cultural Studies 1983*; Slack, "Theory and Method"; Grossberg, *Cultural Studies in the Future Tense*.

3 Ellcessor, *Restricted Access*, 17.

4 Wylie, "Single Day's Walking," 245.

5 Further research on this question is clearly necessary. See Peterson, "Dear Reviewer 2."

BIBLIOGRAPHY

Abrams, Thomas. "Cartesian Dualism and Disabled Phenomenology." *Scandinavian Journal of Disability Research* 18, no. 2 (April 2, 2016): 118–28.

Adair, Cassius. "Bathrooms and Beyond: Expanding a Pedagogy of Access in Trans/Disability Studies." *TSQ: Transgender Studies Quarterly* 2, no. 3 (August 1, 2015): 464–68.

Ahmed, Sara. *Living a Feminist Life*. Durham, NC: Duke University Press, 2017.

Ahmed, Sara. *Queer Phenomenology: Orientations, Objects, Others*. Durham, NC: Duke University Press, 2006.

Akiyama, Mitchell. "Silent Alarm: The Mosquito Youth Deterrent and the Politics of Frequency." *Canadian Journal of Communication* 35, no. 3 (2010): 455–71.

Alexander, Neta. "Rage against the Machine: Buffering, Noise, and Perpetual Anxiety in the Age of Connected Viewing." *Cinema Journal* 56, no. 2 (January 7, 2017): 1–24.

"All about Audio Description." *The Audio Description Project: An Initiative of the American Council of the Blind*. Accessed October 19, 2020. https://acb.org/adp/ad.html.

Alper, Meryl. *Giving Voice: Mobile Communication, Disability, and Inequality*. Cambridge, MA: MIT Press, 2017.

Al-Saji, Alia. "Bodies and Sensings: On the Uses of Husserlian Phenomenology for Feminist Theory." *Continental Philosophy Review* 43, no. 1 (April 2010): 13–37.

Amundson, Ron. "Disability, Handicap, and the Environment." *Journal of Social Philosophy* 23, no. 1 (1992): 105–19.

Anastasia, Andrew. "Voice." *TSQ: Transgender Studies Quarterly* 1, nos. 1–2 (May 1, 2014): 262–63.

Anderson, Ben. *Encountering Affect: Capacities, Apparatuses, Conditions*. New York: Routledge, 2017.

Anthes, Emily. "Outside In: It's So Loud, I Can't Hear My Budget!" *Psychology Today* 43, no. 5 (October 9, 2010). https://www.psychologytoday.com/ca/articles/201009/outside-in-its-so-loud-i-cant-hear-my-budget.

Arruzza, Cinzia. *Dangerous Liaisons: Marriages and Divorces of Marxism and Feminism.* London: Merlin Press, 2013.

Attali, Jacques. *Noise: The Political Economy of Music.* Translated by Brian Massumi. Minneapolis: University of Minnesota Press, 1985.

Audiology Online. "Interview with Mead Killion Ph.D., Founder of Etymotic." *Audiology Online* (blog), August 18, 2003. https://www.audiologyonline.com/interviews /interview-with-mead-killion-ph-1673.

Bargu, Banu. "The Silent Exception: Hunger Striking and Lip-Sewing." *Law, Culture and the Humanities* (May 24, 2017): 1–28.

Barney, Darin. "Withdrawal Symptoms: Refusal, Sabotage, Suspension." In *Politics of Withdrawal: Media, Arts, Theory*, edited by Pepita Hesselberth and Joost de Bloois, 115–31. New York: Rowman and Littlefield, 2020.

Bartley, S. Howard. "Conflict, Frustration, and Fatigue." *Psychosomatic Medicine* 5, no. 1 (1943): 160–63.

Bartley, S. Howard, and Eloise Chute. *Fatigue and Impairment in Man.* New York: McGraw-Hill, 1947.

Battersby, Christine. *The Sublime, Terror and Human Difference.* London: Routledge, 2007.

Baumeister, Roy. *Self-Regulation and Self-Control: Selected Works of Roy F. Baumeister.* London: Routledge, 2018.

Baynton, Douglas. *Forbidden Signs: American Culture and the Campaign against Sign Language.* Chicago: University of Chicago Press, 1996.

Bayton, Mavis. "Women and the Electric Guitar." In *Sexing the Groove*, edited by Sheila Whitely, 37–49. New York: Routledge, 1997.

Beach, E. F., Warwick Williams, and Megan Gilliver. "A Qualitative Study of Earplug Use as a Health Behavior: The Role of Noise Injury Symptoms, Self-Efficacy and an Affinity for Music." *Journal of Health Psychology* 17, no. 2 (2012): 237–46.

Beauvoir, Simone de. *The Second Sex.* Translated by H. M. Parshley. New York: Vintage Books, 1974.

Ben-Moshe, Liat. *Decarcerating Disability: Deinstitutionalization and Prison Abolition.* Minneapolis: University of Minnesota Press, 2021.

Bennett, Tony. "The Exhibitionary Complex." *New Formations: A Journal of Culture/ Theory/Politics* 4 (Spring 1988): 73–102.

Bennion, Elisabeth. *Antique Hearing Devices.* London: Vernier Press, 1994.

Benthien, Claudia. *Skin: On the Cultural Border between Self and the World.* Translated by Thomas Dunlap. New York: Columbia University Press, 2002.

Berger, Elliott H. "History and Development of the E-A-R Foam Earplug." *Canadian Hearing Report / Revue Canadienne d'Audition* 5, no. 1 (2010): 28–34.

Berkowitz, Shari. "Hand Dryer Noise in Public Restrooms Exceeds 80 DBA at 10 Ft (3 m)." *Noise and Health* 17, no. 75 (April 2015): 90–92.

Berland, Jody. "Contradicting Media: Towards a Political Phenomenology of Listening." *Border/Lines* 1, no. 1 (Fall 1984): 32–35.

Berland, Jody. "The Elephant in the Classroom." *International Journal of Inclusive Education* 13, no. 7 (November 2009): 699–711.

Berlant, Lauren. *Cruel Optimism*. Durham, NC: Duke University Press, 2011.

Bérubé, Michael. "Autism Aesthetics." *Public Books*, September 23, 2019. https://wwwn.publicbooks.org/autism-aesthetics/.

Bérubé, Michael. "Disability and Citizenship." *Dissent*, Spring 2003. http://www.dissentmagazine.org/article/?article=506%5D.

Bérubé, Michael. *Life as We Know It: A Father, a Family and an Exceptional Child*. New York: Pantheon Books, 1996.

Best, Beverly. "Wages for Housework Redux: Feminist Marxism, Social Reproduction, and the Utopian Dialectic of the Value Form." Presentation to the Critical Social Theory Working Group, McGill University, Montreal, October 11, 2019.

Bhattacharya, Tithi. "Introduction: Mapping Social Reproduction Theory." In *Social Reproduction Theory*, edited by Tithi Bhattacharya, 1–20. London: Pluto Press, 2017.

Bischoff, Petra, and Ingrid Rundshagen. "Awareness under General Anesthesia." *Deutsches Ärzteblatt International* 108, nos. 1–2 (January 2011): 1–7.

Biss, Eula. "The Pain Scale." *Creative Nonfiction*, no. 32 (2007): 65–84.

Blake, Art. "Finding My Voice while Listening to John Cage." *Sounding Out! The Sound Studies Blog*, February 23, 2015. https://soundstudiesblog.com/2015/02/23/finding-my-voice-while-listening-to-john-cage/.

Blesser, Barry. "The Seductive (yet Destructive) Appeal of Very Loud Music." *EContact!* 9, no. 4 (2007). https://econtact.ca/9_4/blesser.html.

Bloechl, Jeffrey. "The Difficulty of Being: A Partial Reading of E. Levinas, *De l'existence à l'existant*." *European Journal of Psychotherapy and Counselling* 7, nos. 1–2 (March 1, 2005): 77–87.

Blue V, Alex. "Hear What You Want." *Current Musicology* 99–100 (Spring 2017): 87–106.

Boas, Franz. "On Alternating Sounds." *American Anthropologist* 2, no. 1 (1889): 47–54.

Boone, Elizabeth Hill. "Introduction: Writing and Recording Knowledge." In *Writing without Words: Alternative Literacies in Mesoamerica and the Andes*, edited by Elizabeth Hill Boone and Walter D. Mignolo, 3–26. Durham, NC: Duke University Press, 1994.

Boring, Edwin. *A History of Experimental Psychology*. 2nd ed. New York: Century Company, 1950.

Born, Georgina, and Kyle Devine. "Gender, Creativity and Education in Digital Musics and Sound Art." *Contemporary Music Review* 35, no. 1 (January 2, 2016): 1–20.

Bouk, Dan. "The History and Political Economy of Personal Data over the Last Two Centuries in Three Acts." *Osiris* 32, no. 1 (2017): 85–106.

Bourdieu, Pierre. *Distinction: A Social Critique of the Judgement of Taste*. Translated by Richard Nice. Cambridge, MA: Harvard University Press, 1984.

Bourdieu, Pierre. *The Logic of Practice*. Translated by Richard Nice. Stanford: Stanford University Press, 1990.

Bousquet, Marc. *How the University Works: Higher Education and the Low Wage Nation*. New York: New York University Press, 2008.

Bowen, Alison. "Doctor Recommends 60/60 Rule for Music Listening to Prevent Hearing Loss." *Chicago Tribune*, October 26, 2015.

Brain, Robert Michael. *The Pulse of Modernism: Physiological Aesthetics in Fin-de-Siècle Europe*. Seattle: University of Washington Press, 2015.

Brain, Robert Michael. "Representation on the Line: The Graphic Method and the Instruments of Scientific Modernism." In *From Energy to Information: Representation in Science, Art, and Literature*, edited by Bruce Clark and Linda Dalrymple Henderson, 155–78. Stanford: Stanford University Press, 2002.

Braithwaite, Frederick. "On the Fatigue and Consequent Fracture of Metals." *Institute of Civil Engineers, Minutes of Proceedings* 13 (1854): 463–74.

Brillhart, Barbara. "Predictors of Self-Acceptance." *Rehabilitation Nursing* 11, no. 2 (March–April 1986): 8–12.

Bronfman, Alejandra. *Isles of Noise: Sonic Media in the Caribbean*. Chapel Hill: University of North Carolina Press, 2016.

Brooks, Daphne A. "'All That You Can't Leave Behind': Black Female Soul Singing and the Politics of Surrogation in the Age of Catastrophe." *Meridians* 8, no. 1 (2008): 180–204.

Brooks, Daphne. *Bodies in Dissent: Spectacular Performances of Race and Freedom, 1850–1910*. Durham, NC: Duke University Press, 2006.

Brooks, Daphne A. *Liner Notes for the Revolution: The Intellectual Life of Black Feminist Sound*. Cambridge, MA: Harvard University Press, 2021.

Brout, Jennifer J., Miren Edelstein, Mercede Erfanian, Michael Mannino, Lucy J. Miller, Romke Rouw, Sukhbinder Kumer, and M. Zachary Rosenthal. "Investigating Misophonia: A Review of the Empirical Literature, Clinical Implications, and a Research Agenda." *Frontiers in Neuroscience* 12 (February 7, 2018). https://doi.org/10.3389/fnins.2018.00036.

Brown, Wendy. *Edgework: Critical Essays on Knowledge and Politics*. Princeton, NJ: Princeton University Press, 2005.

Brown, Wendy. *Regulating Aversion: Tolerance in the Age of Identity and Empire*. Princeton, NJ: Princeton University Press, 2009.

Browne, Simone. *Dark Matters: On the Surveillance of Blackness*. Durham, NC: Duke University Press, 2015.

Brudholm, Thomas. *Resentment's Virtue: Jean Amery and the Refusal to Forgive*. Philadelphia: Temple University Press, 2008.

Brunner, Hannah V. Bingham. "Disability Theory Online." ResearchGate, February 2016. https://www.researchgate.net/publication/323078436_Disability_theory_online.

Buckley, Tess. "Covering a Facial Difference during COVID-19: Comforting and Challenging." *About Face* (blog), November 19, 2020. https://www.aboutface.ca/2020/11/19/covering-a-facial-difference-during-covid-19-comforting-and-challenging/.

Bull, Michael. *Sounding Out the City: Personal Stereos and Everyday Life*. New York: New York University Press, 2000.

Bulut, Zeynep. "A Case of Tactile Speech." Presented as part of the Social Acoustics Series, Errant Sound, Berlin, August 19, 2018.

Burke, Edmund. *A Philosophical Enquiry into the Origin of Our Ideas of the Sublime and Beautiful*. London: Dodsley, 1764.

Bussel, Rachel Kramer. "Beyond Yes or No: Consent as a Sexual Process." In *Yes Means Yes! Visions of Female Sexual Power and a World without Rape*, edited by Jaclyn Friedman and Jessica Valenti, 43–52. Berkeley: Seal Press, 2008.

Butler, Judith. *Bodies That Matter: On the Discursive Limits of "Sex."* New York: Routledge, 1993.

Butler, Judith. *Gender Trouble*. New York: Routledge, 1990.

Butler, Shelly Ruth, and Erica Lehrer, eds. *Curatorial Dreams: Critics Imagine Exhibitions*. Montreal: McGill-Queen's University Press, 2016.

Camille, Michael. "Seeing and Reading: Some Visual Implications of Medieval Literacy and Illiteracy." *Art History* 8, no. 1 (1985): 26–49.

Canguilhem, Georges. *The Normal and the Pathological*. Translated by Carolyn R. Fawcett. New York: Zone Books, 1991.

Carel, Havi. *Phenomenology of Illness*. Oxford: Oxford University Press, 2016.

Carlson, Elmer V. "Passive Ear Protector." U.S. Patent 4,807,612; filed November 9, 1987; granted February 28, 1989.

Carson, Mina, Tisa Lewis, and Susan M. Shaw. *Girls Rock! Fifty Years of Women Making Music*. Lexington: University Press of Kentucky, 2015.

Carter, Lyndal, Warwick Williams, Deborah Black, and Anita Bundy. "The Leisure-Noise Dilemma: Hearing Loss or Hearsay? What Does the Literature Tell Us?" *Ear and Hearing* 35, no. 5 (October 2014): 491–505.

Casselberry, Ian. "Joe Buck Admits That Frequent Hair Plug Treatments Caused Vocal Cord Issues." *Awful Announcing* (blog), November 6, 2016. https://awfulannouncing.com/2016/joe-buck-admits-that-frequent-hair-plug-treatments-caused-vocal-cord-issues.html.

Cattell, Raymond. *General Psychology*. Cambridge, MA: Science-Art, 1941.

Cavarero, Adriana. *For More Than One Voice: Toward a Philosophy of Vocal Expression*. Stanford: Stanford University Press, 2005.

Center for the Study of Language and Information. *Stanford Encyclopedia of Philosophy*. Stanford: Stanford University Press, 1997. https://plato.stanford.edu/archives/.

Chang, Briankle. *Deconstructing Communication: Representation, Subject, and Economies of Exchange*. Minneapolis: University of Minnesota Press, 1996.

Chanter, Tina, ed. *Feminist Interpretations of Emmanuel Levinas*. University Park: Pennsylvania State University Press, 2001.

Chauvin, Max. "In and out of Control: The Consumption of Loudness in the Metal Community." PhD diss., ESSEC Business School, 2014.

Chen, Mel Y. *Animacies: Biopolitics, Racial Mattering, and Queer Affect*. Durham, NC: Duke University Press, 2012.

Cheng, William. *Just Vibrations: The Purpose of Sounding Good.* Ann Arbor: University of Michigan Press, 2016.

Childress, Herb. *The Adjunct Underclass: How America's Colleges Betrayed Their Faculty, Their Students, and Their Mission.* Chicago: University of Chicago Press, 2019.

Chion, Michel. *Audio-Vision.* Translated by Claudia Gorbman. New York: Columbia University Press, 1994.

Claire, Eli. *Exile and Pride: Disability, Queerness and Liberation.* Boston: South End, 1999.

Clifford, James. *The Predicament of Culture: Twentieth-Century Ethnography, Literature, and Art.* Cambridge, MA: Harvard University Press, 1988.

Conrad, Sarah. "Consider the Spoons: An Embodied Approach to Incorporating Fatigue in Eco-Activism." In *The Intersectionality of Critical Animal, Disability, and Environmental Studies: Toward Eco-Ability, Justice, and Liberation,* edited by Anthony J. Nocella II, Amber E. George, and J. L. Schatz, 79–98. New York: Lexington Books, 2017.

Copjec, Joan. "Battle Fatigue: Klarostami and Capitalism." In *Lacan contra Foucault: Subjectivity, Sex and Politics,* edited by Nadia Bou Ali and Rohit Goel, 139–59. New York: Bloomsbury Academic, 2018.

Coulthard, Glen Sean. *Red Skin, White Masks: Rejecting the Colonial Politics of Recognition.* Minneapolis: University of Minnesota Press, 2014.

Cowen, Deborah. *The Deadly Life of Logistics: Mapping Violence in Global Trade.* Minneapolis: University of Minnesota Press, 2014.

Cox, Christoph. "Beyond Representation and Signification: Toward a Sonic Materialism." *Journal of Visual Culture* 10, no. 2 (2011): 145–61.

Cox, Christoph. "Sonic Realism and Auditory Culture: A Reply to Marie Thompson and Annie Goh." *Parallax* 24, no. 2 (2018): 234–42.

Crary, Jonathan. *24/7: Late Capitalism and the Ends of Sleep.* New York: Verso, 2014.

Crawley, Ashon T. *Blackpentecostal Breath: The Aesthetics of Possibility.* New York: Fordham University Press, 2016.

Crimp, Douglas, ed. *AIDS: Cultural Analysis / Cultural Activism.* Cambridge, MA: MIT Press, 1988.

Critical Disability Studies Working Group. "VIBE Art Night." YouTube, December 1, 2018. https://youtu.be/mcRgyKd5ljc?t=4108.

Crosby, Christina. "Articulating Disability and Debility: Dissenting from the Realist Consensus." Conference presentation, American Studies Association, November 17, 2012.

Crosby, Christina. *A Body Undone: Living On after Great Pain.* New York: New York University Press, 2016.

Cusick, Suzanne G. Afterword to "'You Are in a Place That Is out of the World . . .': Music in the Detention Camps of the 'Global War on Terror.'" *Transposition: Musique et Sciences Sociales* 4 (2014).

Cusick, Suzanne G., and Branden W. Joseph. "Across an Invisible Line: A Conversation about Music and Torture." *Grey Room,* no. 42 (Winter 2011): 6–21.

Cvetkovich, Ann. *Depression: A Public Feeling*. Durham, NC: Duke University Press, 2012.

Danziger, Kurt. *Constructing the Subject: Historical Origins of Psychological Research*. New York: Cambridge University Press, 1990.

Daughtry, J. Martin. *Listening to War: Sound, Music, Trauma and Survival in Wartime Iraq*. New York: Oxford University Press, 2015.

Davis, Jeffrey Edward. *Hand Talk: Sign Language among American Indian Nations*. New York: Cambridge University Press, 2010.

Davis, Lennard. *The End of Normal: Identity in a Biocultural Era*. Ann Arbor: University of Michigan Press, 2013.

Davis, Lennard. *Enforcing Normalcy*. New York: Verso, 1995.

Davison, W. Phillips. "The Third Person Effect in Communication." *Public Opinion Quarterly* 47, no. 1 (1983): 1–15.

Deleuze, Gilles. *Cinema 2: The Time-Image*. Translated by Hugh Tomlinson and Robert Gaieta. Minneapolis: University of Minnesota Press, 1989.

Deleuze, Gilles. *Foucault*. Collection "Critique." Paris: Editions de Minuit, 1986.

Deleuze, Gilles, and Félix Guattari. *A Thousand Plateaus: Capitalism and Schizophrenia*. Translated by Brian Massumi. Minneapolis: University of Minnesota Press, 1987.

Derickson, Alan. *Dangerously Sleepy: Overworked Americans and the Cult of Manly Wakefulness*. Philadelphia: University of Pennsylvania Press, 2013.

Derrida, Jacques. *Speech and Phenomena: And Other Essays on Husserl's Theory of Signs*. Translated by David B. Allison. Evanston, IL: Northwestern University Press, 1973.

Descartes, René. *Discourse on Methods and Meditations on First Philosophy*. Translated by Donald A. Cress. 4th ed. Indianapolis: Hackett, 1999.

Devine, Kyle. *Decomposed: The Political Ecology of Music*. Cambridge, MA: MIT Press, 2019.

Devine, Kyle. "Imperfect Sound Forever: Loudness Wars, Listening Formations and the History of Sound Reproduction." *Popular Music* 32, no. 2 (May 2013): 159–76.

Diawara, Manthia. "One World in Relation: Édouard Glissant in Conversation with Manthia Diawara." *Nka: Journal of Contemporary African Art* 2011, no. 28 (March 2011): 4–19.

Dolar, Mladen. *A Voice and Nothing More*. Cambridge, MA: MIT Press, 2006.

Dolmage, Jay. *Academic Ableism: Disability and Higher Education*. Ann Arbor: University of Michigan Press, 2017.

Dolmage, Jay. *Disabled upon Arrival: Eugenics, Immigration, and the Construction of Race and Disability*. Columbus: Ohio State University Press, 2018.

Dong, Hua, Stephen Green, and Neil Thomas. "Redesigning Earplugs: Issues Relating to Desirability and Universal Access." In *International Conference on Universal Access in Human-Computer Interaction*, 137–46. New York: Springer, 2007.

Downey, Gregory John. *Closed Captioning: Subtitling, Stenography, and the Digital Convergence of Text with Television*. Baltimore: Johns Hopkins University Press, 2008.

Drever, John. "The Case for Auraldiversity in Acoustic Regulations and Practice: The

Hand Dryer Noise Story." Presentation, International Congress on Sound and Vibration, London, July 23–27, 2017. http://research.gold.ac.uk/id/eprint/20814/.

Drever, John. "Sanitary Soundscapes: The Noise Effects from Ultra-Rapid 'Ecological' Hand Dryers on Vulnerable Subgroups in Publicly Accessible Toilets." In *Proceedings, AIA-DAGA 2013, The Joint Conference on Acoustics, European Acoustics Association, 29th Annual Congress of the Deutsche Gesellschaft für Akustic and the 40th Annual Congress of the Associazione Italiana di Acustica*. Berlin: German Acoustical Society, 2013.

D'Sousa, Arouna. *Whitewalling: Art, Race and Protest in 3 Acts*. New York: Badlands Unlimited, 2018.

Du Bois, W. E. B. *The Souls of Black Folk: Authoritative Text, Contexts, Criticism*. New York: Norton, 1999.

Duggan, Lisa. "The New Homonormativity: The Sexual Politics of Neoliberalism." In *Materializing Democracy*, edited by Russ Castronovo and Dana D. Nelson, 175–94. Durham, NC: Duke University Press, 2002.

Edwards, Steven D. "The Body as Object versus the Body as Subject: The Case of Disability." *Medicine, Health Care, and Philosophy* 1, no. 1 (1998): 46–56.

Eggermont, Jos J. *Hearing Loss: Causes, Prevention, and Treatment*. London: Academic Press, 2017.

Eggermont, Jos J. *Noise and the Brain*. London: Academic Press, 2014.

Ehrenreich, Barbara, and Deirdre English. *Complaints and Disorders: The Sexual Politics of Sickness*. New York: Feminist Press, 2011.

Eidsheim, Nina Sun. *The Race of Sound: Listening, Timbre, and Vocality in African American Music*. Durham, NC: Duke University Press, 2019.

Eidsheim, Nina Sun. *Sensing Sound: Singing and Listening as Vibrational Practice*. Durham, NC: Duke University Press, 2015.

Elias, Norbert. *The Civilizing Process: Sociogenetic and Psychogenetic Investigations*. Edited by Stephen Mennell. Translated by Eric Dunning and Johan Goudsblom. Malden, MA: Blackwell, 2000.

Ellcessor, Elizabeth. *Restricted Access: Media, Disability and the Politics of Participation*. New York: New York University Press, 2016.

English, Lawrence, and James Parker. "'People's Lives Are at Stake': A Conversation about Law, Listening, and Sound between James Parker and Lawrence English." *Sounding Out!* (blog), August 21, 2017. https://soundstudiesblog.com/2017/08/21/peoples-lives-are-at-stake-a-conversation-about-law-listening-and-sound-between-james-parker-and-lawrence-english/.

Ernst, Wolfgang. "From Media History to Zeitkritik." *Theory, Culture and Society* 30, no. 6 (November 1, 2013): 132–46.

Eshun, Kodwo. *More Brilliant Than the Sun: Adventures in Sonic Fiction*. London: Quartet Books, 1999.

Everest, F. Alton, and Ken C. Pohlmann. *Master Handbook of Acoustics*. 6th ed. New York: McGraw-Hill, 2015.

Eyken, E. Van, L. Van Laer, E. Fransen, V. Topsakal, N. Lemkens, W. Laureys, N. Nelissen, A. Vandevelde, T. Wienker, P. Van De Heyning, and G. Van Camp. "KCNQ4: A Gene for Age-Related Hearing Impairment?" *Human Mutation* 27, no. 10 (2006): 1007–16.

Fanon, Frantz. *Black Skin, White Masks.* Translated by Charles Lam Markmann and Ziauddin Sardar. New York: Grove, 2008.

Fazackerley, Anna. "'It's Cut-Throat': Half of UK Academics Stressed and 40% Thinking of Leaving." *Guardian*, May 21, 2019.

Feaster, Patrick. "Édouard-Léon Scott de Martinville: An Annotated Discography." *ARSC Journal* 41, no. 1 (2010): 43–82.

Feaster, Patrick. "Enigmatic Proofs: The Archiving of Édouard-Léon Scott de Martinville's Phonautograms." *Technology and Culture* 60, no. 2 (June 18, 2019): S14–38.

Feaster, Patrick. "What Is Eduction?" *Griffonage* (blog), January 17, 2015. https://griffon agedotcom.wordpress.com/2015/01/17/what-is-eduction/.

Feaster, Patrick. "What Is Paleospectrophony?" *Griffonage* (blog), October 15, 2014. https://griffonagedotcom.wordpress.com/2014/10/15/what-is-paleospectrophony/.

Federici, Silvia. *Revolution at Point Zero: Housework, Reproduction, and Feminist Struggle.* Oakland, CA: PM Press, 2012.

Federici, Silvia. *Wages against Housework.* Bristol: Falling Wall, 1975.

Feld, Steven. "Acoustemology." In *Keywords in Sound*, edited by David Novak and Matt Sakakeeny, 12–28. Durham, NC: Duke University Press, 2015.

Feld, Steven. "Orality and Consciousness." In *The Oral and the Literate in Music*, edited by Yoshiko Tokumaru and Osamu Yamaguti, 18–29. Tokyo: Academia Music, 1986.

Feldman, Jessica. "'The Problem of the Adjective': Affective Computing of the Speaking Voice." *Transposition: Musique et Sciences Sociales* 6 (December 15, 2016).

Felsch, Philipp. "Mountains of Sublimity, Mountains of Fatigue: Towards a History of Speechlessness in the Alps." *Science in Context* 22, no. 3 (September 2009): 341–64.

Fernandez, Ramez. "Others Need Not Suffer My Living Hell." *Sydney Morning Herald*, April 20, 2013.

Figley, Charles R. "Compassion Fatigue: Psychotherapists' Chronic Lack of Self Care." *Journal of Clinical Psychology* 58, no. 11 (November 2002): 1433–41.

Fink, Daniel. "Will Kids Face an Epidemic of Hearing Loss?" *The Quiet Coalition* (blog), March 21, 2019. https://thequietcoalition.org/will-kids-face-an-epidemic-of -hearing-loss/.

Fink, Marty. "It Will Feel Really Bad Unromantically Soon: Cripping Insomnia through Imogen Binnie's *Nevada*." *TSQ: Transgender Studies Quarterly* 6, no. 1 (February 1, 2019): 4–19.

Fink, Robert. "Below 100hz: Toward a Musicology of Bass Culture." In *The Relentless Pursuit of Tone: Timbre in Popular Music*, edited by Robert Fink, Melinda Latour, and Zachary Wallmark, 88–112. New York: Oxford University Press, 2018.

Finsterer, Josef, and Sinda Zarrouk Mahjoub. "Fatigue in Healthy and Diseased Individuals." *American Journal of Hospice and Palliative Care* 31, no. 5 (August 2014): 562–75.

Fleet, Chancy. "Accessibility, Augmented." *Urban Omnibus* (blog), November 6, 2019. https://urbanomnibus.net/2019/11/accessibility-augmented/.

Fleras, Augie, and Shane Michael Dixon. "Cutting, Driving, Digging, and Harvesting: Re-masculinizing the Working-Class Heroic." *Canadian Journal of Communication* 36, no. 4 (January 17, 2012): 579–97.

Flett, Alison R. "The Significance of Text Scrolls: Towards a Descriptive Terminology." In *Medieval Texts and Images: Studies of Manuscripts from the Middle Ages*, edited by Margaret M. Manion and Bernard J. Muir, 43–56. Philadelphia: Harwood Academic, 1991.

Foucault, Michel. *The History of Sexuality*. Vol. 1, *An Introduction*. Translated by Robert Hurley. New York: Vintage Books, 1978.

Foucault, Michel. "Of Other Spaces." Translated by Jay Miskowiec. *Diacritics* 16, no. 1 (1986): 22–27.

Fox, Aaron. *Real Country: Music and Language in Working-Class Culture*. Durham, NC: Duke University Press, 2004.

Frank, Gelya. *Venus on Wheels: Two Decades of Dialogue on Disability, Biography, and Being Female in America*. Berkeley: University of California Press, 2000.

Fransen, Erik, Nele Lemkens, Lut Van Laer, and Guy Van Camp. "Age-Related Hearing Impairment (ARHI): Environmental Risk Factors and Genetic Prospects." *Experimental Gerontology* 38, no. 4 (April 1, 2003): 353–59.

Fraser, Nancy. "Crisis of Care? On the Social-Reproductive Contradictions of Contemporary Capitalism." In *Social Reproduction Theory*, edited by Tithi Bhattacharya, 21–36. London: Pluto Press, 2017.

Fraser, Nancy. "From Redistribution to Recognition? Dilemmas of Justice in a 'Postsocialist' Age." In *Justice Interruptus: Critical Reflections on the "Postsocialist Condition,"* 11–39. New York: Routledge, 1997.

Frederick, Christine. *Household Engineering: Scientific Management in the Home*. Chicago: American School of Home Economics, 1923.

Freeman, Elizabeth. *Time Binds: Queer Temporalities, Queer Histories*. Durham, NC: Duke University Press, 2010.

Friedan, Betty. *The Feminine Mystique*. New York: Norton, 1963.

Friedner, Michele Ilana. *Valuing Deaf Worlds in Urban India*. New Brunswick, NJ: Rutgers University Press, 2015.

Friedner, Michele, and Stefan Helmreich. "Sound Studies Meets Deaf Studies." *Senses and Society* 7, no. 1 (2012): 72–86.

Frith, Simon, and Simon Zagorski-Thomas. *The Art of Record Production: An Introductory Reader for a New Academic Field*. Burlington, VT: Ashgate, 2012.

Fukuda, Keiji, Stephen E. Straus, Ian Hickie, Michael C. Sharpe, James G. Dobbins, and Anthony Komaroff. "The Chronic Fatigue Syndrome: A Comprehensive Approach to Its Definition and Study." *Annals of Internal Medicine* 121, no. 12 (1994): 953–59.

Fuller, Matthew. *How to Sleep: The Art, Biology and Culture of Unconsciousness*. New York: Bloomsbury Academic, 2018.

Furness, Zack. *One Less Car: Bicycling and the Politics of Automobility*. Philadelphia: Temple University Press, 2010.

Gallope, Michael. *Deep Refrains: Music, Philosophy, and the Ineffable*. Chicago: University of Chicago Press, 2017.

García, Manuel. "Observations on the Human Voice." *Laryngoscope* 15, no. 3 (1905): 185–94.

Gardner, Ross, and Elliott H. Berger. "History and Development of the E-A-R Foam Earplug." *Journal of the Acoustical Society of America* 95, no. 5 (May 1, 1994): 2914.

Garlin, Francine V., and Katherine Owen. "Setting the Tone with the Tune: A Meta-Analytic Review of the Effects of Background Music in Retail Settings." *Journal of Business Research* 59, no. 6 (June 2006): 755–64.

Gates, George, and John H. Mills. "Presbycusis." *Lancet* 366, no. 9491 (2005): 1111–20.

Gaver, Bill, Tony Dunne, and Elena Pacenti. "Design: Cultural Probes." *Interactions* 6, no. 1 (February 1999): 21–29.

Gaver, William W., Andrew Boucher, Sarah Pennington, and Brendan Walker. "Cultural Probes and the Value of Uncertainty." *Interactions* 11, no. 5 (September 2004): 53–56.

Gee, Erin. *Larynx Series* (2014). Website, January 29, 2016. Accessed October 19, 2020. https://eringee.net/larynx-series/.

Geoghegan, B. D. "From Information Theory to French Theory: Jakobson, Lévi-Strauss, and the Cybernetic Apparatus." *Critical Inquiry* 38, no. 1 (2011): 96–126.

Gierke, H. E. vin, H. Davis, D. H. Eldridge, and J. H. Hardy. "Aural Pain Produced by Sound." In *BENOX Report: An Exploratory Study of the Biological Effects of Noise*, edited by H. W. Ades, 29–36. Chicago: University of Chicago, 1953.

Gilbreth, Frank B., and Lillian Moller Gilbreth. *Fatigue Study: The Elimination of Humanity's Greatest Unnecessary Waste, a First Step in Motion Study*. New York: Macmillan, 1919.

Gillespie, Richard. "Industrial Fatigue and the Discipline of Physiology." In *Physiology in the American Context, 1850–1940*, edited by Gerald L. Geison, 237–62. New York: Springer New York, 1987.

Gilroy, Paul. *The Black Atlantic: Modernity and Double Consciousness*. Cambridge, MA: Harvard University Press, 1994.

Ginsberg, Elaine K., ed. *Passing and the Fictions of Identity*. Durham, NC: Duke University Press, 1996.

Goffman, Erving. *Stigma: Notes on the Management of Spoiled Identity*. Englewood Cliffs, NJ: Prentice-Hall, 1963.

Goh, Annie. "On Noisy Femininities in 2018." In *The Sonic Cyberfeminisms Zine*, edited by Annie Goh and Marie Thompson, 48–49. Cambridge, UK: Wysing Arts Centre, 2018.

Goh, Annie. "Sounding Situated Knowledges: Echo in Archaeoacoustics." *Parallax* 23, no. 3 (2017): 283–304.

Goldmark, Josephine Clara. *Fatigue and Efficiency: A Study in Industry*. New York: Charities Publication Committee, 1912.

Gómez-Barris, Macarena. *The Extractive Zone*. Durham, NC: Duke University Press, 2017.

Gonzalez-Polledo, Elena. "Chronic Media Worlds: Social Media and the Problem of Pain Communication on Tumblr." *Social Media + Society* 2, no. 1 (January 6, 2016).

Goodman, Steve. *Sonic Warfare: Sound, Affect and the Ecology of Fear*. Cambridge, MA: MIT Press, 2010.

Goodyear, John. "Escaping the Urban Din: A Comparative Study of Theodor Antiärmverein (1908) and Maximilian Negwer's Ohropax (1908)." In *Germany in the Loud Twentieth Century: An Introduction*, edited by Florence Feiereisen and Alexandra Merley Hill, 19–34. New York: Oxford University Press, 2012.

Gorfinkel, Elena. "Weariness, Waiting: Enduration and Art Cinema's Tired Bodies." *Discourse* 34, no. 2 (2012): 311–47.

Gould, Stephen J., and Richard Lewontin. "The Spandrels of San Marco and the Panglossian Paradigm: A Critique of the Adaptationist Programme." *Proceedings of the Royal Society of London, Series B, Biological Sciences* 205, no. 1161 (September 21, 1979): 581–98.

Graham, Laurel D. "Lillian Gilbreth's Psychologically Enriched Scientific Management of Women Consumers." *Journal of Historical Research in Marketing* 5, no. 3 (2013): 351–69.

Gramsci, Antonio. *Prison Notebooks*. Translated by Joseph A. Buttigieg and Antonio Callari. New York: Columbia University Press, 1992.

Grant, Melissa. *Playing the Whore: The Work of Sex Work*. New York: Verso, 2014.

Gregg, Melissa. *Counterproductive: Time Management in the Knowledge Economy*. Durham, NC: Duke University Press, 2018.

Groeneveld, Elizabeth, and Carrie Rentschler. "Consent." In *Rethinking Gender and Women's Studies II*, edited by Ann Braithwaite and Catherine M. Orr. New York: Routledge, forthcoming.

Grossberg, Lawrence. *Cultural Studies in the Future Tense*. Durham, NC: Duke University Press, 2010.

Guardiola-Rivera, Oscar. "Gayatri Spivak, Interviewed by Oscar Guardiola-Rivera." *Naked Punch* (blog), August 28, 2009. http://www.nakedpunch.com/articles/21.

Guffey, Elizabeth. "The Disabling Art Museum." *Journal of Visual Culture* 14, no. 1 (April 2015): 61–73.

Guffey, Elizabeth, and Kate C. Lemay. "Retrofuturism and Steampunk." In *The Oxford Handbook of Science Fiction*, edited by Rob Latham. Accessed April 2, 2021. New York: Oxford University Press, 2014. https://www-oxfordhandbooks-com.proxy3.library.mcgill.ca/view/10.1093/oxfordhb/9780199838844.001.0001/oxfordhb-9780199838844-e-42.

Gumbrecht, Hans Ulrich. *Production of Presence: What Meaning Cannot Convey*. Stanford: Stanford University Press, 2004.

Gyenge, Andrea. "Laocoon's Scream; or, Lessing Redux." *New German Critique*, no. 142 (February 2021): 41–70.

Gyenge, Andrea. "Res Oralis: Mouths of Philosophy." PhD diss., University of Minnesota, 2018.

Hagood, Mack. "Disability and Biomediation: Tinnitus as Phantom Disability." In *Disability Media Studies*, edited by Elizabeth Ellcessor and Bill Kirkpatrick, 311–29. New York: New York University Press, 2017.

Hagood, Mack. *Hush: Media and Sonic Self-Control*. Durham, NC: Duke University Press, 2019.

Hagood, Mack. "Quiet Comfort: Noise, Otherness and the Mobile Production of Personal Space." *American Studies* 63, no. 3 (2011): 573–89.

Hagood, Mack, and Travis Vogan. "The 12th Man: Fan Noise in the Contemporary NFL." *Popular Communication* 14, no. 1 (January 2, 2016): 30–38.

Hainge, Greg. "Of Glitch and Men: The Place of the Human in the Successful Integration of Failure and Noise in the Digital Realm." *Communication Theory* 17, no. 1 (2007): 26–42.

Halberstam, Jack. *Female Masculinity*. Durham, NC: Duke University Press, 1998.

Hall, Stuart. *Cultural Studies 1983: A Theoretical History*. Edited by Jennifer Daryl Slack and Lawrence Grossberg. Durham, NC: Duke University Press, 2016.

Hall, Stuart. "Marx's Notes on Method: A 'Reading' of the '1857 Introduction.'" *Cultural Studies* 17, no. 2 (2003): 113–49.

Hamper, Ben. *Rivethead: Tales from the Assembly Line*. New York: Warner Books, 1986.

Hamraie, Aimi. *Building Access: Universal Design and the Politics of Disability*. Minneapolis: University of Minnesota Press, 2017.

Haraway, Donna. *Simians, Cyborgs and Women*. New York: Routledge, 1991.

Haraway, Donna. "Situated Knowledges: The Science Question in Feminism and the Privilege of Partial Perspective." *Feminist Studies* 14, no. 3 (1988): 575–99.

Hardt, Michael. "Affective Labor." *boundary 2* 26, no. 2 (1999): 89–100.

Hardt, Michael, and Antonio Negri. *Multitude: War and Democracy in the Age of Empire*. New York: Penguin Books, 2005.

Harmon, Kristen. "Addressing Deafness: From Hearing Loss to Deaf Gain." *Profession*, 2010, 124–30.

Harney, Stefano, and Fred Moten. *The Undercommons: Fugitive Planning and Black Study*. New York: Autonomedia, 2013.

Harsin, Jayson. "Toxic White Masculinity, Post-truth Politics and the COVID-19 Infodemic." *European Journal of Cultural Studies* 23, no. 6 (2020): 1–9.

Heidegger, Martin. *Being and Time*. New York: Harper and Row, 1962.

Heller, Michael C. "Between Silence and Pain: Loudness and the Affective Encounter." *Sound Studies* 1, no. 1 (January 2015): 40–58.

Hendren, Sara. *What Can a Body Do? How We Meet the Built World*. New York: Riverhead Books, 2020.

Henville, Letitia. "Your Reader Is a Little Bit Drunk." *University Affairs* (blog), October 16, 2018. https://www.universityaffairs.ca/career-advice/ask-dr-editor/your-reader-is-a-little-bit-drunk/.

Herndl, Diane Price. "Disease versus Disability: The Medical Humanities and Disability Studies." *PMLA* 120, no. 2 (2005): 593–98.

Herrera, C. D. "Ethics, Deception and 'Those Milgram Experiments.'" *Journal of Applied Philosophy* 18, no. 3 (2001): 245–56.

Heyes, Cressida. *Anaesthetics of Existence: Essays on Experience at the Edge*. Durham, NC: Duke University Press, 2020.

Hilderbrand, Lucas. *Inherent Vice: Bootleg Histories of Videotape and Copyright*. Durham, NC: Duke University Press, 2009.

Hochschild, Arlie. *The Managed Heart: Commercialization of Human Feeling*. 2nd ed. Berkeley: University of California Press, 2012.

Hockey, Robert. *The Psychology of Fatigue: Work, Effort and Control*. Cambridge: Cambridge University Press, 2013.

Hoffmann, Anette, and Phindezwa Mnyaka. "Hearing Voices in the Archive." *Social Dynamics* 41, no. 1 (January 2, 2015): 140–65.

Holmes, Jessica A. "Expert Listening beyond the Limits of Hearing: Music and Deafness." *Journal of the American Musicological Society* 70, no. 1 (April 1, 2017): 171–220.

Hook, Derek. "Racism as Abjection: A Psychoanalytic Conceptualization for a Post-apartheid South Africa." *South African Journal of Psychology* 34, no. 4 (2004): 672–703.

Hosokawa, Shuhei. "The Walkman Effect." *Popular Music* 4 (1984): 165–80.

Howe, Blake, Stephanie Jensen-Moulton, Neil William Lerner, and Joseph Nathan Straus, eds. *The Oxford Handbook of Music and Disability Studies*. New York: Oxford University Press, 2016.

Hu, Tung-Hui. *A Prehistory of the Cloud*. Cambridge, MA: MIT Press, 2015.

Hu, Tung-Hui. "Wait, Then Give Up: Lethargy and the Reticence of Digital Art." *Journal of Visual Culture* 16, no. 3 (2017): 337–54.

Hui, Alexandra. *The Psychophysical Ear: Musical Experiments, Experimental Sounds, 1840–1910*. Cambridge, MA: MIT Press, 2013.

Husserl, Edmund. "'Phenomenology': Edmund Husserl's Article for the Encyclopaedia Britannica (1927): New Complete Translation by Richard E. Palmer." *Journal of the British Society for Phenomenology* 2, no. 2 (1971): 77–90.

Igloliorte, Heather. "Curating Inuit Qaujimajatuqangit: Inuit Knowledge in the Qallunaat Art Museum." *Art Journal* 76, no. 2 (2017): 100–113.

Ihde, Don. *Listening and Voice: A Phenomenology of Sound*. Athens: Ohio University Press, 1974.

Ihde, Don. *Listening and Voice: Phenomenologies of Sound*. 2nd ed. Albany: State University of New York Press, 2007.

"Interview with Dr. Mead Killion: Founder, Etymotic Research, Inc." Etymotic. Accessed May 28, 2020. https://www.etymotic.com/about-us/interview-with-mead.

Jain, S. Lochlann. *Malignant: How Cancer Becomes Us*. Berkeley: University of California Press, 2013.

James, Robin. "Acousmatic Surveillance and Big Data." *Sounding Out!* (blog), October 20, 2014. https://soundstudiesblog.com/2014/10/20/the-acousmatic-era-of-surveillance/.

James, Robin. "Affective Resonance: On the Uses and Abuses of Music in and for Philosophy." *PhaenEx* 7, no. 2 (December 16, 2012): 59–95.

Jason, Leonard, Jason Meredyth Evans, Molly Brown, Nicole Porter, Abigail Brown, Jessica Hunnell, Valerie Anderson, and Athena Lerch. "Fatigue Scales and Chronic Fatigue Syndrome: Issues of Sensitivity and Specificity." *Disability Studies Quarterly* 31, no. 1 (February 4, 2011). https://dsq-sds.org/article/view/1375/1540.

Jason, Leonard, Tricia Jessen, Nicole Porter, Aaron Boulton, and Mary Gloria-Njoku. "Examining Types of Fatigue among Individuals with ME/CFS." *Disability Studies Quarterly* 29, no. 3 (July 16, 2009). https://dsq-sds.org/article/view/938/1113.

Jason, Leonard A., Judith A. Richman, Alfred W. Rademaker, Karen M. Jordan, Audrius V. Plioplys, Renee R. Taylor, William McCready, Cheng-Fang Huang, and Sigita Plioplys. "A Community-Based Study of Chronic Fatigue Syndrome." *Archives of Internal Medicine* 159, no. 18 (October 11, 1999): 2129–37.

Jenrose. "Fork Theory." Blog, December 15, 2018. https://jenrose.com/fork-theory/.

Johnson, Andi. "Measuring Fatigue: The Politics of Innovation and Standardization in a South African Lab." *BioSocieties* 8, no. 3 (September 1, 2013): 289–310.

Johnson, Andi. "'They Sweat for Science': The Harvard Fatigue Laboratory and Self-Experimentation in American Exercise Physiology." *Journal of the History of Biology* 48, no. 3 (August 1, 2015): 425–54.

Jones, Amelia. *Body Art / Performing the Subject*. Minneapolis: University of Minnesota Press, 1998.

Jones, Amelia. "Performing the Wounded Body: Pain, Affect and the Radical Relationality of Meaning." *Parallax* 15, no. 4 (November 1, 2009): 45–67.

Jones, Amelia. *Self/Image: Technology, Representation, and the Contemporary Subject*. New York: Routledge, 2006.

Junka-Aikio, Laura, and Catalina Cortes-Severino. "Cultural Studies of Extraction." *Cultural Studies* 31, nos. 2–3 (May 4, 2017): 175–84.

Kafai, Shayda. "Spoons, Spoons, Spoons." *CripFemmeCrafts* (blog), August 31, 2018. https://cripfemmecrafts.com/blogs/news/spoons-spoons-spoons.

Kafer, Alison. "Crip Kin, Manifesting." *Catalyst: Feminism, Theory, Technoscience* 5, no. 1 (April 1, 2019): 1–37.

Kafer, Alison. *Feminist, Queer, Crip*. Bloomington: Indiana University Press, 2013.

Kahn, Douglas. *Earth Sound Earth Signal: Energies and Earth Magnitude in the Arts*. Berkeley: University of California Press, 2013.

Kahneman, Daniel, and Amos Tversky. "Prospect Theory: An Analysis of Decision under Risk." *Econometrica* 47, no. 2 (1979): 263–91.

Kane, Brian. "Sound Studies without Auditory Culture: A Critique of the Ontological Turn." *Sound Studies* 1, no. 1 (January 2015): 2–21.

Kant, Immanuel. *Critique of Judgement*. Edited by Nicholas Walker. Translated by James Creed Meredith. New York: Oxford University Press, 2007.

Kantorowicz, Ernst H. *The King's Two Bodies: A Study in Medieval Political Theology*. Princeton, NJ: Princeton University Press, 1997.

Kellaris, James J., Susan Powell Mantel, and Moses B. Altsech. "Decibels, Disposition, and Duration: The Impact of Musical Loudness and Internal States on Time Perceptions." *Advances in Consumer Research* 23 (1996): 498–503.

Kelly, Aoife C., Sara M. Boyd, Gary T. M. Henehan, and Gordon Chambers. "Occupational Noise Exposure of Nightclub Bar Employees in Ireland." *Noise and Health* 14, no. 59 (January 7, 2012): 148–54.

Kelly, Caleb. *Cracked Media: The Sound of Malfunction*. Cambridge, MA: MIT Press, 2009.

Kelly, Caleb. *Gallery Sound*. New York: Bloomsbury Academic, 2017.

Kerby-Fulton, Kathryn. Introduction to *Medieval Images, Icons and Illustrated English Literary Texts*, by Madie Hilmo, xix–xxv. Aldershot: Ashgate, 2004.

Kerr, Madeleine J., Richard L. Neitzel, OiSaeng Hong, and Robert T. Sataloff. "Historical Review of Efforts to Reduce Noise-Induced Hearing Loss in the United States." *American Journal of Industrial Medicine* 60, no. 6 (2017): 569–77.

Kezar, Adrianna, Tom DePaola, and Daniel T. Scott. *The Gig Academy: Mapping Labor in the Neoliberal University*. Baltimore: Johns Hopkins University Press, 2019.

Kheshti, Roshanak. *Modernity's Ear: Listening to Race and Gender in World Music*. New York: New York University Press, 2015.

Killion, Mead C. "The Parvum Bonum, Plus Melius Fallacy in Earplug Selection." In *Recent Developments in Hearing Instrument Technology: Proceedings of the 15th Danavox Symposium*, 415–33. Taastrup: Danavox Jubilee Foundation, 1993.

Killion, Mead C., Jonathan K. Stewart, Robert Falco, and Elliott H. Berger. "Audibility Earplug." U.S. Patent 5,113,967; submitted May 7, 1992; granted May 19, 1992.

King, Mark B. "Hearing the Echoes of Verbal Art in Mixtec Writing." In *Writing without Words: Alternative Literacies in Mesoamerica and the Andes*, edited by Elizabeth Hill Boone and Walter D. Mignolo, 102–36. Durham, NC: Duke University Press, 1994.

Kirkpatrick, Bill. "'A Blessed Boon': Radio, Disability, Governmentality, and the Discourse of the 'Shut-In,' 1920–1930." *Critical Studies in Media Communication* 29, no. 3 (August 2012): 165–84.

Kirkpatrick, Bill. "'A Voice Made for Print': Crip Voices on Radio." In *Radio's New Wave*, edited by Michele Hilmes and Jason Loviglio, 106–25. New York: Routledge, 2013.

Kittay, Eve Feder. "Ah! My Foolish Heart: A Reply to Alan Soble's 'Antioch's "Sexual Offense Policy"': A Philosophical Exploration.'" *Journal of Social Philosophy* 28, no. 2 (1997): 153–59.

Kittler, Friedrich. *Gramophone-Film-Typewriter*. Translated by Geoffrey Winthrop-Young. Stanford: Stanford University Press, 1999.

Kleege, Georgina. *More Than Meets the Eye: What Blindness Brings to Art*. New York: Oxford University Press, 2018.

Kleege, Georgina. *Sight Unseen*. New Haven, CT: Yale University Press, 1999.

Kraaijenga, Véronique J. C., Geerte G. J. Ramakers, and Wilko Grolman. "The Effect of Earplugs in Preventing Hearing Loss from Recreational Noise Exposure: A Systematic Review." *JAMA Otolaryngology–Head and Neck Surgery* 142, no. 4 (April 1, 2016): 389–94.

Krenn, Mario. "From Scientific Management to Homemaking: Lillian M. Gilbreth's

Contributions to the Development of Management Thought." *Management and Organizational History* 6, no. 2 (May 1, 2011): 145–61.

Krentz, Christopher. "The Hearing Line: How Literature Gains from Deaf People." In *Deaf Gain: Raising the Stakes for Human Diversity*, edited by H-Dirksen L. Bauman and Joseph J. Murray, 421–35. Minneapolis: University of Minnesota Press, 2014.

Kunreuther, Laura. "Earwitnesses and Transparent Conduits of Voice: On the Labor of Field Interpreters for UN Missions." *Humanity* 11, no. 3 (Winter 2020): 298–316.

Kunreuther, Laura. *Voicing Subjects: Public Intimacy and Mediation in Kathmandu.* Berkeley: University of California Press, 2014.

Kurakata, Kenji, and Tazu Mizunami. "Reexamination of the Age-Related Sensitivity Decrease in ISO 7029: Do the Japanese Have Better Hearing Sensitivity?" *Acoustical Science and Technology* 26, no. 4 (2005): 381–83.

Kwakkel, Erik. "Medieval Speech Bubbles." *Medievalbooks* (blog), January 23, 2015. https://medievalbooks.nl/2015/01/23/medieval-speech-bubbles/.

Labelle, Brandon. *Lexicon of the Mouth.* New York: Bloomsbury, 2014.

Lagerkvist, Amanda. "Existential Media: Toward a Theorization of Digital Thrownness." *New Media and Society* 19, no. 1 (2017): 1–15.

Latham, Rob. "Our Jaded Tomorrows." Edited by Eric Dregni, Jonathan Dregni, Elizabeth E. Guffey, David Heckman, Mac Montandon, Ann Vandermeer, Jeff Vandermeer, and Daniel H. Wilson. *Science Fiction Studies* 36, no. 2 (2009): 339–49.

Lazard, Carolyn. "How to Be a Person in the Age of Autoimmunity." Accessed March 15, 2021. https://static1.squarespace.com/static/55c40d69e4b0a45eb985d566 /t/58cebc9dc534a59fbdbf98c2/1489943709737/HowtobeaPersonintheAgeof Autoimmunity+%281%29.pdf.

Le Breton, David. "Understanding Skin-Cutting in Adolescence: Sacrificing a Part to Save the Whole." *Body and Society* 24, no. 2 (2018): 33–54.

Leone, Stephanie S., Simon Wessely, Marcus J. H. Huibers, J. André Knottnerus, and Ijmert Kant. "Two Sides of the Same Coin? On the History and Phenomenology of Chronic Fatigue and Burnout." *Psychology and Health* 26, no. 4 (April 1, 2011): 449–64.

Levinas, Emmanuel. *Existence and Existents.* Translated by Alphonso Lingis. Boston: Kluwer, 1988.

Levinas, Emmanuel. *Totality and Infinity: An Essay on Exteriority.* Translated by Alphonso Lingis. London: Kluwer, 1991.

Levy, Karen E. C. "Digital Surveillance in the Hypermasculine Workplace." *Feminist Media Studies* 16, no. 2 (March 3, 2016): 361–65.

Lewis, G., and S. Wessely. "The Epidemiology of Fatigue: More Questions Than Answers." *Journal of Epidemiology and Community Health* 46, no. 2 (April 1, 1992): 92–97.

Li, Xiaochang, and Mara Mills. "Vocal Features: From Voice Identification to Speech Recognition by Machine." *Technology and Culture* 60, no. 2 (June 18, 2019): S129–60.

Lingis, Alphonso. "Irrevocable Loss." In *Non-representational Methodologies: Re-*

envisioning Research, edited by Phillip Vannini, 165–75. New York: Routledge, 2015.

Linton, Simi. *Claiming Disability: Knowledge and Identity*. New York: New York University Press, 1998.

Linton, Simi. "Disability Studies / Not Disability Studies." *Disability and Society* 13, no. 4 (1998): 525–40.

Livingston, Julie. *Debility and the Moral Imagination in Botswana*. Bloomington: Indiana University Press, 2005.

Livingston, Julie. "Insights from an African History of Disability." *Radical History Review*, no. 94 (Winter 2006): 111–26.

Llewelyn, John. *Emmanuel Levinas: The Genealogy of Ethics*. London: Routledge, 1995.

Lloyd, Stephanie, and Alexandre Tremblay. "No Hearing without Signals." *Senses and Society*, forthcoming.

Lochhead, Judy. "The Sublime, the Ineffable, and Other Dangerous Aesthetics." *Women and Music: A Journal of Gender and Culture* 12, no. 1 (October 29, 2008): 63–74.

Lord, Alexandra M. *Condom Nation: The U.S. Government's Sex Education Campaign from World War I to the Internet*. Baltimore: Johns Hopkins University Press, 2010.

Loughridge, Dierdre. "Technologies of the Invisible: Optical Instruments and Musical Romanticism." PhD diss., University of Pennsylvania, 2011.

Lucas, Olivia. "Loudness, Rhythm and Environment: Analytical Issues in Extreme Metal Music." PhD diss., Harvard University, 2016.

Ludwig, Bob. "The Loudness Wars: Musical Dynamics versus Volume." In *Less Noise, More Soul: The Search for Balance in the Art, Technology, and Commerce of Music*, edited by David Flitner, 57–66. New York: Hal Leonard, 2013.

MacMillan, M. B. "Beard's Concept of Neurasthenia and Freud's Concept of the Actual Neuroses." *Journal of the History of the Behavioral Sciences* 12, no. 4 (1976): 376–90.

Maginnis, Hayden. *Painting in the Age of Giotto: A Historical Reevaluation*. University Park: Pennsylvania State University Press, 1997.

Mahmood, Saba. *Politics of Piety: The Islamic Revival and the Feminist Subject*. Princeton, NJ: Princeton University Press, 2011.

Maldonado, Tomás. "Taking Eyeglasses Seriously." *Design Issues* 17, no. 4 (October 2001): 32–43.

Mallur, Pavan S., and Clark A. Rosen. "Vocal Fold Injection: Review of Indications, Techniques, and Materials for Augmentation." *Clinical and Experimental Otorhinolaryngology* 3, no. 4 (December 2010): 177–82.

Marks, Laura U. *The Skin of the Film: Intercultural Cinema, Embodiment, and the Senses*. Durham, NC: Duke University Press, 2000.

Marra, Pedro Silva, and Felipe Trotta. "Sound, Music and Magic in Football Stadiums." *Popular Music* 38, no. 1 (January 2019): 73–89.

Marshall, Caitlin. "Crippled Speech." *Postmodern Culture* 24, no. 3 (2014).

Marshall, Edward. "The Future Man Will Spend Less Time in Bed." *New York Times*, October 11, 1914, Sunday edition, sec. 4.

Marx, Karl. *Capital.* Vol. 1, *A Critique of Political Economy.* New York: Penguin Classics, 1992.

Mauss, Marcel. *Sociology and Psychology: Essays.* Translated by Ben Brewster. Boston: Routledge and Kegan Paul, 1979.

Maxwell, James C. "On Governors." *Proceedings of the Royal Society of London* 16 (1868): 270–83.

Maxwell, Richard, and Toby Miller. *Greening the Media.* New York: Oxford University Press, 2012.

McChesney, Robert. *Telecommunications, Mass Media, and Democracy: The Battle for Control over U.S. Public Broadcasting, 1928–1935.* New York: Oxford University Press, 1993.

McClelland, Clive. *Tempesta: Stormy Music in the Eighteenth Century.* Lanham, MD: Lexington Books, 2017.

McEnaney, Tom. *Acoustic Properties: Radio, Narrative and the New Neighborhood of the Americas.* Evanston, IL: Northwestern University Press, 2017.

McKay, Anne. "Speaking Up: Voice Amplification and Women's Struggle for Public Expression." In *Technology and Women's Voices,* edited by Cheris Kramarae, 187–206. New York: Routledge and Kegan Paul, 1988.

McKinnon, Susan. *Neo-liberal Genetics: The Myths and Moral Tales of Evolutionary Psychology.* Chicago: Prickly Paradigm, 2005.

McKittrick, Katherine, and Alexander Weheliye. "808s & Heartbreak." *Propter* 2, no. 1 (Fall 2017): 13–42.

McRuer, Robert. "Any Day Now: Queerness, Disability, and the Trouble with Homonormativity." In *Disability Media Studies,* edited by Elizabeth Ellcessor and Bill Kirkpatrick, 272–91. New York: New York University Press, 2017.

McRuer, Robert. *Crip Theory: Cultural Signs of Queerness and Disability.* New York: New York University Press, 2006.

Medina, Eden. *Cybernetic Revolutionaries: Technology and Politics in Allende's Chile.* Cambridge, MA: MIT Press, 2011.

Meintjes, Louise. *Sound of Africa! Making Music Zulu in a South African Studio.* Durham, NC: Duke University Press, 2003.

Meizel, Katherine. *Multivocality: Singing on the Borders of Identity.* New York: Oxford University Press, 2020.

Merleau-Ponty, Maurice. *Phenomenology of Perception.* London: Routledge and Kegan Paul, 1962.

Merleau-Ponty, Maurice. *The Primacy of Perception: And Other Essays on Phenomenological Psychology, the Philosophy of Art, History, and Politics.* Evanston, IL: Northwestern University Press, 1964.

Mezzadra, Sandro, and Brett Neilson. "On the Multiple Frontiers of Extraction: Excavating Contemporary Capitalism." *Cultural Studies* 31, nos. 2–3 (May 4, 2017): 185–204.

Mezzadri, Alessandra. "On the Value of Social Reproduction: Informal Labor, the Majority World, and the Need for Inclusive Theories and Politics." *Radical Philosophy*

2, no. 4 (Spring 2019): 33–41. https://www.radicalphilosophy.com/article/on-the
-value-of-social-reproduction.

Michaud, Alyssa. "No One in the Spotlight: Holographic Performance, East and West."
International Musicological Society, Tokyo, Japan, March 23, 2017.

Mills, Mara. "Deafening: Noise and the Engineering of Communication in the Telephone System." *Grey Room*, no. 43 (Spring 2011): 118–43.

Mills, Mara. "Deaf Jam: From Inscription to Reproduction to Information." *Social Text*
28, no. 1 (Summer 2010): 35–58.

Mills, Mara. "Do Signals Have Politics? Inscribing Abilities in Cochlear Implants." In
Oxford Handbook of Sound Studies, edited by Karin Bijsterveld and Trevor Pinch,
320–46. New York: Oxford University Press, 2011.

Mills, Mara. "Evocative Object: Auditory Inkblot." *Continent* 5, no. 1 (2016): 15–23.

Mills, Mara. "Hearing Aids and the History of Electronics Miniaturization." *IEEE Annals
of the History of Computing* 33, no. 2 (April 2011): 24–44.

Mills, Mara. *Hearing Loss and the History of Information Theory*. Durham, NC: Duke
University Press, forthcoming.

Mills, Mara. "Media and Prosthesis: The Vocoder, the Artificial Larynx, and the History
of Signal Processing." *Qui Parle* 21, no. 1 (2012): 107–49.

Mirzoeff, Nicholas. *Silent Poetry: Deafness, Sign, and Visual Culture in Modern France*.
Princeton, NJ: Princeton University Press, 1995.

Miserandino, Christine. "The Spoon Theory." *But You Don't Look Sick* (blog), April 25,
2013. https://butyoudontlooksick.com/articles/written-by-christine/the-spoon
-theory/.

Moeller, Susan D. *Compassion Fatigue: How the Media Sell Disease, Famine, War and
Death*. New York: Routledge, 2002.

Monaghan, John. "The Text in the Body, the Body in the Text: The Embodied Sign in
Mixtec Writing." In *Writing without Words: Alternative Literacies in Mesoamerica
and the Andes*, edited by Elizabeth Hill Boone and Walter D. Mignolo, 87–101.
Durham, NC: Duke University Press, 1994.

Montgomery, Cal. "A Hard Look at Invisible Disability." *Ragged Edge* 1, no. 2 (2001).
http://www.raggededgemagazine.com/0301/0301ft1.htm.

Moren, Lisa. "'Talking Popcorn' and 'Indecision on the Moon' by Nina Katchadourian."
YouTube, August 22, 2012. https://youtu.be/YTMkzYofShc?t=204.

Moreno, Jairo. "Antenatal Aurality in Pacific Afro-Colombian Midwifery." In *Remapping
Sound Studies*, edited by Gavin Steingo and Jim Sykes, 109–34. Durham, NC: Duke
University Press, 2019.

Morris, Jeremy. "Sounds in the Cloud: Cloud Computing and the Digital Music Com-
modity." *First Monday* 16, no. 5 (2011). https://firstmonday.org/ojs/index.php/fm
/article/view/3391.

Morton, Timothy. "Sublime Objects." *Speculations* 2 (2011): 207–27.

Moten, Fred. *Black and Blur*. Durham, NC: Duke University Press, 2017.

Moten, Fred. *In the Break: The Aesthetics of the Black Radical Tradition*. Minneapolis:
University of Minnesota Press, 2003.

Mowitt, John. "The Sound of Music in the Era of Its Electronic Reproducibility." In *Music and Society: The Politics of Composition, Performance and Reception*, edited by Richard Leppert and Susan McClary, 173–97. New York: Cambridge University Press, 1987.

Mulvin, Dylan. "Media Prophylaxis: Night Modes and the Politics of Preventing Harm." *Information and Culture* 53, no. 2 (May 2018): 175–202.

Muñoz, José. *Cruising Utopia: The Then and There of Queer Futurity*. New York: New York University Press, 2009.

Murphy, Michelle. *Sick Building Syndrome and the Problem of Uncertainty: Environmental Politics, Technoscience, and Women Workers*. Durham, NC: Duke University Press, 2006.

Nakamura, Karen. *Deaf in Japan: Signing and the Politics of Identity*. Ithaca, NY: Cornell University Press, 2006.

Nancy, Jean-Luc. *The Fall of Sleep*. New York: Fordham University Press, 2009.

Nancy, Jean-Luc. *Listening*. Translated by Charlotte Mandell. New York: Fordham University Press, 2007.

The Nap Ministry. "About." Accessed April 7, 2021. https://thenapministry.wordpress.com/about/.

Napolin, Julie Beth. *The Fact of Resonance: Modernist Acoustics and Narrative Form*. New York: Fordham University Press, 2020.

Noise and Vibration Editors. "Earplugs and Condoms." *Noise and Vibration Worldwide* 36, no. 6 (2005): 2.

Noll, A. Michael. *Introduction to Telephones and Telephone Systems*. 3rd ed. Boston: Artech House, 1998.

Nordmarken, Sonny. "Microaggressions." *TSQ: Transgender Studies Quarterly* 1, nos. 1–2 (May 2014): 129–34.

Norris, Heather. "Colonialism and the Rupturing of Indigenous Worldviews of Impairment and Relational Independence: A Beginning Dialogue towards Reclamation and Social Transformation." *Critical Disability Discourse / Discours Critiques dans le Champ du Handicap* 6 (2014): 53–79.

Novak, David. *Japanoise: Music at the Edge of Circulation*. Durham, NC: Duke University Press, 2013.

Nudelman, Franny. *Fighting Sleep: The War for the Mind and the US Military*. New York: Verso, 2019.

O'Brien, Ian, and Elizabeth Beach. "Hearing Loss, Earplug Use, and Attitudes to Hearing Protection among Non-orchestral Ensemble Musicians." *Journal of the Audio Engineering Society* 64, no. 3 (2016): 132–37.

Ochoa Gauthier, Ana María. *Aurality: Listening and Knowledge in Nineteenth-Century Colombia*. Durham, NC: Duke University Press, 2014.

Ott, Katherine. *Artificial Parts, Practical Lives: Modern Histories of Prosthetics*. New York: New York University Press, 2002.

"Our Vibrating Hands." *Vibrations*, November 13, 2018. http://vibrations.participatorymedia.ca/our-vibrating-hands-2018/.

Ouzounian, Gascia. *Stereophonica: Sound and Space in Science, Technology, and the Arts.* Cambridge, MA: MIT Press, 2021.

Packer, Jeremy. *Mobility without Mayhem: Safety, Cars, and Citizenship.* Durham, NC: Duke University Press, 2007.

Pateman, Carole. *The Sexual Contract.* Stanford: Stanford University Press, 1988.

Patra, Kevin. "Atlanta Falcons Lose 2016 Pick for Pumping Fake Noise." *Around the NFL* (blog), March 30, 2015. http://www.nfl.com/news/story/0ap3000000482500 /article/atlanta-falcons-lose-2016-pick-for-pumping-fake-noise.

Patton, Cindy. *Fatal Advice: How Safe-Sex Education Went Wrong.* Durham, NC: Duke University Press, 1996.

Patton, Cindy, and Sue O'Sullivan. "Mapping: Lesbians, AIDS and Sexuality." *Feminist Review*, no. 34 (1990): 120–33.

Pattyn, Nathalie, Jeroen Van Cutsem, Emilie Dessy, and Olivier Mairesse. "Bridging Exercise Science, Cognitive Psychology, and Medical Practice: Is 'Cognitive Fatigue' a Remake of 'The Emperor's New Clothes'?" *Frontiers in Psychology* 9 (September 10, 2018).

Paulsen, Roland. *Empty Labor: Idleness and Workplace Resistance.* Cambridge: Cambridge University Press, 2014.

Peake, Bryce. "Listening like White Nationalists at a Civil Rights Rally." *Journal of Sonic Studies*, no. 14 (2017). https://www.researchcatalogue.net/view/375960/375961.

Pearson, Robert. "Described Video Best Practices." Accessible Digital Media and Accessible Media Inc., July 2013. https://ecfsapi.fcc.gov/file/7520940294.pdf.

Peck, Kathy. "Oral History Interview." National Association of Music Merchants (NAMM), January 17, 2008. https://www.namm.org/library/oral-history/kathy -peck.

Peirce, Charles S. *Philosophical Writings of Peirce.* New York: Dover, 1955.

Peters, John Durham. "Cloud." In *Digital Keywords: A Vocabulary of Information, Society, and Culture*, edited by Benjamin Peters, 54–62. Princeton, NJ: Princeton University Press, 2016.

Peters, John Durham. *The Marvelous Clouds.* Chicago: University of Chicago Press, 2015.

Peters, John Durham. *Speaking into the Air: A History of the Idea of Communication.* Chicago: University of Chicago Press, 1999.

Peterson, David A. M. "Dear Reviewer 2: Go F' Yourself." *Social Science Quarterly* 101, no. 4 (2020): 1648–52.

Piekut, Benjamin. *Experimentalism Otherwise: The New York Avant-Garde and Its Limits.* Berkeley: University of California Press, 2011.

Piepzna-Samarasinha, Leah Lakshmi. *Care Work: Dreaming Disability Justice.* Vancouver: Arsenal Pulp Press, 2018.

Pierce, John R. "The Early Days of Information Theory." *IEEE Transactions in Information Theory* 19, no. 1 (1973): 3–8.

Pieters, B. M., G. B. Eindhoven, C. Acott, and A. A. J. Van Zundert. "Pioneers of Laryngoscopy: Indirect, Direct and Video Laryngoscopy." *Anaesthesia and Intensive Care* 43, no. 1 suppl. (July 2015): 4–11.

Pinch, Trevor, and Karin Bijsterveld. "New Keys to the World of Sound." In *The Oxford Handbook of Sound Studies*, edited by Trevor Pinch and Karin Bijsterveld, 3–35. New York: Oxford University Press, 2011.

Pinch, Trevor, and Frank Trocco. *Analog Days: The Invention and Impact of the Moog Synthesizer*. Cambridge, MA: Harvard University Press, 2002.

Pinchevski, Amit. "Bartleby's Autism: Wandering along Incommunicability." *Cultural Critique*, no. 78 (Spring 2011): 27–59.

Pinchevski, Amit, and John Durham Peters. "Autism and New Media: Disability between Technology and Society." *New Media and Society*, July 8, 2015.

Pitts-Taylor, Victoria. *In the Flesh: The Cultural Politics of Body Modification*. New York: Palgrave Macmillan, 2003.

Pliner, Susan Marcia. "Listening to the Learning Disabled: Self-Perceptions of Learning Disabled Identity among College Students." PhD diss., University of Massachusetts, 1999.

Pohl, Mary E. D., Kevin O. Pope, and Christopher von Nagy. "Olmec Origins of Mesoamerican Writing." *Science* 298, no. 5600 (2002): 1984–87.

Poss, Robert. "Distortion Is Truth." *Leonardo Music Journal* 8, no. 1 (1998): 45–48.

Powell, Anastasia. *Sex, Power, and Consent: Youth Culture and the Unwritten Rules*. Cambridge: Cambridge University Press, 2010.

Price, Margaret. *Mad at School: Rhetorics of Mental Disability and Academic Life*. Ann Arbor: University of Michigan Press, 2011.

Puar, Jasbir. *The Right to Maim: Debility, Capacity, Disability*. Durham, NC: Duke University Press, 2017.

Puar, Jasbir. *Terrorist Assemblages: Homonationalism in Queer Times*. Durham, NC: Duke University Press, 2017.

Pugliese, Joseph. "Penal Asylum: Refugees, Ethics, Hospitality." *Borderlands E-Journal* 1, no. 1 (2002). https://webarchive.nla.gov.au/awa/20021021002338/http://www .borderlandsejournal.adelaide.edu.au/vol1no1_2002/pugliese.html.

Pugliese, Joseph. "Subcutaneous Law: Embodying the Migration Amendment Act 1992." *Australian Feminist Law Journal* 21, no. 23 (July 2004): 23–34.

Pullin, Graham. *Design Meets Disability*. Cambridge, MA: MIT Press, 2009.

Pullin, Graham, and Andrew Cook. "Six Speaking Chairs (Not Directly) for People Who Cannot Speak." *ACM Interactions Magazine* 17, no. 5 (October 2010): 39–42.

Quetelet, Lambert Adolphe. *A Treatise on Man and the Development of His Faculties*. Edinburgh: Chambers, 1842.

Quine, Oscar. "Calais Jungle Refugees Sew Mouths Shut in Protest at Camp Clearance." *The Independent*, March 4, 2016.

Quintero, Michael. "Loudness, Excess, Power: A Political Liminology of a Global City of the South." In *Remapping Sound Studies*, edited by Gavin Steingo and Jim Sykes, 135–55. Durham, NC: Duke University Press, 2019.

Rabinbach, Anson. *The Human Motor: Energy, Fatigue and the Origins of Modernity*. Berkeley: University of California Press, 1990.

Radovac, Lilian. "Muting Dissent: New York City's Sound Device Ordinance and the

Liberalization of the Public Sphere." *Radical History Review*, no. 121 (January 2015): 32–50.

Ragg, Mark. "Epidemic of Hearing Loss Predicted." *Lancet* 344, no. 8923 (September 3, 1994): 675.

Rai, Sonali, Joan Greening, and Leen Petré. "A Comparative Study of Audio Description Guidelines Prevalent in Different Countries." Media and Culture Department, Royal National Institute of Blind People, December 15, 2010. http://audiodescription.co.uk/uploads/general/RNIB._AD_standards.pdf.

Raine, Emily. "On Waiting: A Political Economy of Affect in Restaurant Service." PhD diss., McGill University, 2012.

Rajan, Nithya. "What Do Refugees Want? Reading Refugee Lip-Sewing Protests through a Critical Lens." *International Feminist Journal of Politics* 21, no. 4 (August 2019): 527–43.

Ramsey, Eric. *The Long Path to Nearness: A Contribution to a Corporeal Philosophy of Communication and the Groundwork for an Ethics of Relief.* Atlantic Highlands, NJ: Humanities Press, 1998.

Rangan, Pooja, Akshya Saxena, Ragini Tharoor Srinivasan, and Pavitra Sundar, eds. *Thinking with an Accent.* Berkeley: University of California Press, forthcoming.

Rath, Richard Cullen. *How Early America Sounded.* Ithaca, NY: Cornell University Press, 2003.

"Refugees Sew Lips Together in Border Protest." *Al Jazeera*, November 24, 2015. https://www.aljazeera.com/gallery/2015/11/24/refugees-sew-lips-together-in-border-protest/.

Reim Ifrach, Emily, and Abbe Miller. "Social Action Art Therapy as an Intervention for Compassion Fatigue." *Arts in Psychotherapy* 50 (September 1, 2016): 34–39.

Robinson, Dylan. *Hungry Listening: Resonant Theory for Indigenous Sound Studies.* Minneapolis: University of Minnesota Press, 2020.

Rodgers, Tara. *Pink Noises: Women on Electronic Music and Sound.* Durham, NC: Duke University Press, 2010.

Rose, Sarah F. *No Right to Be Idle: The Invention of Disability, 1840s–1930s.* Chapel Hill: University of North Carolina Press, 2017.

Rosen, Steven. "Rock Fans Fighting Hearing Loss Insist: Not So Loud, Please!" *New York Times*, September 7, 1988, sec. C.

Roy, Jeff. "Remapping the Voice through Transgender-Hījṛā Performance." In *Remapping Sound Studies*, edited by Gavin Steingo and Jim Sykes, 173–82. Durham, NC: Duke University Press, 2019.

Rubin, Gayle. "The Traffic in Women: Notes on the 'Political Economy' of Sex." In *Feminist Anthropology*, edited by Ellen Lewin, 87–106. Malden, MA: Blackwell, 2006.

Salamon, Gayle. "'The Place Where Life Hides Away': Merleau-Ponty, Fanon, and the Location of Bodily Being." *Differences* 17, no. 2 (2006): 96–112.

Samuels, Ellen Jean. "My Body, My Closet: Invisible Disability and the Limits of Coming-Out Discourse." *GLQ: A Journal of Lesbian and Gay Studies* 9, no. 1 (April 10, 2003): 233–55.

Samuels, Ellen Jean. "Sick and Well Time." *Brevity Magazine* 65 (September 12, 2020). https://brevitymag.com/nonfiction/sick-and-well-time/.

Samuels, Ellen Jean. "Six Ways of Looking at Crip Time." *Disability Studies Quarterly* 37, no. 3 (August 31, 2017). https://dsq-sds.org/article/view/5824/4684.

Sargent, Lydia, ed. *Women and Revolution: A Discussion of the Unhappy Marriage of Marxism and Feminism.* Boston: South End, 1981.

Sauter, Dan. "HEAR This: Kathy Peck." *Music Life Radio: Stories at the Intersection of Music and Life*, June 30, 2012. http://www.musicliferadio.com/2012/06/059-hear-this-kathy-peck/.

Scarry, Elaine. *The Body in Pain: The Making and Unmaking of the World.* New York: Oxford University Press, 1987.

Scheffler, Robin Wolfe. "The Fate of a Progressive Science: The Harvard Fatigue Laboratory, Athletes, the Science of Work and the Politics of Reform." *Endeavour* 35, no. 2 (June 1, 2011): 48–54.

Scheffler, Robin Wolfe. "The Power of Exercise and the Exercise of Power: The Harvard Fatigue Laboratory, Distance Running, and the Disappearance of Work, 1919–1947." *Journal of the History of Biology* 48, no. 3 (August 2015): 391–423.

Schieber, David. "Money, Morals, and Condom Use: The Politics of Health in Gay and Straight Adult Film Production." *Social Problems* 65, no. 3 (August 1, 2018): 377–94.

Schildkrout, Enid. "Inscribing the Body." *Annual Review of Anthropology* 33 (2004): 319–44.

Schivelbusch, Wolfgang. *The Railway Journey: The Industrialization of Time and Space in the Nineteenth Century.* Berkeley: University of California Press, 1986.

Schlichter, Annette. "Un/voicing the Self: Vocal Pedagogy and the Discourse-Practices of Subjectivation." *Postmodern Culture* 24, no. 3 (2014). doi:10.1353/pmc.2014.0011.

Schmidgen, Henning. *Horn, or The Counterside of Media.* Durham, NC: Duke University Press, 2022. Originally published as *Horn: Oder Die Gegenseite der Medien.* Berlin: Matthes and Seitz, 2018.

Schuknecht, Harold F. M. D. "Presbycusis." *Laryngoscope* 65, no. 6 (June 1955): 402–19.

Schulten, Susan. *Mapping the Nation: History and Cartography in Nineteenth-Century America.* Chicago: University of Chicago Press, 2012.

Schulze, Holger. *Sonic Fiction.* New York: Bloomsbury, 2020.

Schütz, Walter. "A History of Fatigue." *Engineering Fracture Mechanics* 54, no. 2 (May 1, 1996): 263–300.

Schwartz, Hillel. *Making Noise: From Babel to the Big Bang and Beyond.* New York: Zone Books, 2011.

Scott, James C. *Domination and the Arts of Resistance: Hidden Transcripts.* New Haven, CT: Yale University Press, 2008.

Seagrave, Kerry. *Vision Aids in America: A Social History of Eyewear and Sight Correction since 1900.* Jefferson, NC: McFarland, 2011.

Sedgwick, Eve Kosofsky. *Touching Feeling: Affect, Pedagogy, Performativity.* Durham, NC: Duke University Press, 2003.

Shakespeare, Tom. Comment on Michael Bérubé, "On Humans, Disability, and the

Humanities?" *On the Human: A Project of the National Humanities Center* (blog), January 29, 2011. https://nationalhumanitiescenter.org/on-the-human/2011/01/humans-disabilities-humanities/#comment-4573.

Sharma, Sarah. "A Manifesto for the Broken Machine." *Camera Obscura: Feminism, Culture, and Media Studies* 35, no. 2 (2020): 171–79.

Sheller, Mimi. *Aluminum Dreams: The Making of Light Modernity*. Cambridge, MA: MIT Press, 2014.

Shorter, Edward. "Chronic Fatigue in Historical Perspective." In *Ciba Foundation Symposium 173—Chronic Fatigue Syndrome*, 6–22. Hoboken, NJ: John Wiley and Sons, 2007.

Shukaitis, Stevphen. "Learning Not to Labor." *Rethinking Marxism* 26, no. 2 (April 3, 2014): 193–205.

Siebers, Tobin. *Disability Aesthetics*. Ann Arbor: University of Michigan Press, 2013.

Siebers, Tobin. *Disability Theory*. Ann Arbor: University of Michigan Press, 2008.

Silverman, S. R. "LVI Tolerance for Pure Tones and Speech in Normal and Defective Hearing." *Annals of Otology, Rhinology and Laryngology* 56, no. 3 (September 1, 1947): 658–77.

Simmel, Georg. "The Metropolis and Mental Life." In *Georg Simmel: On Individuality and Social Forms*, edited by Donald Levine, translated by Kurt Wolff, 409–24. Chicago: University of Chicago Press, 1971.

Simpson, Audra. *Mohawk Interruptus: Political Life across the Borders of Settler States*. Durham, NC: Duke University Press, 2014.

Simpson, Leanne Betasamosake. *As We Have Always Done: Indigenous Freedom through Radical Resistance*. Minneapolis: University of Minnesota Press, 2017.

Slack, Jennifer Daryl. "The Theory and Method of Articulation in Cultural Studies." In *Stuart Hall: Critical Dialogues*, edited by David Morley and Kuan-Hsing Chen, 113–29. New York: Routledge, 1996.

Sloterdijk, Peter. *Critique of Cynical Reason*. Minneapolis: University of Minnesota Press, 1987.

Small, Christopher. *Musicking: The Meanings of Performing and Listening*. Hanover, NH: Wesleyan University Press, 1998.

Smeds, Karolina, and Arne Leijon. "Loudness and Hearing Loss." In *Loudness*, edited by Mary Florentine, Arthur N. Popper, and Richard R. Fay, 223–59. New York: Springer, 2011.

Smith, William A., Walter R. Allen, and Lynette L. Danley. "'Assume the Position . . . You Fit the Description': Psychosocial Experiences and Racial Battle Fatigue among African American Male College Students." *American Behavioral Scientist* 51, no. 4 (December 1, 2007): 551–78.

Snoddon, Kristin. "Baby Sign as Deaf Gain." In *Deaf Gain: Raising the Stakes for Human Diversity*, edited by H-Dirksen L. Bauman and Joseph J. Murray, 146–58. Minneapolis: University of Minnesota Press, 2014.

Sobchack, Vivian. *Carnal Thoughts: Embodiment and Moving Image Culture*. Berkeley: University of California Press, 2004.

Socialist Patients' Collective. *Turn Illness into a Weapon.* Translated by Wolfgang Huber. Preface by Jean-Paul Sartre. Heidelberg, Germany: KRRIM-PF-Verlag für Krankheit, 1993.

Somers, Julie. "Listening to the Text: The Medieval Speech Bubble." *Medievalfragments* (blog), June 6, 2014. https://medievalfragments.wordpress.com/2014/06/06 /listening-to-the-text-the-medieval-speech-bubble/.

"SoundBuddy Portable Speaker Kit with Bodypack Transmitter." Special Needs Computers. Accessed October 7, 2019. https://www.specialneedscomputers.ca/index .php?l=product_detail&p=5605.

Southworth, Michael. "The Sonic Environment of Cities." *Environment and Behavior* 1, no. 1 (June 1969): 49–70.

Spankovich, Christopher, and James W. Hall III. "The Misunderstood Misophonia." *Audiology Today* 26, no. 4 (August 2014): 15–23.

Spencer, Danielle. *Metagnosis: Revelatory Narratives of Health and Identity.* New York: Oxford University Press, 2021.

"Spokeman Personal Voice Amplifier." Luminaud. Accessed October 7, 2019. https:// www.luminaud.com/spokeman_amp.

Stanyek, Jason. "If There's a Place in Your Voice: 'Corcovado' and Corpaural Politics of Accent in the United States." Unpublished paper delivered at the "Voice Workshop," UC Humanities Research Institute, University of California, Irvine, September 17. 2010.

Stanyek, Jason, and Benjamin Piekut. "Deadness: Technologies of the Intermundane." *TDR: The Drama Review* 54, no. 1 (2010): 14–38.

Steingo, Gavin, and Jim Sykes. "Introduction: Remapping Sound Studies in the Global South." In *Remapping Sound Studies*, edited by Gavin Steingo and Jim Sykes, 1–36. Durham, NC: Duke University Press, 2019.

Stenklev, Niels Christian, and Einar Laukli. "Presbyacusis—Hearing Thresholds and the Iso 7029." *International Journal of Audiology* 43, no. 5 (January 1, 2004): 295–306.

Sterne, Jonathan. *The Audible Past: Cultural Origins of Sound Reproduction.* Durham, NC: Duke University Press, 2003.

Sterne, Jonathan. "Ballad of the Dork-o-Phone: Toward a Crip Vocal Technoscience." *Journal of Interdisciplinary Voice Studies* 4, no. 2 (2019): 179–89.

Sterne, Jonathan. "Cancer Crawl Feb 20th." *Super Bon!* (blog), February 20, 2010. https://superbon.net/2010/02/20/cancer-crawl-feb-20th/.

Sterne, Jonathan. "Disability Studies 101: Saturday Night Practicum." *Super Bon!* (blog), January 11, 2010. https://superbon.net/2010/01/11/disability-studies-101-saturday -night-practicum/.

Sterne, Jonathan. "Headset Culture, Audile Technique and Sound Space as Private Space." *Tijdschrift Voor Mediageschiedenis* 6, no. 2 (2003): 57–82.

Sterne, Jonathan. "The Loaner." *Super Bon!* (blog), March 21, 2010. https://superbon.net /2010/03/21/the-loaner/.

Sterne, Jonathan. *MP3: The Meaning of a Format.* Durham, NC: Duke University Press, 2012.

Sterne, Jonathan. "Player Hater." *FlowTV*, October 30, 2011. http://www.flowjournal.org
/2011/10/player-hater/.

Sterne, Jonathan. "Space within Space: Artificial Reverb and the Detachable Echo." *Grey
Room*, no. 60 (Summer 2015): 110–31.

Sterne, Jonathan. "10." *Super Bon!* (blog), June 20, 2010. https://superbon.net/2010
/06/10/10/.

Sterne, Jonathan. "Voice Lift Review or Laryngology Phenomenology (Not Really but It
Rhymes)." *Super Bon!* (blog), September 24, 2011. https://superbon.net/2011/09
/24/voice-lift-review-or-laryngology-phenomenology-not-really-but-it-rhymes/.

Sterne, Jonathan. "'What Do We Want? Materiality! When Do We Want It? Now!'"
In *Media Technologies: Essays on Communication, Materiality and Society*, edited by
Tarleton Gillespie, Pablo J. Boczkowski, and Kirsten A. Foot, 119–28. Cambridge,
MA: MIT Press, 2014.

Sterne, Jonathan, and Mitchell Akiyama. "The Recording That Never Wanted to Be
Heard and Other Stories of Sonification." In *The Oxford Handbook of Sound Studies*, edited by Trevor Pinch and Karin Bijsterveld, 544–60. New York: Oxford University Press, 2011.

Stevens, Sarah E. "Care Time." *Disability Studies Quarterly* 38, no. 4 (December 21,
2018). https://dsq-sds.org/article/view/6090/5136.

Stoever, Jennifer. *The Sonic Color Line: Race and the Cultural Politics of Listening*. New
York: New York University Press, 2016.

"Stokowski Seeks True Tone Colors." *New York Times*, October 26, 1932, 23.

Strachan, Robert. *Sonic Technologies: Popular Music, Digital Culture and the Creative
Process*. New York: Bloomsbury Academic, 2017.

Straus, Joseph Nathan. *Extraordinary Measures: Disability in Music*. New York: Oxford
University Press, 2011.

Suisman, David. "The Oklahoma City Sonic Boom Experiment and the Politics of Su-
personic Aviation." *Radical History Review*, no. 121 (January 2015): 169–95.

Szeman, Imre, and Dominic Boyer, eds. *Energy Humanities: An Anthology*. Baltimore:
Johns Hopkins University Press, 2017.

Szendy, Peter. *All Ears: The Aesthetics of Espionage*. New York: Fordham University Press,
2017.

Tahmahkera, Dustin. "Becoming Sound: Tubitsinakukuru from Mt. Scott to
Standing Rock." *Sounding Out!* (blog), October 9, 2017. https://soundstudiesblog
.com/2017/10/09/becoming-sound-tubitsinakukuru-from-mt-scott-to
-standing-rock/.

Thompson, Emily. *The Soundscape of Modernity: Architectural Acoustics and the Culture
of Listening in America, 1900–1930*. Cambridge, MA: MIT Press, 2002.

Thompson, E. P. "Time, Work-Discipline, and Industrial Capitalism." *Past and Present*,
no. 38 (1967): 56–97.

Thompson, Marie. *Beyond Unwanted Sound: Noise, Affect and Aesthetic Moralism*. New
York: Bloomsbury, 2017.

Thompson, Marie. "Whiteness and the Ontological Turn in Sound Studies." *Parallax* 23, no. 3 (2017): 266–82.

Timoshenko, Stephen P. *History of Strength of Materials*. New York: Dover, 1983.

Tkaczyk, Viktoria. "The Shot Is Fired Unheard: Sigmund Exner and the Physiology of Reverberation." *Grey Room*, no. 60 (Summer 2015): 66–81.

Tkaczyk, Viktoria. "Whose Larynx Is It? Fields of Scholarly Competence around 1900." *History of Humanities* 3, no. 1 (2018): 57–73.

Tomlinson, Gary. *A Million Years of Music: The Emergence of Human Modernity*. Cambridge, MA: MIT Press, 2015.

Tomlinson, Gary. *The Singing of the New World: Indigenous Voices in the Era of European Contact*. Cambridge: Cambridge University Press, 2007.

Toombs, S. Kay. *The Meaning of Illness: A Phenomenological Account of the Different Perspectives of Physician and Patient*. Dordrecht: Kluwer Academic, 1993.

Torres-Harding, Susan, and Leonard A. Jason. "What Is Fatigue? History and Epidemiology." In *Fatigue as a Window to the Brain*, edited by John DeLuca, 3–17. Cambridge, MA: MIT Press, 2003.

Tracy, Sarah J., and Karen Tracy. "Emotion Labor at 911: A Case Study and Theoretical Critique." *Journal of Applied Communication Research* 26, no. 4 (November 1998): 390–411.

Tracy, Sarah W. "The Physiology of Extremes: Ancel Keys and the International High Altitude Expedition of 1935." *Bulletin of the History of Medicine* 86, no. 4 (December 23, 2012): 627–60.

Treichler, Paula A. *How to Have a Theory in an Epidemic: Cultural Chronicles of AIDS*. Durham, NC: Duke University Press, 1999.

Treichler, Paula A. "'When Pirates Feast . . . Who Pays?': Condoms, Advertising, and the Visibility Paradox, 1920s and 1930s." *Journal of Bioethical Inquiry* 11, no. 4 (2014): 479–505.

Truța, Camelia. "Emotional Labor Strategies Adopted by School Psychologists." In "PSIWORLD 2011," special issue, *Procedia—Social and Behavioral Sciences* 33 (January 1, 2012): 796–800.

Tsing, Anna Lowenhaupt. *The Mushroom at the End of the World*. Princeton, NJ: Princeton University Press, 2017.

Turino, Thomas. "Signs of Imagination, Identity and Experience: A Peircean Semiotics Theory for Music." *Ethnomusicology* 43, no. 2 (1999): 221–55.

Useem, Jerry. "Bring Back the Nervous Breakdown: It Used to Be Okay to Admit That the World Had Simply Become Too Much." *The Atlantic*, March 2021. https://www.theatlantic.com/magazine/archive/2021/03/bring-back-the-nervous-breakdown/617788/.

Vallee, Mickey. *Sounding Bodies Sounding Worlds: An Exploration of Embodiments in Sound*. New York: Palgrave Macmillan, 2020.

Vallee, Mickey. "Technology, Embodiment, and Affect in Voice Sciences: The Voice Is an Imaginary Organ." *Body and Society* 23, no. 2 (June 2017): 83–105.

Vasey, Craig R. "*Existence and Existents* by Emmanuel Levinas." *The Thomist: A Speculative Quarterly Review* 44, no. 3 (1980): 466–73.

Virdi, Jaipreet. *Hearing Happiness: Deafness Cures in History*. Chicago: University of Chicago Press, 2021.

Voegelin, Salomé. *Sonic Possible Worlds: Hearing the Continuum of Sound*. New York: Bloomsbury Academic, 2014.

Voigt, Kristin, and Nicholas B. King. "Disability Weights in the Global Burden of Disease 2010 Study: Two Steps Forward, One Step Back?" *Bulletin of the World Health Organization* 92, no. 3 (March 1, 2014): 226–28.

Voigt, Kristin, and Nicholas B. King. "Out of Alignment? Limitations of the Global Burden of Disease in Assessing the Allocation of Global Health Aid." *Public Health Ethics* 10, no. 3 (November 1, 2017): 244–56.

Volmar, Axel. "Listening to the Cold War: The Nuclear Test Ban Negotiations, Seismology, and Psychoacoustics, 1958–1963." *Osiris* 28 (2013): 80–102.

Waddell, J. P. "Considering Commercial Advertisement Loudness Mitigation and Its Side Effects [Standards in a Nutshell]." *IEEE Signal Processing Magazine* 29, no. 4 (2012): 102–6.

Waksman, Steve. "California Noise: Tinkering with Hardcore and Heavy Metal in Southern California." *Social Studies of Science* 34, no. 5 (October 2004): 675–702.

Wall, Dorothy. *Encounters with the Invisible: Unseen Illness, Controversy, and Chronic Fatigue*. University Park, TX: Southern Methodist University Press, 2005.

Walsh, Martin, Edward Stein, and Jean-Marc Jot. "Dynamic Compensation of Audio Signal for Improved Perceived Spectral Imbalances." U.S. Patent No. U.S. 2012/0063616 (March 15, 2012). https://patents.google.com/patent/EP2614586A2/en.

Warner, Bernhard. "Why Do Stars like Adele Keep Losing Their Voices?" *Guardian*, August 10, 2017.

Warszawa, Anna, and Robert T. Sataloff. "Noise Exposure in Movie Theaters: A Preliminary Study of Sound Levels during the Showing of 25 Films." *Ear Nose Throat* 89, no. 9 (September 2010): 444–50.

Weber, Max. *The Protestant Ethic and the Spirit of Capitalism*. New York: Charles Scribner's Sons, 1958.

Wegel, R. L. "LVIII: Physical Data and Physiology of Excitation of the Auditory Nerve." *Annals of Otology, Rhinology and Laryngology* 41, no. 3 (September 1, 1932): 740–79.

Weheliye, Alexander. "'Feenin': Posthuman Voices in Contemporary Black Popular Music." *Social Text* 20, no. 2 (2002): 21–47.

Weidman, Amanda. *Singing the Classical, Voicing the Modern: The Postcolonial Politics of Music in South India*. Durham, NC: Duke University Press, 2006.

Wendell, Susan. "Toward a Feminist Theory of Disability." *Hypatia* 4, no. 2 (1989): 104–24.

Wendell, Susan. "Unhealthy Disabled: Treating Chronic Illnesses as Disabilities." *Hypatia* 16, no. 4 (2001): 17–33.

Whiteley, Sheila. "Progressive Rock and Psychedelic Coding in the Work of Jimi Hendrix." *Popular Music* 9, no. 1 (1990): 37–60.

Wik, Reynold Millard. "Henry Ford's Science and Technology for Rural America." *Technology and Culture* 3, no. 3 (Summer 1962): 247–58.

Wilde, Oscar. *The Uncensored Picture of Dorian Gray: A Reader's Edition*. Edited by Nicholas Frankel. Cambridge, MA: Harvard University Press, 2012.

Williamson, Bess. *Accessible America: A History of Disability and Design*. New York: New York University Press, 2019.

Wilson, Robin. "Why Are Associate Professors So Unhappy?" *Chronicle of Higher Education*, June 3, 2012. https://www.chronicle.com/article/Why-Are-Associate -Professors/132071.

Winter, Alison. *Memory: Fragments of a Modern History*. Chicago: University of Chicago Press, 2012.

Winthrop-Young, Geoffrey. *Kittler and the Media*. Cambridge, UK: Polity, 2011.

Wishart, Trevor. *On Sonic Art*. Amsterdam: Harwood Academic, 1996.

Woodforde, John. *The Strange Story of False Teeth*. London: Routledge and Kegan Paul, 1968.

Wurth, Kiene Brillenburg. *Musically Sublime: Indeterminacy, Infinity, Irresolvability*. New York: Fordham University Press, 2009.

Wylie, John. "A Single Day's Walking: Narrating Self and Landscape on the South West Coast Path." *Transactions of the Institute of British Geographers* 30, no. 2 (June 2005): 234–47.

Wyschogrod, Edith. *Emmanuel Levinas: The Problem of Ethical Metaphysics*. 2nd ed. New York: Fordham University Press, 2000.

Yergeau, M. Remi. *Authoring Autism: On Rhetoric and Neurological Queerness*. Durham, NC: Duke University Press, 2018.

Young, Iris Marion. "Throwing like a Girl: A Phenomenology of Feminine Comportment, Motility and Spatiality." In *On Female Body Experience: "Throwing like a Girl" and Other Essays*, 27–45. New York: Oxford University Press, 2005.

Zak, Albin J. *The Poetics of Rock: Cutting Tracks, Making Records*. Berkeley: University of California Press, 2001.

INDEX

ing others, 16–17, 219n19; user manual, 15, 218n17; variability of, 36–37. *See also* phenomenology

impairment theory (user's guide), 193–205; backward compatibility and future versions, 205; defining impairment, 194–95; disposal instructions, 204; how to use, 197–202; limited liability, 203–4; theory, defining, 196–97; troubleshooting, 202–3

incapacity, 119, 120

inequality, theory of, 172

information fatigue, 179

injection medialization laryngoplasty, 92, 93–95, 231n52, 231n54

interdependence, 171

International Organization for Standardization (ISO), Standard 7029 (2000), 130, 132

interpretation, impairment and, 154–56, 231n56

interpreters, sign language, 70

intersectionality, 162, 199–200, 236n36

intersubjectivity, 142, 143

intoxication, 157–58, 177, 195

invisible disability, 182, 226n31. *See also* coming out as disabled; disability; passing

"It's So Loud, I Can't Hear My Budget" (*Psychology Today*), 137, 236n46

Jain, S. Lochlann, 24, 238n82

Jenrose, 169–70, 242n30

Jones, Amelia, 76–77

justice, 164, 171, 190, 201, 229n27

Kafer, Alison, 19, 25–26, 184, 221n55

Kafka, Franz, 143

Kallman syndrome, 97–98

Kant, Immanuel, 136, 138, 236n42

Katchadourian, Nina, 106–9

Kelly, Caleb, 140

Killion, Mead C., 147–48, 149

Kirkpatrick, Bill, 73, 235n32

Kittler, Friedrich, 142

Kleege, Georgina, 13–14

kludge, 53, 63, 64

kookaburras, 184

Krentz, Christopher, 133

Labelle, Brandon, 46, 224n10

labor, 33, 162, 182; academic, 157–58, 240nn1–2; care work, 164–65, 170–72, 179, 247n85; emotional, 171, 179; executive athleticism, 165; expanding the concept of work, 170–71; extractivism, 165–66, 241n17; fatigue, excluding work as a cause of, 173–74; industrial work and fatigue, 166–68; refusal of, 185–86; unemployment, 171; working-class men, 175. *See also* capitalism

Lagerkvist, Amanda, 20

lame, as term, 51, 225n23

Lane, Burl, 149

larynxes, 91–105, 115; author's larynx, open and closed, 92–95; inner imitations, 97; laryngoscope, invention of, 96–97; laryngoscopy, 92–95, 105, 230n52, 231n58; larynx studies 101, 95–98

Larynx Series (Gee), 98–105; *Larynx1—Voice One*, 103, 104; *Larynx3*, 99, 100–101

Lazard, Carolyn, 186–87

Le Breton, David, 122

Leduc, Véro, 113–14

Levinas, Emmanuel, 182–84, 189, 191, 245nn59–60, 246n63, 246nn66–67

Li, Xiaochang, 88

light conductor, 96

limits, 164–65, 170, 172, 181, 194, 200, 202. *See also* ability; disability; finitude; impairment; phenomenology

Linton, Simi, 19, 219n26

listener collapse. *See* consensual desubjectification

listening, 11, 56, 77, 97–98, 104, 142, 153–54, 235n26; *Listening and Voice* (Ihde), 13; *Listening In . . . a Portrait of Charles Graser* (Martin), 110–13

Livingston, Julie, 34–35, 126, 222n61

Lloyd, Stephanie, 133

Lochhead, Judy, 136

long-range acoustic devices (LRADs), 123

muteness, 18, 62, 77, 224n10. *See also* d/
  Deafness
myalgic encephalomyelitis/chronic fatigue
  syndrome (ME/CFS), 175–76, 182, 243n43,
  244n47, 244n49. *See also* chronic fatigue;
  fatigue
My Bloody Valentine (band), 238n73

Nakamura, Karen, 112
Nancy, Jean-Luc, 142
Nap Ministry, 186
national culture, loudness and, 137–38
National Science Foundation, 148
naturalization, critique of, 11
Nazis, 174, 242n27
negative phenomenologies, 162, 180
Negwer, Maximilian, 143–44
nerd, as term, 49, 225n17
neurasthenia, 175
New York League of the Hard of Hearing, 126
New York Times (newspaper), 157
Nishnaabeg people, 185–86
noise, 234n18; Japanese noise music, 136; as
  metaphor for violence, 138; urban antinoise
  crusades, 143–44
Noise and Vibration (journal), 151–52
nondepletionist approach to fatigue, 162,
  180–81, 182–91; phenomenology of fatigue,
  189–91; refusal and withdrawal, 185–88;
  time, relationship to, 182–87. *See also*
  depletionism
normal impairments, 15, 35, 141, 154–56, 195,
  199, 235n23, 235n32; audile scarification as,
  118–19, 125–26; expected impairments, 47,
  126–34, 155. *See also* audile scarification;
  fatigue
normalization, 73
Novak, David, 136
Nudelman, Franny, 189, 247n84

Ohropax, 143–44
#120db campaign, 140
oralism, 112
oral voice, 46, 66, 79–80, 115
orientation, change in, 12, 36, 37

orphic media technologies, 152–54
Our Vibrating Hands (video project), 113–14
Oxford English Dictionary, 31, 49, 179, 242n20

Packer, Jeremy, 145, 147
pain, 136, 159, 161–62, 177, 182, 190, 225n15,
  244n49; emotional, 153; threshold of,
  117–18, 123, 125, 134, 138, 233n4. *See also*
  chronic illness
Parr, Mike, 77
passing, 35, 46, 56, 95, 226n31. *See also* coming
  out as disabled; invisible disability
Patton, Cindy, 152, 238n82, 239n89
Peabody Museum of Archaeology and Ethnology, Harvard University, 81
Peck, Kathy, 147–48, 149
perception, 11, 18–20, 45, 153, 154–56, 183,
  232n1
personhood, 38, 78, 90, 228n25. *See also*
  subjecthood
phenomenology: anti-, 73–74; of apperception, 128; of fatigue, 189–91; feminist,
  21–22; of loudness, 138; negative, 162, 180;
  The Phenomenology of Perception (Merleau-
  Ponty), 18; of policy, 32–35; political, 11–13,
  18–19, 36–37, 189–90, 196, 218n8, 233n1;
  positive, 162; of subjectivity, 155; tradition of, 10–11, 13, 18. *See also* impairment
  phenomenology
phonautograms, 84–86; phonautographs, 86,
  230n46
Piekut, Ben, 90
Piepzna-Samarasinha, Leah Lakshmi, 164, 171,
  246n71
piezoelectric transducer, 142
Pinch, Trevor, 137
pinna, 79
pleasure, 79, 118–19, 129–30, 133, 136, 153; loudness and, 137–38, 151
police sublime, 140
policy, phenomenology of, 32–35
political economy, 168–72
political phenomenology, 11–13, 18–19, 36–37,
  189–90, 196, 218n8, 233n1. *See also* fatigue;
  impairment phenomenology